The Leader in You
Developing Your Leadership Potential

Peter Miller
Carol Dalglish

The Leader in You
Developing Your Leadership Potential
1st edition, 1st printing

Authors
Peter Miller • Carol Dalglish

Cover designer
Christopher Besley, Besley Design.

ISBN: 978-0-7346-1138-3

Disclaimer

All reasonable efforts have been made to ensure the quality and accuracy of this publication. Tilde University Press assumes no responsibility for any errors or omissions and no warranties are made with regard to this publication. Neither Tilde University Press nor any authorised distributors shall be held responsible for any direct, incidental or consequential damages resulting from the use of this publication.

Published in Australia by:
Tilde University Press
PO Box 72
Prahran VIC 3181, Australia
Tel: 1300 880 935
www.tup.net.au

Contents

About the authors

Peter Miller

Peter has more than 30 years experience working in senior management roles in the public sector, the mining industry and higher education. He has had a lifelong interest in studying how people and organisations interact. Peter's goal is to understand how to shape organisations so that people can be truly engaged and productive. He achieves this by observing how things get done and who makes them happen within an organisation.

Peter was CEO for two start-up companies and been on the board of directors of several organisations. He has worked with CEOs and executive teams as a coach and with boards of directors to undertake performance evaluations. He has been a consultant to a number of national organisations and is the author/co-author of ten books.

Currently an Associate Professor in the Graduate College of Management at Southern Cross University, NSW, Australia, Peter also teaches and undertakes research in leadership.

Carol Dalglish

For over 30 years, Carol has worked in senior management roles in the public sector and education in Australia and the United Kingdom. She also spent five years as an independent management consultant in Queensland, specialising in the management of change in both the public and private sectors.

Carol has a particular interest in how individuals can learn to be effective by improving their understanding of themselves and the impact of cultural diversity on organisations. She was instrumental in establishing a not-for-profit agency, Awaken Mozambique, to support and research entrepreneurship in Africa. She has taught in countries as diverse as Taiwan, Denmark and South Africa and is the author/co-author of ten books.

Carol is currently an Associate Professor in the School of Management at the Queensland University of Technology, Queensland, Australia where she teaches and researches leadership and micro-entrepreneurship in developing economies.

Acknowledgements

We would like to acknowledge many people for assisting us with the development of this book. Our gratitude and thanks go to our colleagues for their encouraging comments and views on the various drafts.

We would also like to show appreciation to the leadership professionals and reviewers who provided input and contributed comments as the chapters developed.

Our very special thanks go to the many leaders who agreed to have their profiles included in the book. Effective leaders love to share their experiences and to mentor others, and your insights and lessons provide valuable tools from which other leaders can learn.

We would especially like to thank the team at Tilde University Press, and in particular Rick Ryan and Sally Keohane, for the professional way they work with authors like us, and for their patience and guidance.

Introduction

We, the authors of this book, have both held leadership positions in various contexts for many decades in the private, public, tertiary education and community sectors – and in different cultural settings. But more than this, we have also been students of leadership with lifelong ambitions to study people and organisations.

We seek to understand the people who get things done in organisations, along with

- how people in organisations interact
- how to best shape organisations to allow people to be truly engaged and productive
- how things get done in organisations.

Our leadership experience and research suggests that there is a serious shortcoming in the quality and competence of leaders in our organisations, and that the concept of leadership in our societies requires renewal.

Leading people in any organisational setting, whether it's in a traditional organisational management role, a community organisation of volunteers, a sporting context or any other context where people are in groups, is an exciting challenge. It is a great opportunity for those willing to step up and a very serious responsibility. Leadership can also be difficult and lonely in times of turbulence and change.

All cultures and civilisations throughout history have focused attention on their leaders. Some leaders are revered and others despised. Ancient writers like Confucius, Socrates and Plato were among the first to recognise the importance of good leadership in society. Spiritual leaders like Jesus and Mohammed spoke often about the subject of leadership. Philosophers and historians like Lao Tzu, Homer and Machiavelli provided advice for leaders that is still used today.

The recent global financial crisis (GFC) has once again focused our attention on the leaders of large corporations around the globe and on government and political leaders. If people were once complacent about the competence of our leaders in these settings – thinking leaders at these levels do not impact on them personally – then their attention has now been refocused on the significant impact that leaders everywhere can have on all aspects of our existence. Most importantly, the GFC has reminded us that if our society and economies are to move forward successfully, we must have the right kind of leaders and the right kind of leadership throughout our organisations.

One of the philosophies about leadership that underpins the approach taken in this book is that becoming a leader in an organisation (or any other setting) is a privilege, but this privilege comes with certain obligations. A prime obligation is that leaders are morally obliged to serve first the organisation and its people rather than their own self-interests. Over the last few years there has been a trend for the leaders (particularly the senior leaders) of many organisations to develop a culture of greed and abuse of organisational resources and assets, and a pattern of self-indulgence. The occurrence of the GFC, which at least partially resulted from these tendencies, has confirmed this trend.

Another of this book's underlying philosophies is that most of us can learn to become better leaders. However some people, because of personality flaws like narcissism, Machiavellianism and psychopathic personality disorders, should never be allowed to lead others. Unfortunately, some organisations in more recent times have mistakenly attributed these tendencies to leadership ability. The result has been promotions of inappropriate people to senior leadership positions where these behaviours are potentially very destructive.

The other important philosophy grounding this book is about the importance of leaders being self-aware and reflective. Reflection is possibly a leader or manager's least favourite activity. Leadership development is based on the premise that self-learning is fundamental to improving leadership effectiveness. If you are to improve your leadership skills and practices, then it is important that you are aware of your current level of skills, your values and behavioural patterns and the predominant ways you attempt to influence others, that is, your leadership style. Self-awareness is therefore a key to being a more effective leader.

Self-awareness is really about self-discovery and our aim in this book is to assist you to move on that path. However, genuine self-awareness can be confronting and will therefore require your patience and perseverance.

Statements from philosophers about the need for self-awareness for those in leadership positions go back thousands of years to the ancient writers mentioned previously. There are two more recent statements, however, that seem to best sum up the need for leader self-awareness. Writing in 1623 about a slave revolt in the Greek city of Syracuse, Philip Massinger (1583–1640) said in *The Bondman*, 'He that would govern others must first master himself'.

In other words (excusing the sexist language of the time), if you are to lead other people well, you must first have a mature understanding of who you are and why you behave in the ways you do and be secure in self-acceptance.

The second statement comes from Segal and Horne (1997, p.56):

> *The pursuit of self-knowledge is the work of a developed personality and a characteristic of an enlightened leader. Self-understanding is the most secure bed-rock on which to shape one's life. Nothing is more important in conditions of turbulence and change than a secure sense of self. Self-understanding also provides a basis for understanding others – it is difficult to be conscious of another's need, motivation, and processes without first having awareness of one's own.*

The book has been framed to be useful to all individuals who are currently in leadership roles, from chief executives to frontline managers, as well as community leaders and leaders of volunteer groups. Government, business, education, sports and religious leaders will improve their leadership potential if they work through the process in this book. Those who wish to step up to a leadership role will also find this book relevant to their development. Organisations can utilise this book to assist their leaders at all levels to increase their leadership potential.

While we focus attention in this book on leaders, we recognise that leaders alone will not accomplish much. It is the followers of leaders that are a leaders' strength, and it is the hard work of non-leaders that turns a profit, or the initiative of volunteers that achieves a non-profit organisation's goals.

If you want to search for and develop leadership qualities in yourself, then this book is for you. If you feel the responsibility to lead more effectively and to reach your own personal potential, then this book is for you. If you want to set a higher standard in your organisation and you think leadership is a serious matter in the lives of other people, then this book is for you. In the process of self-reflection, this book will enable you to develop an *individual leadership profile* and an *individual skills profile*, culminating in the development of a plan for leadership improvement. And we aim to couple these outcomes with exposure to some practical skills that leaders need in everyday environments.

In order to proceed with the leadership development process, the book is structured into 12 chapters. Chapter 1 attempts to place the study of leadership in the global context. It provides guidance on the meaning of leadership, the difference between leadership and management, the importance of leadership in our society and a framework for understanding it.

Chapter 2 explores the concept of values and ethics and their relevance to business leadership. In the light of the excesses of business in the past few years and the failure of so many substantial organisations due to improper and even criminal behaviour on the part of organisational leaders, the role of values and ethics in business has been thrown into sharp relief. Understanding values is important because the leader's personal values may be one of the most important determinants of how power is exercised or constrained. The leader's perceptions and behaviour will also set the tone for how the organisation conducts itself.

Chapter 3 is about exploring the role of the person as leader — how his or her characteristics and behaviour impact on leadership effectiveness. It suggests that understanding yourself, your strengths and weaknesses, and your own values and culture are an integral part of being able to respond effectively in a range of leadership situations. Not being self-aware may lead to action that destroys confidence; it may even lead followers into harm.

Chapter 4 continues the theme of assisting leaders to understand who they are and why they do the things they do, and provides further guidance on understanding yourself. By having a better understanding of yourself, you will begin to have a better understanding of others and therefore be in a better position to lead them. This chapter examines what are known as the 'big five' personality traits and the cognitive factors that are said to underpin effective leadership behaviour and act as the building blocks of a person's self-concept.

At the end of Chapter 4, we will pause to allow you to build your *individual leadership profile.*

Chapter 5 examines leadership development and some of the theories that underpin it. Research examining leadership development has consistently shown that less than ten per cent of the experiences leaders reported as 'key events' and 'shaping events' originated from traditional education or training programs. The chapter demonstrates that on-the-job experience is a significant contributor to leadership development, but it should be framed in wider learning processes like action learning, succession planning, coaching and mentoring.

Chapter 6 reviews charismatic and transformational leadership models that move beyond simple consideration of personality — they explore the impact of leadership characteristics and behaviour on followers. They explore the relationship between leaders and their situations, bringing together aspects of traits theory and contingency theories. Transformational leadership and breakthrough leadership, an Australian model, also explore the impact of the leader's behaviour on the followers' behaviour and development.

Chapter 7 explores the concept of cultural diversity and its relevance to leadership. What is seen as appropriate in one context may be seen as inappropriate in another. Leaders can be seen as the creators of organisational culture. This is not about the purpose of leadership or the particular functions that leaders fill, but rather how they go about leading; how they create an environment where cultural diversity is seen as strength rather than grounds for suspicion.

Chapter 8 looks at power and influence, which are at the very heart of what leadership is about. Power is the *potential* or *capacity* of the leader to influence followers while influence is the *ability* of the leader to gain acceptance of requests and ideas. The exercising of power and influence in a workplace context is a complex phenomenon dependent on many factors, and leaders need to recognise the types of power that effective leaders can draw upon to influence others.

Chapter 9 examines the communication skills that are critical for leaders. The leader's main roles are to influence others towards the organisation's vision and to assist others in understanding their roles within the organisation. This gives followers meaning for their work. Everything a leader does when influencing others involves communicating. Good communication skills, when compared with other leadership skills, are foundational to effective leadership. Good communication skills alone, however, do not make an effective leader. Communication is viewed from three levels including core communication skills, team communication skills, and strategic and external communication skills.

Chapter 10 explores teams and teamwork. There are many different types of teams, with a trend in modern organisations to the development of self-managed teams. The chapter concentrates on the leadership of teams and the need for leaders to understand the role they play in developing successful and effective team work in organisations. The chapter also examines why organisations and teams decline.

Chapter 11 concentrates on change. Leaders of organisations need to manage change effectively. This chapter provides frameworks for the way leaders can successfully implement change in their organisations. Leaders must first develop an understanding of the effects of change on individuals, and then extend that understanding to the effect change has in the organisational context.

Chapter 12 focuses on the third dimension of the leadership process, the external environment, exploring how leaders interact with it and the challenges they face. The chapter provides a more detailed look at the leadership environment and the crucial importance of strategic thinking in today's rapidly changing environment. Because strategic leadership deals with the major purposes of an organisation, its perspective is often different from that of leadership at other levels in an organisation.

At the end of Chapter 12, we will again pause to allow you to build your *individual skills profile*. Then, in the Summary section of the book, we provide you with the opportunity to develop a 2–3 year *leadership development plan*.

We trust that this book enables you to explore the nature and practice of leadership. We hope you can truly reflect upon who you are as a leader, and that you are inspired and moved to greater capacities by this book. We believe, whatever your current leadership style and effectiveness, this book will help you examine your leadership style and will motivate you to work towards becoming a more effective leader. Research shows that only about one third of leaders have a realistic understanding of their own leadership style and impact on others. Using this book you can assess whether your perception of your own leadership style agrees with the perceptions of others.

Peter Miller
Carol Dalglish
September 2010

Reference

Segal, S & Horne, D 1997, *Human Dynamics*, Pegasus, Cambridge, MA.

Chapter 1

LEADERSHIP IN THE GLOBAL CONTEXT

CHAPTER CONTENTS

- ☐ Spotlight: Karen Stanton
- ☐ The meaning of leadership
- ☐ The difference between leadership and management
- ☐ The global context of leadership
- ☐ Leader in action: Herman Chinery-Hesse
- ☐ The impact and importance of leadership
- ☐ A framework for understanding leadership
- ☐ Summary
- ☐ Reflection on your leadership practice

Spotlight: Karen Stanton

The illusory quality we call 'leadership' is evident in Karen Stanton from the first conversation with her. Although a successful business woman, there are no airs or affectations. She is calm, intelligent, witty and very honest in her conversation—all the while putting you at ease. Karen Stanton has been the managing director of Heat Treatment Australia for the past eight years. The company has grown from a relatively small Queensland business to a national company—a leader in its field—with plans to expand internationally.

Karen says that education has been one of the main contributors to her success. She said that she 'realised that when you work hard and try hard, and learn as much as you can, you can have a big impact on whatever you are trying to achieve'. Karen has a Bachelor of Commerce, an MBA, a Master of Technology, and is currently working towards a doctorate. She feels that study opens her mind and, as it is closely related to her work, will help her make the business even more successful.

While her business success is important to her, family is paramount for Karen. She is married with children aged 3, 10 and 13. Karen's regular holidays with her family and the time she takes to be with them only adds to her success rather than taking from it. She says that this balance gives her time to think and relax.

Karen does not like the term 'followers', and does not think of others in this way. She leads people by showing them what she expects and by setting an example for them. No one is seen as being below or above her. Karen sees her role as supporting those who run the day-to-day operations of the business. She sets the direction and the targets, and then monitors the progress of the whole organisation. Karen sees it as her responsibility to align the values, goals and ideas of the staff with solid business goals.

Karen has an international growth strategy. The partners and managers are on board with this. Karen says that she talks about it all the time. Together they have spent a lot of time deciding how to move forward, as Karen's leadership style is inclusive. She tailors her communication to the situation and to her audience. She uses all manner of communication methods—from face-to-face through to print, telephone and email. There is a staff barbeque on the same Friday every month, where for an hour Karen spends the time talking to as many people as she can. This is an informal way of getting to know her employees individually and of showing that she enjoys their company.

Karen feels that her own enthusiasm *does* translate to her staff. Her aim is to create a friendly environment so that people will want to come to work. She does not expect employees to work long hours, but while they are there she expects them to work hard, smart and efficiently. And, she provides just such an example and expects others to do the same. She works hard to create a positive culture where each staff member is valued. For example, each person receives a card for every anniversary of their being with company, with a personal note from her about their achievements. She also keeps birthday lists and notes of spouses and children's names to jog her memory.

Karen has identified some characteristics that she thinks are important for effective leadership. These include:

- creativity,
- self confidence,
- the ability to communicate at all levels, and
- being interested in and concerned for people.

She attributes her success to her willingness to make each member of her staff feel that they have the same right to speak to her as anyone else, the simple things she does to reward her staff, her reliability, and her clearly articulated values.

Her leadership advice is to

Give it a go! If you have some confidence and you are willing to work hard, why not try? If it doesn't work out, you haven't lost anything.

Sources: Personal interview; Dawn Galvin in Dalglish C & Evans P 2007, *Leadership in the Australian Context*, Tilde University Press, Melbourne.

The above description of Karen Stanton touches on many leadership topics that will be covered in this book. Karen demonstrates the leadership skills she uses to be effective in a rapidly growing business that has international ambitions. This short profile also identifies some critical issues for leaders in the contemporary world, and highlights an Australian way of dealing with these issues. They exist for all leaders, and include:

- the importance of having a clear vision that inspires and motivates others,
- the importance of local understanding and sensitivity, and
- a willingness to be determined and consistent so that trust develops.

Karen is leading in an industry where women are still a minority, and yet she has overcome this disadvantage to lead her company through rapid growth. Leadership happens in a wide range of contexts, and everyone who wants to make a difference can make a difference.

The meaning of leadership

Stories of leaders come from the earliest human writings. From ancient Egypt to the Chinese classics advice is given to the country's leaders on how to be successful. Machiavelli's *The Prince* provides comment on leadership that is as current today as it was when he wrote it in 1514 in medieval Europe. The concept of the leader, therefore, is as old as history. All societies have leaders. Some people become leaders as a result of heredity, others through acts of war. In modern society leaders can emerge through the political process, through career progression to the head of a business or other organisation, or from within a community with a mission to make some aspect of that society better.

The modern concept of leadership, however, developed during the twentieth century. Whereas in the past leaders came by their positions in a variety of ways, e.g. inheritance or strength of arms, their position was accepted because it couldn't be changed. Today, however, most people have a choice. Leadership, therefore, is the study of what makes a leader effective; however he or she came by that position. So what is effective leadership?

Over the past century, academics in a variety of disciplines have tried to identify what makes some leaders effective and others not. They have looked to explain the nature of leadership by looking at a range of aspects of the phenomenon. Below are brief descriptions of the ways in which different theories have evolved over the past century. While these will be described in much greater detail in subsequent chapters, this section simply puts the ideas in context.

The great man theory

One of the earliest theories of leadership is the 'great man' theory. This theory, which was popular in the early 1900s and still holds currency today, holds that leaders and followers are fundamentally different. According to this theory, leaders have different personal attributes and act in ways fundamentally different to followers because leaders are born to be leaders. This theory generated much research, the general conclusion of which was that leaders and followers are not fundamentally different (Wren 1995).

The big five model

More recent research shows that possessing certain personality traits generally helps leaders but that personality traits alone are no guarantee of success. The 'big five' model of personality is a categorisation scheme that seeks to encapsulate all possible personality traits. Five traits were found to be consistently related to leadership success. These included:

- dominance and extraversion,
- sociability and warmth,
- achievement orientation and organisational ability,
- self acceptance, and
- self control (Deary 1996).

Charismatic leadership

We often associate charisma with leadership. *Charisma* is a Greek word meaning 'divinely inspired gift', but there are a number of different views as to how charisma is derived. Some argue that charismatic individuals come from the margins of society and emerge as leaders during times of great social crises; others argue that 'charismatic leadership' is primarily a function of the leader's extraordinary qualities and not the situation. Often charisma is attributed to those leaders who can develop particularly strong emotional attachments with followers (Weber 1947; Burns 1978; Bass 1990).

Contingency theories

'Contingency theories' hold that effective leadership is contingent on the situation. These theories look at the leader's behaviour as it directly relates either to the specific work situation or the abilities and characteristics of the followers or subordinates. Here it is the 'fit' that matters rather than the charismatic personality of the leader (Hersey & Blanchard 1982; Fiedler, Chemers & Mahar 1994).

Power and leadership

The focus returned to the persona of the leader and his or her behaviour in the transformational/transaction framework that was first articulated by Burns in 1978, but the relevance of the situation and of the followers was also recognised. 'Power' and 'leadership' were seen as two distinct entities. *Power wielders* were those individuals who used their power to influence followers so as to accomplish the leader's goals, and who often saw their followers as a means to an end. *Leadership*, on the other hand, is inseparable from the follower's needs and goals. All leaders are power wielders, but not all power wielders are leaders (Burns 1978). This is a distinction not made in all the theories.

Transactional leadership and transformational leadership

Leadership was also seen to take two forms which are very familiar to us today — transactional leadership and transformational leadership. 'Transactional leadership' is characterised by the leader and follower being in an exchange relationship. 'Transformational leadership', however, seeks to change the *status quo* by appealing to followers' values and their sense of higher purpose, reframing issues so that they align with the leader's vision and the followers' values, and operating at a higher stage of moral development than their followers (Burns 1978; Bass 1990).

Servant leadership

Another perspective on leadership, and one which has been adopted in the not-for-profit sector and appears to be of increasing interest in today's business environment, is 'servant leadership'. These leaders lead because they want to serve others. People follow servant leaders freely because they trust them. The test of servant leadership is whether those served grow as people (Greenleaf 1977; Spears 1997).

Leadership roles

So there appear to be leadership perspectives to suit all tastes and contexts. These ways of viewing leadership and gaining a better understanding of the leadership process are all covered in greater detail in the chapters of this book.

Most of the leadership literature referred to above emanates from the United States (US), and was written during the second half of the twentieth century. Different theorists studied samples from politics and business in North America that were largely based on Caucasian male samples. How relevant, then, is this picture of leadership effectiveness in an Australian/New Zealand, European, African or Asian context where political and business systems, languages and cultures are very different? Is there a 'one size fits all' version of leadership effectiveness, or do effective leaders in different contexts in fact behave differently from their North American counterparts?

One useful way of gaining an understanding of leadership is to examine the various roles carried out by leaders. A 'role' in this context is an expected set of activities or behaviours stemming from one's job or position. It is important to remember that leadership does not only happen at the top of business organisations; it can happen at all levels of an organisation. Leadership happens in business, political, public sector and not-for-profit organisations. It also happens in every community. In fact, leadership as a process of influencing others to achieve an objective can occur in any aspect of life—from the sporting field through to team leadership in large or small organisations.

What do leaders do?

So, what exactly is it that leaders do? Whilst the discussion of the origins of leadership and the personal styles and characteristics of leaders continues in many hundreds of journals, business magazines and texts, there is a perspective emerging based on what leaders do and the roles/functions they fulfil in any organisation or community. This is different to considering their personal characteristics and leadership styles. These roles, tasks or functions include:

- creating a vision, direction or goals (Gardner 1990; Bennis 1989; Kotter 1990; Conger 1992; Gardner 1997; Mariotti 1999);

- communicating with followers (Gardner 1990; Bennis 1989; Mariotti 1999);

- motivating and empowering (Gardner 1990; Kotter 1990);

- affirming/re-affirming values (Gardener 1990; Freiberg 1998);

- aligning people (i.e. the management of meaning) and achieving workable unity (Gardner 1990; Bennis 1989; Kotter 1990; Conger 1992; Gardner 1997);

- serving as a symbol (Gardner 1990; Conger 1992; Freiberg 1998);

- the management of trust (Bennis 1989; Gardner 1997); and

- the management of self (Bennis 1989; Freiberg 1998).

So, whilst there are leadership perspectives to suit all tastes and contexts, there appears to be a growing consensus about some of the things that effective leaders do, if not how they do them. Effective leaders:

- focus attention through a compelling vision;

- communicate meaning to their followers;

- develop trust through reliability and integrity; and

- manage themselves through self-awareness and positive self-regard.

John Gardner (1989), in his book *On Leadership*, identifies what he believes to be the tasks and roles of leaders. These nine tasks and roles are worth thinking about and are listed below. Do all these roles need to be fulfilled? If so, the path to effective leadership can be found by identifying the most appropriate ways of undertaking these various roles.

- *Envisioning goals.* Leaders look into the future. They can create a vision, identify goals or provide solutions to problems. They can see things that others cannot yet see. They provide a focus which unites various individuals and groups in action.

- *Affirming values.* Articulating and affirming values is a very important role performed by leaders. They revitalise shared beliefs and values. Each generation must rediscover the living elements in their own tradition and adapt these to current realities. How can the old values be articulated in a new and very different society?

- *Motivating.* Different individuals and groups are motivated by many different things. Effective leaders identify those motives that can assist with collective action in pursuit of shared goals.

- *Managing.* Much more will be said about the difference between leadership and management later in this chapter. For goals to be achieved, both leadership and management are required, and if the leader does not manage, he/she must ensure that someone else does.

- *Achieving workable unity.* In most modern situations there are many different purposes and many different ways of doing things. One of the greatest challenges for leaders is to reduce conflict and to develop a level of mutual tolerance. This requires leaders to have the capacity to inspire trust in themselves.

- *Explaining.* This may appear self-evident, but it is nevertheless critical that leaders explain what they want and why. In some cultures, such as in Australia and New Zealand, this explanation is critical to success (Dalglish & Evans 2007).

- *Serving as a symbol.* This is perhaps the most obvious role of leaders; however, it can also create a heavy burden for leaders. Everything they do, whether related to their position as leader or not, will be a reflection of their leadership and the group that they lead. Expectations will be high and unavoidable.

- *Representing the group.* Virtually all leaders, wherever they are in the organisation, have tasks that involve dealing with external groups—be these negotiations, public relations, or defending the integrity or activities of the group.

- *Renewing.* Leaders must foster the process of renewal, challenge the status quo, and encourage responsiveness to change.

You will read about many effective leaders throughout this book. A down-to-earth definition of what leaders do was put forward by John Kotter in 1990:

> *...it (leadership) produces movement. Throughout the ages, individuals who have been seen as leaders have created change, sometimes for the better and sometimes not. They have done so in a variety of ways, though their actions often seem to boil down to establishing where a group of people should go, getting them lined up in that direction and committed to movement, and then energizing them to overcome the inevitable obstacles they will encounter along the way (Kotter 1990).*

This definition of leadership offers leaders a framework for developing their own 'ways'—ways that work in the wide variety of social, organisational and cultural contexts.

The difference between leadership and management

Leadership

To be able to understand leadership and the attributes needed to be an effective leader, it is important to grasp the differences between leadership and management. These terms are often used interchangeably, but there is increasing recognition that they are not the same thing. Broadly speaking, 'leadership' deals with interpersonal matters and focuses on the people who need to be motivated to complete the task in hand. It is also often connected with change and the introduction of the new. Managers, however, focus on planning, organising and controlling the whole range of resources required to achieve stated objectives.

According to JP Kotter, a prominent leadership theorist, managers must know how to lead as well as manage. As seen earlier in Gardener's description of leadership roles, management was considered one of the leadership roles. There is ongoing debate about whether leadership and management skills can exist in the same person. What is clear is that without being led as well as being managed, organisations face the threat of irrelevance leading to extinction.

Management

'Management' can be defined as the attainment of organisational goals in an effective and efficient manner through planning, organising, directing staff and controlling organisational resources. Leadership does not replace management; it is an addition to it. In the debate about the difference between leadership and management the importance of management has often been underestimated. The two roles are complementary and both are necessary.

Distinctions between management and leadership

The following are several key distinctions between management and leadership that the literature has identified:

- Management is an explicit set of tools and techniques, based on reasoning and testing, that can be used in a variety of situations. It involves specific skills like planning and budgeting.

- Leadership involves having a vision of what the organisation can become, creating a different future, and having the strategy to get there. Leadership is about creating organisational culture, renewing values and helping others to grow (Kotter 1990; Gardner & Schein 1985).

- Leadership focuses on people, eliciting cooperation and teamwork, and inspiring and motivating those required to achieve stated objectives.

- Leadership produces change, e.g. spearheading the launch of a new product, or opening a new market for an old product. Management is about stability, and is more likely to produce a degree of predictability and order. It is about making the best of what is.

- A leader creates a vision to direct the organisation. In contrast, the key function of the manager is to implement the vision. The manager and his/her team choose the means to achieve the end that the leader formulates (Kotter 1990; Whetton & Cameron 1995; Leonard 1999; Locke 1991).

If these views are taken to the extreme, the leader becomes an inspirational figure and the manager a bureaucrat mired in the *status quo*. But we must be careful not to downplay the importance of management. Effective leaders have to be good managers themselves, or be supported by good managers. A germane example is the inspirational entrepreneur who is so preoccupied with motivating employees and captivating customers that internal administration is neglected, resulting in costs growing beyond revenues and matters such as remitting employees' superannuation and paying bills and taxes on time being overlooked.

Activity 1.1 Self assessment

Think about the various roles you have played in organisations. This can be as part of the workforce, through involvement with a community organisation or sporting team, at school, or at a college or university. Leadership and management happen in all these contexts. This short activity provides an opportunity to reflect on the experience you have already had in leadership or management, and the types of activity you felt most comfortable with.

Read the type of activity and identify whether you have undertaken this activity often, sometimes or never.

Activity	Often	Sometimes	Never
1. Developed goals			
2. Developed a budget			
3. Produced a vision			
4. Produced a plan of action			
5. Prepared a public speech			
6. Supervised staff			
7. Encouraged participation			
8. Created systems			
9. Supported people			
10. Controlled a budget or staff			
11. Initiated change			
12. Organised an event			

Allocate yourself two points where you have ticked often, one point for sometimes, and no points for never.

Add up the points you have for all the odd numbered questions — these relate to leadership tasks. Add up all the points you have for all the even numbered questions — these relate to management tasks. The higher your score, the more experience you have in both leadership and management.

Reflect on the types of experience you have had and where you had those experiences. If it is early in your career, you may have a low score in leadership in the workplace but more leadership experience from other contexts. Reflect on where the gaps are and consider how you might build up your expertise in leadership and/or management.

The global context of leadership

The external environment in the twenty-first century offers many challenges to effective leadership. These challenges include responding effectively to the changes brought about by the information technology revolution, recognising the cross-cultural nature of much business activity, and being conscious that 'globalisation' brings with it increased concerns about social responsibility and the environment. Leadership in times of change is critical, but it also has its challenges. People are often uncomfortable with, or even resistant to, rapid change. They rely on leaders to point the direction and to help them feel competent and confident in the new circumstances.

The rapid growth of information technology has brought the world together as never before. Globalisation is a reality. Changes in one part of the world can rapidly bring changes everywhere else, and with surprising speed. However, this interaction does not mean that we are becoming more alike. Schneider and Barsoux (1997) point to compelling evidence that, as the world gets smaller, the pressure to preserve difference becomes greater.

> *The pressures to preserve political and economic sovereignty, as well as cultural identity and integrity, have remained, and have grown even stronger as evidenced by regional tensions in Spain, Ireland and Belgium, and most dramatically in the former Yugoslavia. Indeed, it seems that the pressure for convergence or integration may in fact create an equal if not stronger pressure for divergence or fragmentation (Fayerweather & Webber quoted in Schneider & Barsoux 1997).*

Information technology has not only brought people together and enabled them to become more aware of differences, but has highlighted differences in both culture and socio-economic status. The internet has provided a window on the world for many more people. Those in the developed world are aware as never before, and have become increasingly concerned with the impact of change on those who are potentially exploited by the stated imperatives of business and politics. This has given rise to an expectation on the part of many consumers that businesses will be socially and environmentally responsible — that they will be responsible in their relationships with the relatively powerless developing world by not exploiting the people or damaging the environment. The idea of the corporation as a socially responsible citizen, at home and abroad, is one of increasing importance and presents significant challenges for leaders.

It has also led to decreasing tolerance for those who abuse the privileges their positions give them. The corruption of individuals in leadership positions presents a major challenge, not only to countries struggling with the challenges of development and poverty but also to the reputations of those countries among the developed nations who are in a position to help.

The attitudes of many workers toward their leaders have also changed. Across the world they increasingly expect leaders to think and plan for the long term, create motivating visions, communicate effectively, be self-aware, be trustworthy, have integrity and hold an optimistic view of the future.

Leader in action: Herman Chinery-Hesse

Our mission is to provide tropically tolerant software solutions to the West African region. We are committed to ensuring that we are responsive to rapidly changing information technology and to changes in our clients' environments (Chinery-Hesse).

This is a simple mission perhaps, but one that raises many challenges. To be successful it requires that the local conditions and cultures are understood, and that technology developed in very different conditions and cultures is adapted in response to these new circumstances. This is the sort of cross-cultural challenge faced by many businesses throughout Africa and the rest of the world.

Herman Chinery-Hesse comes from the elite within his country, and has benefitted from the opportunities offered by an international education. As a child he moved between Accra and wherever his parents—both career diplomats—were posted, including Tanzania, Sierra Leone and Switzerland. He attended Ghana's prestigious Mfantsipim School (which was also the school that Kofi Annan attended). He left Ghana to attend college, studying industrial technology at Texas State University in San Marcos. Herman is a manufacturing engineer by education but a software engineer by trade, having graduated in industrial technology from Texas State University.

In Texas, Chinery-Hesse was an outsider. He admits that he often felt afraid to talk to strangers or to the police. He remembers this period as the time of his entrepreneurial conversion—when he first understood how business could change an impoverished country. At a time when most of his friends were leaving Ghana, he decided to return to Accra in 1990. He has become a technology entrepreneur on a technologically barren continent. He is an atheist in a deeply religious country, and a capitalist who was brought up in a socialist environment.

Ghana is a small country in a very poor region of the world, but this has not prevented Chinery-Hesse is his entrepreneurial aspirations. Ghana does not appear the ideal place to start a business. It has a population of 23 million and a *per capita* income of $US676 a year. Inflation has been running at approximately 18 per cent a year, and interest rates have reached 25 per cent. According to the World Bank, Ghana is one of the most difficult places in the world in which to start a business, ranking 138th after Venezuela, Serbia and Iran.

Things are changing however. Today, Accra boasts dozens of tech companies and one of the largest internet cafes in Africa. Chinery-Hess was an early investor in the Internet Café, a local business which also serves as an incubator that rents space to start-ups.

With no start-up capital and no equipment other than his old personal computer, his company SOFTtribe was started in his bedroom. The company now employs 70 people and has a client base of more than 250 organisations including major multinationals such as the Ford Foundation, Nestle and Unilever. It is also a Microsoft development partner in the region. The company has annual revenues of $US 1 million a year in a country where a three-bedroom house costs $US20,000.

Chinery-Hesse believes that technology is the only way for Africa to become wealthy:

We don't have proper infrastructure and we can't compete in manufacturing. But if you put me behind a PC and tell me to write software for a Chinese customer, then I can compete brain for brain with anyone trying to do the same in the US.

He recognised that for information systems to be useful they had to be adapted to the reality of the African context. They needed to be people tolerant. The training process and documentation cannot assume *priori* exposure to IT, as most people will have had no opportunity to learn computer literacy prior to accessing this software. Also, Ghana has very little bandwidth, and the software systems need to keep working when the phone lines are down. In Ghana, as in many developing nations, power failures are common, so systems that can recover immediately after a power failure are essential. Most African entrepreneurs are capital poor, and therefore systems need to be inexpensive and cost effective. Systems need to be highly modular so that an enterprise solution need not be installed all at once, but rather as capital becomes available over the medium to long term.

Understanding the reality of the African context is the key to Chinery-Hesse's success. He has found ways of using technology to address the very specific issues confronting business people in tropical Africa; he has not borrowed from another cultural and geographical context. Instead, he has built his business on the realities of life in Ghana, recognising the strengths and limitations of that context.

SOFTtribe has won a number of awards, including the Millennium Excellence Awards for IT in 2005. But SOFTtribe is just the beginning. Chinery-Hesse has many other plans. He appears to have the capacity to use ideas and to adapt them to the reality of his context. He has a vision and is able to manage the frustrations that often confront new ideas and difficult situations.

Sources:
<http://softtribe.com/about_us/index.htm>;
<http://www.bbc.co.uk/worldservice/specials/1631_judges/pge5.shtml>;

<http://inc.com/magazine/20081001/meet-the-bill-gates-of-ghana_Printer_Friend>;
<http://wipo.int/wipo_magazine/en/2005/02/article_0006.html>.

The above profile on Herman Chinery-Hesse demonstrates the difference between leadership and management. Herman is a definitely a leader. He is a leader because he has a vision of where he sees himself and his organisation. This vision inspires others to follow him and assist in implementing his goals. SOFTtribe is like any other organisation - local but impacted on by global forces. Without Herman's leadership, SOFTtribe would be just another idea.

The impact and importance of leadership

The term 'leader' has a positive connotation for most people. There may be different expectations of business, political or community leaders in different contexts. However, in all cases it is important to remember that leaders have followers—that is, people whom they influence.

There is an assumption underlying the study of leadership that leaders affect the performance of organisations. Leaders, through their actions and personal influence, bring about change. People who control organisations—i.e. the highest level executives—make the same assumption, as do many business commentators. It is not uncommon for the share price of a business to be affected—both positively and negatively—by a change in leadership at the top of an organisation. Many boards will even replace leaders in an effort to improve the performance of an organisation.

The belief that leaders actually influence organisational performance and morale is so plausible that very little research has been conducted into the issue. The very existence of leadership throughout time and cultures suggests that leadership is considered critical to most groups of people. A number of studies have supported this view, with the members of organisations responding positively to the influence of their leaders.

Attribution theory

However, there have also been some other attempts to understand this perception of leadership impact. An understanding of such perceptions derives from 'attribution theory', the process of attributing causality to events. Gary Yukl (1994) explains that organisations are complex social systems of interactions between people. In their efforts to understand and simplify organisational events, people interpret events in simple human terms. One especially strong and prevalent explanation of organisational events is to attribute causality to leaders. Leaders are viewed as heroes and heroines who determine the fate of their organisations. So, for example, the extraordinary success of the airline Virgin Blue is attributed to Richard Branson, its chief executive. The question might be: 'Which came first—exceptional leadership ability on the part of Branson or business success which was then attributed to Branson?'

The leadership substitute concept

Arguments are also made that leadership is not required, and that there are a number of substitutes for leadership. These substitutes include:

- a work environment that provides guidance and incentives to perform;
- closely knit teams;
- intrinsic satisfaction with one's job;
- computer technology; and
- professional norms (Howell *et al.* 1990).

Although the 'leadership substitute' concept has some merit, it reflects naïveté about the role of organisational leadership. Bass (1990) notes that self management by groups and individuals requires delegation by a higher authority that sets the direction and provides guidance, encouragement and support.

A framework for understanding leadership

Many different theories and explanations of leadership have been developed over the years because of the interest in leadership as a practice and as a research topic. Several attempts have been made to integrate the large number of leadership theories into one comprehensive framework (Chemers 1997; Locke 1991). The framework presented in Figure 1.1 looks at the three major elements of the leadership process. These elements have been researched widely, and thus we know a great deal about each of them. But it is the way the three come together that leads to effective leadership.

Leadership is a process. For it to be effective all three elements in the diagram have to work together: the characteristics and behaviour of the **leader**, the culture and characteristics of the **followers**, and the **context**, whether industry or politics, in stable or unstable times, in developing or developed economies.

Figure 1.1 Elements of the leadership process

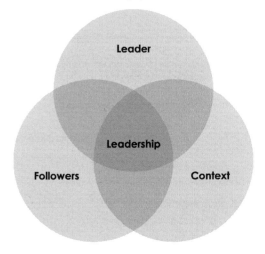

The first element is made up of the leader's characteristics and traits, and the resulting behaviour. These qualities enable the leader to undertake the leadership roles, and often determine how these roles are fulfilled.

The second element is group member/follower characteristics. This refers to the attributes of the people who could have a bearing on how effective the leadership attempt will be. Well-motivated group members, for example, can facilitate the leader's doing an outstanding job. These characteristics may include attitudes, cultural background, educational levels and expectations as well as many other possible attributes.

The third element is the situation — i.e. the internal and external environment — which also influences leadership effectiveness. A leader in a culturally diverse environment, for example, will need to have multicultural skills to be effective. The situation is different in times of war than in times of peace, in times of change rather than times of stability, and in small rather than large organisations. Every situation has its own very specific set of circumstances that can influence leader effectiveness.

Where these three dimensions intersect sits effective leadership. There needs to be synergy between the leader, the followers and the context. The greater the synergy, the greater leadership effectiveness, and the greater the chance of the group achieving their stated objectives in a manner that is rewarding for all those involved.

Summary

Leadership is the ability to inspire confidence in and support among the people who are needed to achieve organisational goals. This may include people over whom the leader has no formal authority. The current international context of leadership — with the advent of information technology, globalisation, concerns about social responsibility, and the environment in a period of rapid change — presents new challenges for today's leaders. Every country and organisation will also have its own particular leadership challenges.

Examining the roles carried out by leaders contributes to an understanding of what leadership is. A general view of what leaders do states that they:

- focus attention through a compelling vision;
- communicate meaning to their followers;
- develop trust through reliability and integrity; and
- manage themselves through self-awareness and positive self-regard.

John Gardner (1989), in his book *On Leadership*, identifies what he believes to be the tasks and roles of leaders. These include:

- envisioning goals,

- affirming values,

- motivating,

- managing,

- achieving workable unity,

- explaining,

- serving as a symbol,

- representing the group, and

- renewing.

What followers expect from leaders can be important in ensuring effectiveness. One study identified that the most significant abilities and attributes that managers wanted from their leaders were (in order of importance starting with the most important):

- the ability to see the long term;

- the ability to communicate well;

- self awareness; trustworthiness;

- the ability to create a vision;

- understanding of the organisational culture;

- enthusiasm;

- integrity;

- optimism; and

- the ability to give and take feedback.

The framework for understanding leadership presented here is based on the idea that the leadership process is a function of the leader, group members, and other situational variables, and that leadership effectiveness is dependent on a synergy between the three sets of variables.

Reflection on your leadership practice

Would you like to be a leader? If you are already in a leadership position, would you like to improve the way you lead others? Why?

What do you think are the particular challenges for leaders in your organisation and also in a rapidly changing world?

References

Bass, BM 1990, *Bass & Stogdill's Handbook of Leadership: Theory, Research, & Managerial Applications*, Free Press, New York.

Bennis, W 1989, *On Becoming a Leader*, Addison Wesley Publishing Company.

Burns, JM 1978, *Leadership*, Harper & Row, New York.

Chemers, MM 1997, *An Integrative Theory of Leadership*, Lawrence Erlbaum Associates, Mahwah, NJ.

Conger, JA 1992, *Learning to Lead*, Jossey Bass Inc, San Francisco.

Dalglish, C & Evans, P 2007, *Leadership in the Australian Context*, Tilde University Press.

Deary, JJA 1996, '(Latent) Big Five Personality Model in 1915? A re-analysis of Webb's Data', *Journal of Applied Psychology* 71, no. 5, 1996 pp. 992-1005.

Farquhar, L 2007, 'Doug Hargreaves' in *Leadership in the Australian Context* by Dalglish, C & Evans, P, Tilde University Press, Melbourne.

Fiedler, FE, Chemers, M & Mahar, L 1994, *Improving Leadership effectiveness: the Leader match concept*, 2nd edn, Wiley, New York.

Freiberg, K 1998, 'Leaders as value shapers', *Executive Excellence*, Provo, November.

Gardner, H 1997, *Leading Minds*, Harper Collins.

Gardner, J 1990, *On Leadership*, The Free Press, Macmillan Inc, New York.

Galvin, D 2007, 'Karen Stanton' in *Leadership in the Australian Context*, Tilde University Press, Melbourne.

Greenleaf, R 1977, *The Power of Servant Leadership*, San Francisco, Berret-Koehler Publisher Inc.

Hersey, P, Blanchard, K & Johnson, DE 1997, *Managing Organizational Behavior, Utilizing Human Resources*, Prentice Hall, Upper Saddle River, NJ.

Kotter, JP 1990, *A Force for Change*, The Free Press NY.

Leonard, B 1999, 'From Management to Leadership', *HR Magazine*, January.

Locke, EA & Associates 1991, *The Essence of Leadership: The Four Keys to Leading Successfully*, Lexington/Macmillan, New York.

Mariotti, J 1999, 'The Role of a Leader', *Industry Week*, Cleveland, Feb1.

Schein, E 1985, *Organisational Culture and Leadership*, Jossey-Bass Publishers, San Francisco.

Schneider, SC & Barsoux, J 1997, *Managing Across Cultures*, Prentice Hall, Hemel Hempstead, UK.

Spears, JT 1997, 'Servant Leadership and the Greenleaf Legacy', In Spears, L ed. *Reflections on Leadership*, New York, John Wiley & Sons Ltd.

Weber, M 1947, *The Theory of Social and Economic Organisation*, Free Press, New York

Whetton, DA & Cameron, K.S 1995, *Developing Management* Skills, 3rd edn, Harper Collins, New York.

Wren, JT 1995, *Leaders Companion*, The Free Press, NY.

Yukl, GA 1994, *Leadership in Organisations*, 3rd edn, Prentice Hall, Upper Saddle River, NJ.

Chapter 2

VALUES-DRIVEN LEADERSHIP

CHAPTER CONTENTS

- □ Spotlight: Tim Costello
- □ Introduction
- □ The development of values
- □ Ethics and leadership
- □ Leading an ethical organisation
- □ Codes of ethics
- □ Leader in action: Lars Kolind
- □ Summary
- □ Reflection on your leadership practice

Spotlight: Tim Costello

Values, and action taken as a result of values, have been the foundation of Tim Costello's leadership. Currently Chief Executive of World Vision Australia, Costello is recognised as one of Australia's leading voices on social justice issues.

After ordination as a Baptist minister in 1984, Tim established a socially active ministry at St Kilda Baptist Church between 1986 and 1994. He went on from there to be minister at the Collins Street Baptist Church in Melbourne where he was also executive director of Urban Seed, a Christian not-for-profit outreach service for the urban poor.

His advocacy for the poor and disadvantaged led him to engage actively in the community in a variety of ways.

He has written several books:

- *Streets of Hope: Finding God in St Kilda;*

- *Tips from a Travelling Soul Searcher; and*

- *Wanna Bet? Winners and Losers in Gambling's Luck Myth.*

All explored values in action in an often unforgiving world, and all were part of his own personal journey. Of his appointment as CEO of World Vision Australia he said:

I had always had a sense that my own development, both in terms of spiritual leaning and passion, might be international issues. This is the first step of that journey. (The Age 2003)

As CEO of World Vision Australia he will oversee 400 staff, revenue of $213 million and 300,000 children around the world sponsored by Australians. His vision and values now also have a much higher profile. Since 2004 he has been instrumental in ensuring that issues surrounding global poverty are placed on the national agenda. World Vision raised $100 million for tsunami relief. He played a prominent role in the Make Poverty History campaign and in April 2008 he chaired the Strengthening Communities, supporting the Families and Social Inclusion Committee of the government's 2020 Summit in Canberra. His values-driven leadership has led to other positions including:

- chairman of the National Australia Bank External Stakeholder Forum,

- member of the Alcohol Education and Rehabilitation Foundation, and

- member of the National Aid Advisory Council.

He is highly regarded by the Australian public, having been voted one of Australia's 100 National Living Treasures. His voice will now be heard on a larger stage. He has been an outstanding advocate on a range of social issues in Australia and now he will be an outstanding advocate for the abolition of world poverty.

He believes that young people understand the concept of the global village and the big moral issues facing the world. December 2008 was the 60th anniversary of the Universal Declaration of Human Rights yet over nine million people died from hunger and poverty in 2008. Under-nourished people were estimated at 848 million in 2003–2005. Even in Australia the price of food has risen steeply. Food prices around the world have increased 83% since 2005, making the issue even more important.

There is no doubt that Tim Costello still speaks out on world poverty and continues to urge those in power to accept the challenge and put an end to poverty. He is no longer just Australia's national living treasure but has the potential to lead in a world where his commitment to a clear set of values may contribute to changes in the way the poor are helped.

Sources: World Vision,
<http://www.worldvision.com.au/AboutUs/OurCEO TimCostello.aspx>, accessed 17/05/09; Monash University <www.monash.edu.au/alumni/prominent-alumni/tim-costello.html >, accessed 15/05/09;
Tim Costello takes on world poverty,
<www.theage.com.au/articles/2003>, accessed 17/05/09;
Speakers for Summit '08,
<www.http:b4md.com.au/sum_spk_17.asp>.

The description of Tim Costello highlights the importance of values in effective leadership. The drive and commitment that come from a clear set of values has taken Tim Costello from the local community to the international community. The short profile above also identifies how values can have a critical role in addressing some of the critical issues for leaders in the contemporary world. Tim Costello demonstrates the importance of having a clear vision and a set of values that inspires and motivates others. Even in a cynical world, often driven by economic factors and self interest, a clearly articulated set of values can make a difference and inspire others.

Introduction

This chapter explores the concept of values and ethics and their relevance to business leadership. In the light of the excesses of business in the past few years and the failure of so many substantial companies due to improper and even criminal behaviour on the part of organisational leaders, the role of values and ethics in business has been thrown into sharp relief.

Understanding values is important because the leader's personal values may be one of the most important determinants of how power is exercised or constrained. The leader's perceptions and behaviour will also set the tone for how the organisation conducts itself.

Are values relevant in business? Business is in fact no different from other sorts of social interaction where values form the foundation for how we deal with each other and as the recent crises in the banking and financial sectors has indicated, business, like society, cannot operate effectively without trust — and trust is built on an understanding of the values that lie behind actions. Values-driven leadership is a term increasingly being used to emphasise values as the driving force behind successful leadership. This is not a new idea but is increasingly being explored and emphasised as a way of offering coherence to leadership in a rapidly changing, diverse working environment.

Ethics concerns right and wrong. In a global environment this raises many challenges, and understanding how we decide on what is right and wrong becomes increasingly important. The idea that knowing right and wrong happens in some instinctive way ignores the impact of upbringing, culture and individual values and can lead to assumptions about how others behave that has little basis in reality.

With concerns about

- global warming,
- high levels of poverty in a resource rich world, and
- concerns about the impact of pollution on both the environment and people,

social and environmental responsibility is a critical topic for leaders and managers around the world. These issues will be dealt with in more detail in chapter 12 in our discussion of strategic leadership.

All of these issues are interrelated. The values that we develop unconsciously will impact on how we respond to each of these issues and the example we set others.

The development of values

Values can be defined as 'constructs representing generalised behaviours or states of affairs that are considered by the individual to be important' (Gordon 1975, p. 2).

Values are assessed, developed and revised throughout life, but many are relatively established by young adulthood. Values are developed by adopting the values of significant others such as our parents, teachers, family or friends. We adopt values portrayed in the media such as television, radio, internet, music, books and magazines. We reflect, often without being aware of it, the dominant values of our culture and sub-cultures.

Our own life experiences shape our values. Values are personally held beliefs, not facts. They are enduring and provide guidance for personal behaviour and personal goals. Often, however, we are not aware of these values—they are hidden assumptions—and how they constrain or facilitate our ability to take advantage of opportunities. Morality and ethics start with values.

It is possible to divide values into two sets: instrumental values and end (terminal) values. Instrumental values include the values that we use on a regular basis to make decisions about our life. These can include values like hard work, honesty, independence, capable, responsible, imaginative, forgiving, polite, clean, cheerful, courageous, logical. These values are given different weight by different individuals. They are a means to an end.

End (terminal) values generally reflect life long aspirations such as becoming wise, bringing about peace or having a sustainable environment. These include things like freedom, self respect, a comfortable life, social recognition, wisdom, contentedness, equality, a world at peace, national security, salvation (Johnson 2009, pp. 90-91).

Reflections

After reading the examples of instrumental and terminal values listed above and thinking about your own set of values, list both the instrumental and terminal values that you hold dear (for example, stability, honesty, achievement).

Can you identify the factors contributing to you holding these particular values?

Despite the cynicism that exists about the ethical practices of people in some leadership positions, managers with a strong sense of right and wrong do appear to be better leaders. Gordon (1975) reported that a leader's personal values correlated positively with leadership effectiveness.

Ethics and leadership

There is discussion about what 'ethics' are and whether they can be taught. Here we define ethics as the study of morality, and that a person begins to 'do' ethics when he or she turns to look at the moral standards that have been absorbed from family, church, friends and society, and begins to ask whether these standards are reasonable or unreasonable.

Ethics and conduct

Lagan (2000, p. 13) takes a particular perspective on ethics which is useful.

Ethics can be defined as "a set of moral principles or values," a definition that portrays ethics as highly personal and relative. I have my moral principles, you have yours, and neither of us should try to impose our ethics on the other. But our definition of ethics – the principles, norms and standards of conduct governing an individual or group – focuses on conduct.

This focus on conduct is particularly important in a global business environment where we may not be familiar with the particular ethical frameworks that our international partners are using. By focussing on behaviour rather than belief, what happens in the organisation can be focussed on without making judgement about possible differences in values. In the business world it is behaviour that talks loudest.

Leaders face ethical dilemmas all the time and the best leaders recognise and face them with a commitment to doing what is right, not just what is expedient. Leaders set a moral example to others that becomes the model for an entire group or organisation, for good or bad. Leaders who themselves do not honour truth do not inspire it in others. Leaders mostly concerned with their own advancement do not inspire selflessness in others. Leaders should have a strong set of ethics, principles of right conduct, or a system of moral values. Ethics and moral values spring from those things in life which are important to the individual. Not all values have an ethical dimension, but all values influence the way leaders behave, their perception of right and wrong and the way they make decisions.

Unethical behaviour

Both Gardner (1990) and Burns (1978) have stressed the centrality and importance of the moral dimension of leadership. Gardner asserts leaders ultimately must be judged on the basis of a framework of values, not just in terms of their effectiveness.

Several researchers have reported that individuals with strong value systems tend to behave more ethically. However, certain types of situations increase the likelihood of unethical behaviour from people, regardless of their value systems. Such situations tend to be highly competitive and unsupervised. Unethical behaviour was found to be more likely to occur when there was no formal ethics policy governing behaviour, when there was no threat of punishment for unethical behaviour, and when unethical behaviour was actually rewarded.

In this context, studies exploring opinions about unethical behaviours or practices in the workplace have yielded fairly disturbing results. A 1988 Harris poll reported that 89% of 1200 workers and managers surveyed believed it was important for leaders to be upright, honest and ethical in their dealings. However, only 41% indicated their current supervisor had these characteristics. Another Harris poll, conducted in 1989, reported that many individuals believed business would purposely sell unsafe products, risk employee health and safety, and harm the environment.

Activity 2.1

Are there businesses with which you work that would knowingly conduct business in a way that harmed the environment, endangered public health, sold unsafe products, sold inferior products, charged inflated prices or risked employee health and safety?

Give examples of this behaviour and discuss why you believe that this behaviour occurs.

If we think of organisations as communities, the need for ethical behaviour becomes apparent. And behaviour is what matters. Ethics in an organisation is learnt by the actions you take, not by the values you espouse. Actions speak louder than words.

Lagan (2000, p. 194) describes what an ethical organisation might look like:

> *When you see an organisation with energised and positive employees who enjoy coming to work; one that has a reputation for customer service and stakeholder involvement; one that is clear about who it is; one that jealously guards its reputation and is at pains to recruit in its own likeness to safeguard its core identity and protect it from contamination – then chances are you have been dealing with an ethical organisation.*

Leading an ethical organisation

An ethical organisation is one that strives to live its values and to make these clear to all who have a relationship with it. It may not be a perfect company but simply one that is still learning and growing, always keen to improve its performance. The leadership of the organisation is critical in developing an ethical culture. Without an example from the top it won't happen.

Rightness and wrongness

So how does a leader create such an organisation and make the appropriate decisions? Velasquez (1998, p. 137) provides an action guiding statement:

An action is morally right if in carrying out the action the agent exercises, exhibits, or develops a morally virtuous character, and it is morally wrong to the extent that by carrying out the action the agent exercises, exhibits, or develops a morally vicious character.

From this perspective, then, the wrongfulness of an action can be determined by examining the kind of character the action tends to produce or the kind of character that tends to produce the action. If the decision to engage in such actions tends to develop a person's character by making them more responsible, more caring, more principled (or any other moral virtue) then such actions are morally right. However, if the decision to engage in such actions tends to make people more self-centred, more selfish, more dishonest (moral vices) then these actions are morally wrong.

We live in a world community and we are all inextricably connected to each other, whether we like it or not, and to the environment around us. A sustainable future depends on our caring about others and our environment. Most human decision making is based on ethical and emotional considerations as well as economic self-interest. This must be reflected in leadership behaviour if it is to be effective over the long term.

Reasons for ethical behaviour

Given recent corporate history, there appear to be compelling reasons to spend more time thinking and talking about ethics — and the importance of ethical behaviour. There are a number of very good reasons for both individuals and organisations to be ethical.

Some of them are listed here. Add other reasons to the list. I am sure that you can identify them.

- People who know that they are working for something larger and more noble than themselves can be expected to be more inspired — and perhaps work harder. Think of all the voluntary work that is done particularly in the not-for-profit sector.

- A reputation for ethics which is beyond reproach is a 'silent partner' in negotiations, between individuals or organisations. Trust is a vital part of any agreement or contract so it is easier to do business with someone who is ethical.

- We all like to feel proud of what we do and the organisation we work for. Reputation counts. As John Akers [cited on page 27 Trevino, Linda K & Nelson, K (2004)] argues:

    No society anywhere will compete very long or successfully with people stabbing each other in the back ... with people trying to steal from each other... There is no escaping this fact; the greater the measure of mutual trust and confidence in the ethics of a society, the greater its economic strength.

There are two major elements to any program to establish ongoing ethical behaviour in an organisation — namely:

- a shared organisation purpose and value system, and

- members who have professional self esteem, self confidence and commitment (Dalglish 1991).

Leaders determine whether these two elements are present in an organisation.

Establishing ethical behaviour in an organisation

If members of any organisation are to behave ethically, the leaders of that organisation must articulate a set of values and standards and these values and standards must be understood and shared by its members. The value system provides a foundation for all the actions in and by the organisation, including action by members, delivery of products and services and the development of organisational practices and policies. To achieve this, the values must be overt and the policies, systems and management practices in the organisation must be consistent with that value system. A code of ethics may be one of the ways in which these values are shared but it is only the first step.

The organisation leader serves as a role model, and actions speak louder than words. What happens at the top of an organisation provides examples for the rest of the members. Appropriate policies can also thwart temptations towards corruption or unethical behaviour and provide support when there are incidents where conflict of interest, discrimination or other dubious behaviour are possible.

One of the most common ways of dealing with misconduct and infringement of ethical codes is trough disciplinary action, after the event when much of the damage has already been done. There are circumstances where this is entirely appropriate. However it is better for everyone if misconduct does not occur. Leadership and management practices need to ensure that everyone is aware of what is expected of them and that ethical behaviour is rewarded.

As indicated by Semler (1994) in the establishment of his business, the ethical route is often not easy and individuals need support and a strong sense of professional identity and self confidence if they are to respond appropriately in difficult and complex situations. There is no easy or certain way to ensure the ethical behaviour of all members of any organisation. A code of conduct or ethics is only the beginning. They set ethical expectations that can help guide people in making decisions in whatever situations they encounter. The way the organisation is led — i.e. the example of the leader — is likely to have a greater impact on behaviour than any set of rules. What is crucial, however, is the development of professional pride in the members of the organisation in living up to the values articulated, and the self confidence and self esteem to enable the individual to behave as he or she would like to behave. Personal mastery (Senge 1990) is a critical element in the development of an ethical organisation.

Codes of ethics

Many ethical choices are easy to make — they clearly pit right against wrong. But this is not always the case; sometimes we are faced with a conflict between two or more values, rights or obligations and we have to choose between two equally unpleasant alternatives. That is when understanding your own values and those of the community you are leading are important.

Ethical dilemmas

When faced with a business decision it is important to recognise that there are a number of layers to any decision-making process. One obviously is the economic outcome, the cost/benefit analysis. However, many decisions also have an ethical dimension. Ethics is the moral perspective that asks you to judge the decision in terms of what is right and wrong, what's decent. The reason to be ethical is simply that it's the right thing to do. You can be fairly certain that during the course of your career, and in fact in other aspects of your life, you'll run into many ethical dilemmas. The solution is not always easy or evident.

There are a number of areas of business where ethical issues are common — namely:

- *Human resource issues.* Managing people is vital to any successful endeavour yet managing human resources can be a minefield of ethical dilemmas. These human resource issues can include privacy, discrimination, sexual and other types of harassment, performance evaluation, and hiring and firing.

- *Conflict of interest.* A conflict of interest occurs when your judgment or objectivity is compromised. The appearance of a conflict of interest can be just as damaging as an actual conflict.

- *Use of corporate resources.* This can vary from the misuse of travel expenses, to using corporate property for private use, and to exploiting the company's reputation.

Activity 2.2

With a small group of peer managers or colleagues identify an ethical issue that has arisen in your organisation and the factors contributing to it. How was it resolved? How would you resolve it?

Thoughtful managers/leaders often face business problems that raise difficult, deeply personal questions. The modern world does not always make it easy for individual managers or leaders to choose the 'right' course of action from those available. How much of yourself—of what you care about and believe in—do you have to sacrifice to get ahead?

Codes of conduct

One way that organisations assist their employees to deal with ethical issues is through a code of conduct or code of ethics.

Codes of ethics are among the most common ethics tools. Most large organisations have such a code, though often staff are not aware of it—nor does it necessarily coincide with custom, practice and policy. Sceptics make some of these criticisms (Johnson 2009):

- Codes are often too vague to be useful.

- Codes are often not distributed widely or read and understood.

- Codes can become the final word on the subject of ethics and remove the incentive for responsible decision making in different contexts.

- Codes can be difficult to apply across cultures and in different situations.

- Codes often lack adequate enforcement.

- Adherence to codes often goes unrewarded.

Johnson (2009) cites the example of Enron. Company officials had a code of ethics that specifically prohibited the kinds of off-the-books financial deals that led to its bankruptcy. Enron often claimed the ethical high ground and yet these executives convinced the board of directors to waive this prohibition.

Defenders of codes point to their potential benefits. A code describes the organisation's ethical stance towards both its members and the outside world. It can provide guidance for behaviour and improve the organisation's image with customers and regulators. However, ethical behaviour must be supported by organisational processes; ethical behaviour rewarded and unethical behaviour punished if the code is to have any real meaning.

Most codes of ethics address the following aspects of organisational behaviour.

- *Conflict of interest.* Conflict of interest arises when an employee cannot exercise independent judgement because of association with another party which could lead to the employee benefiting at the cost of the organisation. Even the appearance of conflicts of interest can be problematic.

- *Confidentiality of information.* Even in the public sector where freedom of information encourages the sharing of information with the public, confidentiality if some matter remains important.

- *Employment practices.* Practices like sexual harassment, discrimination and other human resource issues.

- *Relationships with outside organisations.* Relationships with outside organisations like contractors, customers, suppliers and competitors.

- *The protection of organisational assets.* Organisations must keep accurate records and protect funds and other assets.

Increasingly they may also include elements related to environmental and social responsibility.

Activity 2.3

With a small group of peer managers or colleagues examine the code of conduct for your organisation. How useful do you believe the code to be? How would you change it? What would the organisation need to do to ensure that the code of ethics provided the real basis for organisational member behaviour?

Leader in action: Lars Kolind

The knowledge-based corporation is not only a vision. For me it is a reality. (Lars Kolind)

From 1988 to 1998 Lars Kolind was CEO of Oticon Holdin A/S (now William Dermant Holdin A/A), a hearing-aid company. Lars initiated a complete reorganisation of the company, which led to a dramatic increase in turnover and profits. These changes were driven by a clearly articulated set of values.

Lars Kolind was born in 1947 in Denmark. He is an entrepreneur who has worked in Europe, Latin America, the USA and the Asia Pacific Region, and saw his market as global. He transformed Oticon, a traditional manufacturing business, into a knowledge-based organisation using values rather that structure as the basis for growth. He now chairs his own business discovery fund, Preventure A/A. He has received several awards including Denmark's *Man of the Year* in 1976.

So what did the transformation involve? What was Lars Kolind's leadership role in leading the changes at Oticon?

Oticion tripled its return on investment, increased sales growth, reduced time to market, opened new markets for existing products and launched two new product lines in two-and-a-half years—a desirable set of traditional outcomes. To do this, however, Oticon broke with tradition. Kolind lead Oticon to redefine its business, shifting the emphasis from medical hearing-aids for people with hearing impairments to a focus on hearing and quality of life for everyone. Kolind introduced a value proposition about using the organisation's core competencies related to filtering out background noise (a key element in a successful hearing-aid) to identify a whole new potential market.

Values were also a very important part of how the change came about. These values emerged after hundreds of hours of discussions and became the framework which guided the changes. Four principles were identified as critical to bringing about successful change—namely:

- *Choice*. Employees may choose their projects, the training they need and the hours they work.

- *Multi-job*. Everyone is expected to work on a project outside of his or her core competence. This is seen as a way of developing people and enabling them to see their primary competency in a different light.

- *Transparency*. Almost all information is available to everyone.

- *No controls.* Projects emerge based on opportunity, need and interest.

Alignment around these principles gave Oticon the ability to respond rapidly and flexibly to new opportunities.

The articulated values were supported by the actions of the company.

To develop the necessary skills for use of the new computer system, Oticon supplied everyone with a similar computer at home and the employees formed a computer club to support one another's learning <www.kee-inc.com/article 14/9/2004>.

The vision has not been something separate from the day-to-day activity of the organisation. It has involved everyone in the organisation and encouraged different ways of behaving and different ways of looking at their roles and responsibilities within the organisation. The transformation at Oticon involved a rethinking of what working in an organisation involves, and developing systems and processes that support the values and maximise the involvement of everyone concerned.

Sources:
<www.entovation.com/kleadmap/kolind.htm>;
 <www.kee-inc.com/article 14/9/2004>;
<www.zp.dk/company_profiles.ilko.html>;
<www.euintangibles.net/conferences/20_speakeers/view_person_html>

Dubrin, A, Dalglish, C & Miller, P 2006, *Leadership 2nd Asia Pacific Edition*, Milton, Qld, John Wiley and Sons.

The above profile on Lars Kolind shows the critical importance and place of values in modern organisations. There must be an alignment and coherence between the values espoused by the organisation and those of its people, and in particular the leaders of the organisation. But having the right values is just one side of the coin. The values must be supported and role modelled by action and this requires leaders to involve everyone in the organisation.

Managing in a world of conflict

Marcus Aurelius, a Roman emperor, provides some advice for individuals confronting the problems of managing and leading in a world full of conflicts. They appear as valid today as they were when he wrote them. He suggests three lessons for escaping the tyranny of the here-and-now and providing guidance for some of life's more difficult decisions — namely:

- Retreat;
- Search for 'lived truths'; and
- Keep the imagined 'best life' in view.

Retreat

Remove yourself from human interaction and reflect. He writes, 'Are you distracted towards outward cares? Then allow yourself a space of quiet, wherein you can add to your knowledge of the Good and learn to curb your restlessness.' He tells himself 'Nowhere can a man find a quieter or more untroubled retreat than in his own soul.' And again, 'Avail yourself often, then, of this retirement, and so continually renew yourself' (Badaracco 1997, p. 124).

Search for 'lived truths'

Reflect on what you can learn from the lives and experiences of people you know well, work hard at becoming astute, probing, insightful observers of the lives, efforts and experiences of the people around you.

Keep the imagined 'best life' in view

Act now; be concerned with now but in the context of a comprehensive picture of your 'best imagined' life. Marcus created a mental sketch or collage of the virtues, skills, activities, commitments, habits and values he prized and wanted to make his own. The composite picture Marcus created for himself includes:

- ways of being a friend,
- showing affection to children,
- dealing with flatterers,
- showing courtesy,

- practising self-control, and

- worshipping the gods, and serving the community.

The examples often belong to others, but the combination is Marcus's own.

Thus he begins meditations with the picture of an 'imagined best life' — an image of the life he wanted to live (Badaracco 1997, p. 130).

Activity 2.4: Self assessment

Answer the following questions to see whether you are preparing yourself to make hard decisions and be able to take a leadership perspective.

- How do you escape from the stresses of your daily life? Some activities that would help this could include bush walking, fishing, meditation, long walks on the beach, and gardening.

- How often do you 'make your escape'?

- If you don't currently make time for reflection, what could you do and how often?

- Who do you admire?

- What is it about them that you would like to emulate? Be specific.

- How can you go about developing these capabilities?

- What does your 'perfect' life look like? Be specific. Identify the values that you hold most dear. How can these always be part of your life?

The outcome of this activity will provide you with a strong base for value-driven leadership because you will be clear about what is important and have an opportunity to reflect on how to make it happen; and you will have strategies to deal with the many challenges that come your way.

Summary

This chapter has explored values and ethics and their relationship to leadership. As a result of so many corporate scandals over the past few years, the role of values and ethics in business has been thrown into sharp relief.

Understanding values is important because the leader's personal values may be one of the most important determinants of how power is exercised or constrained. The leader's perceptions and behaviour will also set the tone for how the organisation conducts itself. Values are developed by adopting the values of significant others and from our own experience. We are often not aware of how our personal values and the dominant values of our culture and sub-cultures impact on our beliefs and decision making.

Both Gardner (1990) and Burns (1978) have stressed the centrality and importance of the moral dimension of leadership. Although there has been debate about whether effective leadership should be judged on the basis of a framework of moral values, there is an increasing belief within communities at large that ethical behaviour and a clearly articulated value position are important to effective leadership in a changing and ambiguous world.

Given recent corporate history, there appear to be compelling reasons to spend more time thinking and talking about ethics and the importance of ethical behaviour. We all like to feel proud of what we do and the organisation we work for. A reputation for ethical behaviour is a positive partner in any contract or negotiation. Trust is a vital part of any agreement or contract so it is easier to do business with someone who is ethical.

Codes of ethics are among the most common tools for encouraging ethical behaviour in organisations. There are many critics who argue that codes are often not distributed widely and lack adequate enforcement—that they can be simply a public relations exercise, that they cannot cover all eventualities and can remove the incentive for thoughtful, responsible decision making. However, a code can describe the organisation's ethical stance towards both its members and the outside world and provide guidance for behaviour and improve the organisation's image with customers and regulators. For a code to be meaningful, ethical behaviour must be supported by organisational processes, ethical behaviour rewarded and unethical behaviour punished.

Reflection on your leadership practice

Refer back to the set of values you articulated for yourself earlier in this chapter. Do your own values accord with the espoused values of the organisation you work for? If the answer to this question is 'yes', are these values in use in the daily actions of the leaders in the organisation or are the values just recorded on paper in a values or mission statement? If the answer to this question is 'no', there is really only two options for you. The first option is for you to find another organisation to employ you where your values and the values of the organisation are aligned. The second options is that you take action to change (or enforce) the espoused values of the organisation you are in. The second option is only for the brave and you will need to be very senior in the organisation to have any chance of success. It will require a major cultural shift and change program (see chapter 11).

References

ABC News, 2009, *Foodbank braces for rising demand*, viewed 4 May 2009 <http://www.abc.net.au/ news/stories/2009/05/04>.

Badaracco, JL Jr. 1997, *Defining Moments: When Managers Must Choose Between Right and Right*, Harvard Business School Press.

Burns, JM 1978, *Leadership*, New York: Harper and Row.

Dalglish C, 1991, 'Managing for ethical behaviour in the public service'. Paper given as evidence to an EARC committee hearing on ethics in the Public Service.

Dubrin, A, Dalglish, C & Miller, P 2006 *Leadership 2nd Asia Pacific Edition*, Milton, Qld: John Wiley and Sons, Australia England.

Foodbank, 2009, *John Webster to head Foodbank Australia*, viewed 5 June 2009, <http://nqr.farmonline.com.au/news/ accessed 27/7/2009>.

Foodbank, 2009, *An Australia without Hunger*, viewed 27 July 2009, <http://www.foodbank.com.au>.

Gardner, JW 1990, *On Leadership*, New York: The Free Press, A Division of Macmillan.

Gordon, LV 1975, *Measurement of Interpersonal Values*. Chicago, IL: Science Research Associates.

Herbert, B, 2009, *Not for Profit*, viewed 27 July 2009, <http://www.abc.net.au/landline>.

Johnson, CE 2009, *Meeting the Ethical Challenges of Leadership*, 3rd edn, Sage, Los Angeles.

Kruger, A 2008, *World bank and food security*, viewed 11 February 2008, <http://www.abc,net.au/ landline/content/2006/>.

Lagan, A 2000, *Why Ethics Matter*, Information Australia.

Monash University, viewed 15 May 2009 <www.monash.edu.au/ alumni/prominent-alumni/tim-costello.html>.

Palmer, D *Food and grocery industry continues to head toward the floor the need for food relief has gone through the roof*, viewed 27 July 2009, <http:www.ausfoodnews.com.au>.

St. Mary's Food Bank Alliance, viewed 27 July 2009, <http:// www.firstfoodbank.org/ history.html>.

Semler, R 1994, *Maverick*, Arrow, London.

Senge, PM 1994, *The Fifth Discipline*, Random House, Sydney.

Speakers for Summit, 2008, <www.http:b4md.com.au/sum_spk_ 17.asp>.

The Age, *Tim Costello takes on world poverty*, viewed 17 May 2009, <www.theage.com.au /articles/2003>.

Trevino, Linda, K & Nelson, K 2004, *Managing Business Ethics,* 3rd edn, John Wiley & Sons, Milton.

Velasquez, MG 1998, *Business Ethics Concepts and Cases*, 4th edn. Englewood Cliffs, NJ: Prentice-Hall.

World Vision, viewed 17 May 2009, <http://www.worldvision. com.au/AboutUs/ OurCEOTimCostello.aspx>.

www.entovation.com/kleadmap/kolind.htm.

www.kee-inc.com/article 14 September 2004.

www.zp.dk/company_profiles.ilko.html.

www.euintangibles.net/conferences/20_speakeers/view_person_html.

Chapter 3

DEVELOPING SELF AWARENESS

CHAPTER CONTENTS

☐ Introduction

☐ Spotlight: Julie Hammer

☐ Reflective learning

☐ Personal mastery

☐ Emotional intelligence

☐ Leader in action: Charles Handy

☐ Mentoring and coaching

☐ Servant leadership

☐ Summary

☐ Reflection on your leadership practice

Spotlight: Julie Hammer

Julie Hammer was, until her recent retirement, the most senior woman in the Australian Defence Force (ADF), having reached the rank of Air Vice Marshall. She joined the Royal Australian Air Force (RAAF) in 1977 and a year later the RAAF recruited its first female officer. Though there have been many changes over the years, the RAAF remains primarily a male-dominated environment. By being aware of her own skills and the environment in which she worked, Julie had a significant role in making it possible for women to be successful within the defence forces.

Julie graduated from the University of Queensland as a physicist and couldn't find a job. The RAAF offered her a job as an education officer; she thought she would take it until a 'proper' job came along. That was 28 years ago. In 1981 she requested a transfer to the engineering branch. The engineering branch had never before employed either a woman or a person with a physics degree. Because of her studies in physics she was used to a male-dominated environment; the engineering field suited her well.

I'm not one of the boys; that wouldn't work for me. It meant just getting on and doing the job until the troops recognised that I was actually as competent as the male engineers – and maybe a bit more so than some.

In 1985 Julie became the first female engineer to be promoted to squadron leader. In 1992 she became the first woman to command an operational unit in the RAAF, the Electronic Warfare Squadron (EWSQN). This was a controversial appointment. More controversial even than having a woman commanding officer of an operational squadron was having an engineer in an aircrew job. She was promoted to Air Commodore in December 1999, the first time a female serving officer had achieved One Star rank. In 2003, when she was appointed Air Vice Marshall, she became the first woman to reach Two Star rank.

Julie has what appears to be a simple philosophy—be self aware.

Do what you are good at—and do the very best you can. You need to discover what you enjoy and focus on that. What is most important is that you work hard at whatever you do.

She places great emphasis on knowing your own abilities because then you can have confidence in yourself. Her advice to those starting out includes:

- Know your own strengths and weaknesses better than anybody else.

- Have confidence in your abilities, making sure that this confidence is liberally tinged with reality.

- Don't be bound by restrictions others may put in your way. Make sure you don't allow other people to put artificial barriers in your path.

- Set goals for yourself—and set them high.

- Don't adopt a leadership style at odds with your natural character.

- Don't pretend you are perfect, know everything and never make mistakes. Be natural, be yourself.

Even if at the moment you are unsure of where you see your future heading, your goals should be to be the best you possibly can at what you are currently doing.

In 2005 Julie was named Australian Capital Territory Australian of Year.

Source: Adapted from 'Julie Hammer' by Sharlene Roach, in Dalglish C & Evans P, *Leadership in the Australian Context*, Tilde University Press, Melbourne, Australia, 2007.

Overall, the profile on Julie Hammer demonstrates that for effective leadership, Julie emphasises knowing yourself, knowing your values and beliefs, and creating a bond of trust between yourself and team members. This requires a great deal of self awareness and being comfortable in your own skin.

Introduction

In the first section of this book we are exploring the role of the person as leader—how his or her characteristics and behaviour impact on leadership effectiveness. It suggests that understanding yourself, your strengths and weaknesses, and your own values and culture are an integral part of being able to respond effectively in a range of leadership situations. Not being self aware may lead to action that destroys confidence; it may even lead followers into harm.

Characteristics of future leaders

Bennis (1989) identifies what he believes will be the characteristics required of future leaders—leaders who will be able to respond effectively to the rapidly changing circumstances and great diversity of challenges presented by the 21st century. The characteristics include:

- a broad education,
- boundless curiosity,
- boundless enthusiasm,
- belief in people and teamwork,
- willingness to take risks,
- devotion to long-term growth rather than short-term profit,
- commitment to excellence,
- readiness and preparedness for the role or situation,
- virtue, and
- vision.

Education

The challenges of the future will require a range of different perspectives which are provided by a broad rather than a narrow technical education.

Curiosity

Curiosity is the driving force behind innovation and understanding the unfamiliar — both important behaviours in the 21st century.

Enthusiasm

As will be seen from the study undertaken into follower expectations of effective leaders — enthusiasm is considered very important.

Belief in people

No leadership will be viable unless it is founded on a belief in people and teamwork.

Risk taking

Taking risks does not mean being foolhardy — but leadership is often about moving into the unknown.

Devotion to long-term growth

This is a critical and very challenging perspective. Frequently we are judged on our short-term outcomes — but effective leadership often depends on building trust and developing the organisation's ability to respond and grow, rather than the instant success of individuals.

Commitment to excellence

Nobody wants to follow someone who does a poor job — or does not expect good things from them.

Readiness for the role or situation

Leaders often fail because they take on tasks that they are not competent to complete. This failure will stay with them. It is important that any leader is sufficiently self aware to know what they can and cannot take on, so that they can ensure that they have the necessary intellectual resources (theirs or someone else's) necessary to complete the task.

Virtue

People prefer to follow those they believe to be virtuous.

Vision

An ability to see how the future could look is an integral part of being able to lead people there.

What business expects of its leaders

In 2001/2 a study was undertaken in Australia, South Africa and Denmark to identify what business managers expected of their leaders. The questionnaire was framed around Bennis's suppositions about what would be required for effective leaders. The managers were asked to rank the qualities/abilities that they wanted in an effective leader. The following are the top 10 answers.

1. The ability to think long term
2. Good communication skills
3. Self awareness
4. Trustworthiness
5. Having vision
6. Understanding local/organisational culture
7. Enthusiasm
8. Integrity
9. Optimism
10. The ability to give constructive feedback

The biggest surprise in this list was the importance given to self awareness — it is not often a characteristic discussed in the literature or in organisations. It does, however, explain why self awareness has a chapter of its own in this book.

Leadership is not only about understanding concepts but about being able to examine your own behaviours and attitudes, and make adjustments as necessary. As you progress through this chapter and this book, you will be provided with many opportunities to examine yourself as a leader. The last part of the chapter provides a framework for creating a leadership development plan to improve your leadership skills. To move forward and improve, you have to understand where you are. Self awareness provides that insight.

Reflective learning

Underpinning our understanding of the leadership process is the concept that 'to understand leadership is to understand yourself'. Effective leaders are aware of how they respond to different situations, they are aware of their impact on others, they understand human interaction and the role their behaviour and actions play in bringing about effective outcomes.

Reflective learning is a well grounded theory based on the capacity of an individual to reflect on their own words and actions and to undertake a learning process through such reflection. There are various tools available to allow us to develop this skill and attribute.

Double-loop learning

Double-loop learning (Argyris 1991) is an in-depth type of learning that occurs when people use feedback to confront the validity of the goal or values implicit in the situation. So when something occurs that makes you question your role in a particular situation, you not only observe the action, you actually ask yourself: 'What could I have done to improve the outcome?' Double-loop learning enables a leader to profit from setbacks; interpreting the reason why a setback occurs and learning from that experience so that it does not occur again is a desirable outcome.

Single-loop learning

Single-loop learning occurs when a leader observes a negative situation and says: 'that it is interesting'. There is no analysis of why the situation occurred or of their role in the process. Often single-loop learning picks up only on the feedback that substantiates an already held view.

A reflective journal

One way of developing self awareness is through the keeping of a reflective journal, recording personal events. Self awareness and understanding are developed by reflecting or thinking about aspects of these events in terms of one's emotional reactions, and one's behaviours.

A reflective journal can help us highlight those aspects of our behaviour that we may seek to change; it offers us insights into the process of how to bring about change.

In a reflective journal you record:

- the incident,

- your reaction,

- your reflection, and

- your realisation.

The process provides an opportunity to learn from events that happen around you, whether at work or socially. It does not require lots of writing; it is usually more effective as a learning tool if kept to a page in length. Its power comes from brevity and honesty rather than long-winded justifications or discussions where remedial actions get lost in words. The four headings are a guide to help us focus our thoughts in a positive and constructive way.

Incident

Begin by picking any incident where you were surprised or disappointed with the outcome of the encounter. Perhaps you failed to make a point effectively or one of your colleagues reacted unexpectedly to a suggestion you made. You may record the meeting or discussion and identify some particular aspect that you discussed that caused you concern or discomfort — e.g. *'My colleague raised the issue of how I respond to certain staff and suggested that ...'*

Reaction

Write down how you reacted to the incident. It is important here that you are completely honest with yourself. This is often an emotional statement — e.g. *'I felt confronted by my colleague's observation. I became angry and defensive.'*

Reflection

Consider why you reacted as you did. What caused you to have that reaction? Why was it so negative/positive? — e.g. *'Later on I analysed my reaction and realised that I don't like facing up to some of my negative points. By my colleague raising this issue I have to face something that I don't often think about.'*

Realisation

What can you learn from this incident? How can you improve in this situation? What behaviour was identified here? — e.g. *'On reflection I realise that I often respond to staff in such a way and that it is not conducive to better relationships. I need to become aware of this response and to learn to respond differently.'*

The process outlined here requires commitment and time to gain the maximum benefit from it. However, it opens up excellent learning opportunities; it enables learning to become an integral part of your life.

Personal mastery

Peter Senge, a well respected management scholar, placed considerable weight on the importance of personal mastery in the development of a successful organisation. It is of equal importance to the development of effective leadership skills, as leadership implies a group of people whether part of a larger organisation or not.

The term 'mastery' has an association with competence, the capacity to 'master' a particular task — but although it is grounded in them, personal mastery goes beyond competence and skills. Senge (1990) states that when personal mastery becomes a discipline, an activity which we integrate into our lives, it embodies two underlying movements:

- Continually clarifying what is important to us as individuals — i.e. what does our personal vision look like?

- Continually learning to see current reality more clearly.

Personal vision

Many of us set goals for ourselves but remarkably few have a clear vision of what we would like our life to be. To be effective in the achievement of personal mastery, this vision has to be very precise. It is often easier to articulate what we do not want, rather than what we do want. When we articulate what we want it is good to ask ourselves why, and to continue with the why question until we uncover what we truly desire. This is not an instant process and may take many periods of reflection to clarify. Often the insight comes at a time of tragedy or crisis, when the status quo of our lives is challenged. It is also important to recognise that the vision may change — as we experience and achieve new things.

What we want from life can and does change. Be clear about these changes. This is important otherwise we may find ourselves achieving a vision we no longer want. The ability to develop and articulate a vision is a critical task for leaders. It is also important that the leader has 'ownership', a personal commitment, to that vision. Where better to start than with your own vision for yourself?

Reflections

If you had to describe the perfect life, what would it look like? What are the values that you need to live by and the goals you need to set, to achieve this perfect life?

Current reality

The second element in the process of developing personal mastery is learning to hold a clear picture of current reality. This is more difficult than it sounds. Frequently we judge current reality in negative terms, with what it is *not* providing us. Our perceptions, our personal way of viewing the world mean that it is often difficult to see the world and our situation as it truly is. All situations provide an opportunity for learning and for the development of knowledge or skills. Most of the negative things that happen in life are not directed at us personally by some malevolent force — they are simply the way the world is and need to be dealt with according to our values; much can often be learnt even from very negative situations.

Reflections

Describe your current situation. What are the positive and negative elements that constitute your current life style? What needs to change to bring your current life style closer to your vision?

Creative tension

Senge (1990) claims that the essence of personal mastery is learning how to generate and sustain creative tension in our lives. Creative tension is generated by the juxtaposition of our vision, what we want, and a clear picture of where we are relative to what we want. This gap is the source of the energy that will enable us to achieve our vision. Imagine a rubber band stretched between your vision and current reality. There are two ways for the tension to resolve itself: pull the vision towards reality (reduce or change the vision) or pull reality towards the vision.

Tension thus created is not negative tension unless we attach negative emotions to the situation, thereby creating emotional tension, often experienced as anxiety. There are two ways of reducing emotional tension:

- take action to bring reality into line with your vision (this takes time and effort), and

- lower your vision (e.g. we may say: *I really didn't want to achieve that anyway*). This response relieves disappointment and discouragement; the price is that we abandon what we really want.

Reflections

Think about a time when you responded to emotional tension by lowering your vision—perhaps when you went for a job and were not successful.

What did you do? How did you feel when you rationalised what happened? How do you feel now?

It is not the vision that is important, per se, so much as what it does. The gap between vision and current reality generates the energy for change.

Structural conflict

All of this may sound very easy but often the greatest barrier to our own achievement is ourselves and the unconscious way we view the world. We nearly always rationalise our view as 'common sense', or 'obvious', especially when we are attributing our lack of success to external factors.

According to Robert Fritz (quoted in Senge 1990, p. 156)

> As children we learn what our limitations are. Children are rightfully taught limitations essential to their survival. But too often this learning is generalised. We are constantly told we can't have or can't do certain things and we may come to assume that we have an inability to have what we want.

Most of us come to hold one of two beliefs that limit our ability to create what we really want—i.e.

- our powerlessness—our inability to bring into being all the things we really care about (this is the voice in our heads that says 'You aren't any good at figures; you can't ...; you have never been able to ...'), and

- our unworthiness—the feeling that we do not deserve to have what we truly desire.

Reflections

Think about the voices that remain with you, often voices of people who were very significant to you as you were growing up, your teachers, your parents, friends and family. What perceptions of you and your ability did they give you?

How have these people influenced your perception of your ability and of yourself as a worthwhile person who deserves success, riches, love?

These beliefs work against us achieving our vision. In most cases we are our own worst enemy. We can develop the knowledge and skills to attain our vision if we allow ourselves to do so.

Characteristics of personal mastery

People with a high level of personal mastery:

- have a special sense of purpose that lies behind their vision and goals,

- see current reality as an ally rather than an enemy,

- are deeply inquisitive, committed to seeing reality more accurately,

- feel connected to others,

- live in a continual learning mode — they never arrive,

- are aware of their ignorance, their incompetence and their growth areas, and

- are self confident.

These would appear to be desirable characteristics for an effective leader.

Emotional intelligence

Goleman (1998) brought the idea of emotional intelligence to the public consciousness with his best-selling book, but researchers and experienced workers have long known that how well a person manages his or her emotions and those of others influences leadership effectiveness. For example, recognising anger in yourself and others, and being able to empathise with people, can help you be more effective at exerting influence.

Jordan *et al.* (2002) argue that emotional intelligence is an individual difference that is important for both leaders and followers. It is an individual difference that like many leadership skills is not fixed for life and can be improved by training and development.

Elements of emotional intelligence

Emotional intelligence refers to qualities like:

- understanding one's feelings,

- empathy for others, and

- the regulation of emotions to enhance living.

This type of intelligence has to do with the ability to connect with people and understand their emotions. These are not skills that form part of most formal curricula in schools or universities. Nor do they often get mentioned as something that needs to be developed in order to be effective in leadership or in life. Mayer and Salovey (1997) define emotional intelligence as the ability to detect and to manage emotional cues and information.

In his research in a number of companies, Daniel Goleman discovered that the most effective leaders are alike in one essential way: they all have a high degree of emotional intelligence.

General intelligence and technical skills have long been considered the threshold capabilities for success in senior and leadership positions. According to Goleman, however, a person who is innovative, has excellent training and superior analytical skills but does not have a high degree of emotional intelligence may still not make a good leader. His analysis also suggested that emotional intelligence plays an increasingly important role in high-level management positions whereas differences in technical skills are of negligible importance.

Goleman (1995) identified five key factors in emotional intelligence. Rate yourself on how well you display them. They are areas that can be worked on in your leadership development plan at the end of this chapter. They include:

- self-awareness,
- self regulation,
- motivation,
- empathy, and
- social skill.

Self-awareness

Self awareness and it is here described as the ability to understand your moods, emotions and needs as well as their impact on others. Emotions are not often discussed in a work context, yet we all know that if we are upset about something, or angry, it can greatly influence the way we behave in the workplace.

Self regulation

This is the ability to control impulsiveness, reduce anxiety and react to situations with appropriate anger. The right degree of self regulation helps prevent a person from throwing a temper tantrum when activities do not go as planned. Self regulation does not mean that you do not feel angry or anxious or distressed; rather, it means that you control your behaviour and act in ways that are appropriate to the situation and are not harmful to others.

Motivation

Motivation is a passion to work for reasons other than money or status—such as finding joy in the task itself, or helping others. It also includes drive, persistence and optimism in the face of setbacks. As indicated early in the chapter, followers greatly admire optimism as one of the key attributes that they want in their leaders.

Empathy

Empathy is the ability to respond to the unspoken feelings of others. Leadership is not all about you. Empathy is important for leaders in a number of ways. If you empathise with people you can better understand their position on issues and how to communicate with and influence them. A CEO who has empathy for a labour union's demands, for example, might be able to negotiate successfully with the head of the union and avoid a costly strike. Empathy is not about agreeing with the other person, it is about understanding and acknowledging their perspective on the situation and including that understanding in any communication.

Social skill

Social skill is competency in managing relationships, building networks of support, and having a positive relationship with people. A leader with good social skills is able to develop good working relationships with customers, peers and followers. Establishing good working relationships with a diverse range of people can make the difference between success and failure in many leadership positions. It is difficult and time consuming but worth the effort.

Leader in action: Charles Handy—Thought leader

Charles Handy has long been recognised as one of the world's leading business thinkers. He has explored the business world, its values, its structures and its impact on the world in a series of books including *The Hungry Spirit: Beyond capitalism—a Quest for purpose in the Modern World* (1997).

In his most recent book he explores wider issues, both creative and moral, that have been turning points in his long, varied and successful life. He questions his own experience; he shows us how to learn lessons from our own experience, how to reflect on what we really value, the role of work in our lives and what we find fulfilling. In many of his books he challenges the predominant resource-based views of the world; he has described with great insight some of the impacts, good and bad, that the changes in the modern world bring with them. More so than many management writers he has focused on the importance of reflection and self awareness. He has been a thought leader.

In *Myself and More Important Matters*, Handy (2006) explores the concept of identity. He reflects on the nature of identity and the fact that over the years there have been many different Charles Handys. There was the shy son of an Irish clergyman and the classics scholar at Oxford. There was the Shell executive who found himself struggling in the wilds of Borneo, trying to escape from his early life and enter the more exciting world of money, travel and power—only to discover that this was not the Charles Handy he wanted to be. He found that the role of professor was much closer to the 'real' Charles Handy, for teaching and preaching were part of a heritage he had been trying unsuccessfully to ignore.

He became well known in Britain as the voice of 'Thought for the Day' on BBC radio's 'Today' program. His children, he thinks, saw him as a benevolent if slightly impractical dad and a fairly decent cook.

He argues that identity is a puzzling subject; it often changes so there may be different versions of it throughout life. He says that recognising one's identity is one of the most important things in the journey to effective leadership:

> *I am not only different now from the Charles Handy of my youth, I am different from place to place, from one group to another. Are we then the same person or not? Do we confuse ourselves as well as those observing us? (p. 1)*

If you had to choose three images of yourself, what three would you choose? Handy sees himself foremost as an author but also a cook with his family. In the past he would also have included his role as a business person—a doer as well as a thinker. Recognising the complex nature of who we are is important to self awareness.

Handy argues that life is a search for our own identity; it is the yearning to make a mark on the world, to leave the world a little different for us having lived. This contribution does not have to be earth shattering; it may be children you raised, a business you created, lives you saved, kids you taught or even a garden you made.

The sobering thought is that individuals and societies are not in the end remembered for how they made their money, but for how they spent it. (p. 10)

Source: Adapted from Handy, C 2006, *Myself and other more important matters*, William Heinemann, London.

The profile on Charles Handy above shows some of the deep issues embedded in the concept of leadership. Leaders often become leaders because they want to make a difference. As we experience leadership, we become wiser and we learn from our mistakes if we are able to reflect and learn. It's our own experience that is the best platform on which to learn leadership as we search to become more effective.

Mentoring and coaching

The terms mentoring and coaching are often used interchangeably, but they are really quite different, each with a unique role to play in leadership development.

Mentoring

Mentoring is traditionally thought of as an informal relationship based on the compatibility of two personalities. In the business world it is widespread for employers to formally assign a mentor to a new employee to help them adjust to the organisation and succeed in their work.

Research by Belle Rose Ragins (cited in Dubrin, Dalgish & Miller 2006) found that protégés with an informal mentor received greater benefits than protégés with formal mentors. Informal mentors were also *perceived* to be more effective. The protégés reported that mentors provided a wide range of support including career development, psychological support and social support.

Mentors appear to enhance the careers of protégés by recommending them for promotion and helping them establish valuable contacts. In a study by Van Collie in 1998 (cited in Dubrin 2006), 96% of respondents credited mentoring as an important career development method and 75% said that mentoring played a key role in their career success.

Executive coaching

Executive coaching has become very popular as a professional development tool. It differs from mentoring in that it focuses on specific, clearly articulated outcomes for the relationship.

The quality of the relationship between the coach and the person coached distinguishes coaching from other forms of leader–member interactions. The person being coached trusts the leader's judgment and the coach believes in the capacity of the person being coached to learn and profit from advice and support.

Coaching is a way of enabling others to act and to build on their strengths. To coach is to care enough about people to invest time in building a personal relationship with them. There is evidence that workers who are coached deliver increased productivity (Peterson & Hicks). The research suggests that coaching is a way of interacting with followers to help them develop the skills they need to be successful, whatever role they fill. It is also a way to develop leadership skills.

There are a number of false assumptions about coaching that need to be addressed if it is to be used to its full potential — namely:

Assumption	Reality
Coaching only applies in one-to-one work.	A team can be coached.
Coaching is mostly about providing new knowledge and skills.	Coaching is more about addressing underlying habits than about delivering knowledge and skills.

Assumption	Reality
If coaches go beyond giving instructions in knowledge and skills they risk the danger of getting into psychotherapy.	Coaches need to listen to the other person, attempt to understand their real concerns and provide impartial feedback. They operate as a 'critical friend' holding up a mirror and helping the person come to their own conclusions.
Coaches need to be expert in something in order to coach.	An important role for the coach is to ask pertinent questions and listen.
Coaching has to be done face-to-face.	Face-to-face does facilitate coaching as it assists in the development of a trusting and productive relationship. However, the telephone and email can be used as alternatives to overcome distance.

Here are some suggestions for the knowledge and skills required to be an effective coach. These are skills for you to develop; they are also the skills to seek if you want to find an effective executive coach.

- Communicate clear expectations. For people to perform well and to continue to learn and grow, they need a clear perception of what is expected of them. It is also important for the coach to have a clear understanding of the other person's expectation of the relationship.

- Focus on specific areas that require improvement. These may not always be cleat at the beginning of the relationship; they may become apparent as the result of particular situations or activities at work.

- Listen actively.

- Help remove obstacles.

- Give emotional support. Be helpful and constructive.

- Reflect content or meaning.

- Give gentle advice and guidance – but don't overdo it.

- Allow for modelling of desired performance and behaviour. An effective coaching technique is to show the person by example what constitutes desired behaviour. People will take more notice of what you do and how you behave than of what you say.

- Gain commitment to change. It is important that both the coach and the person being coached are committed to the process.

- Applaud good results.

Executive coaching has a number of benefits:

- it can address the specific areas that need improvement rather than undertaking a formal training program, much of which may not be useful;

- it is flexible in terms of time and place; and

- it can be used in a 'just in time' way to assist with new and unfamiliar situations.

Servant leadership

Robert Greenleaf first coined the term 'servant leadership' in 1970; he published widely on the concept over the next twenty years. Yet servant leadership is not a new concept – it is about leaders who want to make the world a better place.

A question of heart

Servant leadership is often misunderstood. The misunderstanding is based on the belief that you cannot lead and serve at the same time. According to Blanchard (2007) servant leadership has two important elements – the leadership component (which involves creating and communicating the vision) and the implementation component (which is about helping people achieve their goals). Servant leaders try constantly to find out what their people need to perform well and live according to the vision. Blanchard goes on to argue that servant leadership is a question of heart.

We have attempted to change leaders from the outside. In recent years we have found that effective leadership is an inside job. It is a question of heart. It's all about leadership character and intention. Why are you leading? Answering this question is so important. You can't fake being a servant leader. (p. 258)

Servant leaders lead because they want to serve others. This motivation is critical to the model and distinguishes it from other models. People follow servant leaders freely because they trust them. The tests of servant leadership are whether those served grow as people, whether they become wiser and more autonomous during the process, and what the effect is on the least privileged in society. These are not dissimilar to the requirements that Burns (1989) placed on true transformational leadership.

Characteristics and behaviours of servant leaders

Because of the need for servant leadership to come from the inside, the characteristics and behaviours of servant leaders make a good framework for developing leadership skills that are based on a sound understanding of yourself — real self awareness.

According to Larry Spears, there are ten critical characteristics of the servant leader. These are:

- listening,
- empathy,
- healing,
- awareness,
- persuasion,
- conceptualisation,
- foresight,
- stewardship,
- commitment to the growth of people, and
- building community.

Listening

Traditionally, leaders have been valued for their communication and decision-making skills. Servant leaders must reinforce these important skills by making a commitment to listen intently to others.

Empathy

Servant leaders strive to understand and empathise with others.

Healing

Learning to heal is a powerful force for transformation and integration. One of the strengths of servant leadership is the potential for healing one's self and others.

Awareness

General awareness, and especially self-awareness, strengthens the servant leader.

Persuasion

Servant leaders rely on persuasion rather than positional authority in making decisions within the organisation.

Conceptualisation

Servant leaders nurture their abilities to dream great dreams. The ability to look at a problem or an organisation from a conceptualising perspective means one must think beyond day-to-day realities.

Foresight

The ability to foresee the likely outcome of a situation is hard to define but easy to identify. Foresight is the characteristic that enables servant leaders to understand the lessons of the past, the realities of the present, and the likely consequences of a decision for the future.

Stewardship

Stewardship is 'holding something in trust for another'. Servant leadership, like stewardship, assumes first and foremost a commitment to serving the needs of others.

Commitment to the growth of people

Servant leaders believe that people have an intrinsic value beyond their tangible contributions as workers. As a result, servant leaders are deeply committed to the personal, professional and spiritual growth of each and every individual within the organisation.

Building community

Servant leaders seek to identify a means for building community among those who work within a given institution. Greenleaf said:

> All that is needed to rebuild community as a viable life form for large numbers of people is for enough servant leaders to show the way, not by mass movements, but by each servant-leader demonstrating his/her own unlimited liability for a quite specific community related group. (Greenleaf, quoted in Spears, 1997)

Servant leadership is one of the dominant philosophies in leadership discussion today. Perhaps, if more leaders of global organisations had adopted this theory of leadership, the world may not have had to suffer the consequences of the global financial crisis. The concept is similar to the recent emergence of 'worldly leadership'. Worldly leadership concerns similar concepts of ethics, sustainability and leadership for the common good.

There are also a range of other theories that place a premium on creating a positive work environment for spiritual growth and development while highlighting self-awareness. These include:

- authentic leadership (Avolio & Gardner 2005),
- principle centred leadership (Covey 1992), and
- value-centred leadership.

A number of diagnostic survey instruments have been designed to measure the components conceptualised to comprise these theories.

Reflections

To get the true meaning of servant leadership and related theories, take a moment to consider the impact of your leadership on others, especially in those times when you are feeling overwhelmed, tired, irritated or impatient.

Summary

Underpinning our understanding of the leadership process is the concept that 'to understand leadership is to understand yourself'. Effective leaders are aware of how they respond to different situations; they are aware of their impact on others; they understand the human interaction and the role their behaviour and actions play in bringing about effective outcomes. This chapter provides a range of insights and tools that can help you gain insight into your own behaviour and attitudes.

Reflective learning

Reflective learning is an important part of this process. Argyris (1991) coined the terms *double-loop learning* and *single-loop learning* to distinguish between the different ways in which feedback is sought and used to improve performance.

Personal mastery

A study undertaken in 2001/2 (Dalglish 2003) found that self awareness was considered a very important attribute of effective leaders by their prospective followers. Senge (1990) provides one useful concept in the development of self awareness—i.e. personal mastery. When personal mastery becomes a part of our lives it involves two underlying movements:

- continually clarifying what is important to us as individuals— i.e. what our personal vision looks like; and

- continually learning to see current reality more clearly.

People with a high level of personal mastery exhibit a range of behaviours. They:

- have a special sense of purpose that lies behind their vision and goals;
- see current reality as an ally not an enemy;
- are deeply inquisitive, committed to seeing reality more accurately;
- feel connected to others;
- live in a continual learning mode — they never arrive;
- are aware of their ignorance, their incompetence and their growth areas; and
- are self-confident.

Emotional intelligence

Leadership is not just about appealing to the head, being rational. It is about connecting with followers in a way that inspires them to undertake tasks that otherwise they may choose not to. This requires emotional intelligence. Emotional intelligence refers to qualities such as understanding one's feelings, empathy for others, and the regulation of emotions to enhance living. This type of intelligence has to do with the ability to connect with people and understand their emotions. These are not skills that form part of most formal curricula in schools or universities. Nor do they often get mentioned as something that needs to be developed in order to be effective in leadership or in life. Mayer and Salovey (1997) define emotional intelligence as the ability to detect and to manage emotional cues and information.

Executive coaching

Executive coaching has become very popular as a professional development tool. It is different from mentoring in that it focuses on specific, clearly articulated outcomes for the relationship. Coaching is a way of enabling others to act and to build on their strengths.

Servant leadership

Robert Greenleaf first coined the term 'servant leadership' in 1970; he published widely on the concept over the next twenty years. Servant leadership is often misunderstood. The misunderstanding is based on the belief that you cannot lead and serve at the same time. According to Blanchard (2007) servant leadership has two important elements—the leadership component (which involves creating and communicating the vision) and the implementation component (which is about helping people achieve their goals). Servant leaders try constantly to find out what their people need to perform well and live according to the vision. Blanchard goes on to argue that servant leadership is a question of heart.

Reflection on your leadership practice

Are there situations where you always behave in the same way whether it is effective or not? For example, often when people are participating in meetings, they regularly speak first or alternatively, they prefer others to always speak first. Often good leadership demands we behave in ways that are not natural to us if we are to bring out the best in others. We need to master these effective behaviours if we wish to improve our leadership. If you wish to experiment, the next time you participate in a meeting, try to behave the opposite to your usual behaviour. It may be difficult to maintain this un-natural behaviour and also difficult for others who might expect you to act in a certain habitual way. However, your actions may allow others at the meeting to come forward that might have otherwise remained unheard.

References

Argyris, C 199,) Teaching smart people how to learn, *Harvard Business Review,* May-June pp. 99-109.

Bennis W 1989, *On becoming a Leader,* Addison Wesley Publishing.

Blanchard, K., Blanchard, S & Zigarmi D 2007, 'Servant Leadership' in Blanchard, K 2007, *Leading at a Higher level,* Pearson.

Burns, J M 1978, *Leadership,* New York: Harper and Row.

Dalglish, C & Therin, F 2003, Leadership perception: generic and specific characteristics of small vs large businesses, *ICSB* June 2003 Belfast.

Dubrin, A, Dalglish, C & Miller, P 2006, *Leadership 2nd Asia Pacific Edition,* Milton, Qld: John Wiley and Sons Australia.

Goleman, Daniel 2002, *The New Leaders,* Time Warner, London.

Greenleaf, RK 1977, *Servant leadership: a journey into the nature of Legitimate Power and Greatness*, Paulist Press, New York.

Handy, C 2006, *Myself and other more important matters* William Heinemann: London.

Handy, C 1997, *The Hungry Spirit: Beyond capitalism – a Quest for purpose in the Modern World,* Hutchinson, London.

Jordan, PJ, Ashkansy, NM & Hartel EJ 2002, 'Emotional intelligence as a moderator of emotional and behavioural reaction to job insecurity', *Academy of Management Review,* vol. 27, no. 3, p 361

Peterson, DB & Hicks, MD 1996, *Leaders as Coach: Strategies for Coaching and Developing Others,* Minneapolis: personal Decisions Inc.

Roach, Sharlene 2007, 'Julie Hammer' by Sharlene Roach, in Dalglish & Evans *'Leadership in the Australian Context,* Tilde University Press, Melbourne.

Senge, PM 1990, *The Fifth Discipline*, Random House, Sydney.

Spears, L 1995, 'Servant leadership and the Greenleaf Legacy' in Spears, L (ed) *Reflections on Leadership*, John Wiley & Sons Inc. N.Y.

Chapter 4

THE PERSON OF THE LEADER

CHAPTER CONTENTS

Spotlight: *BOSS* True Leaders Survey

Each year in August, The Australian Financial Review magazine *BOSS* publishes the *BOSS* True Leaders Survey which identifies those assessed to be the best leaders in Australia and New Zealand over the past year. A highly respected panel of successful leaders is assembled to judge the awards and to choose the twenty identified leaders.

The panellists for 2008 included John Sevior, Head of Equities, Perpetual Ltd, Peter Shergold, former Secretary Department of Prime Minister and Cabinet, Carol Hardy, CEO of UNICEF Australia, Stephen Roberts, CEO of Citi Markets and Banking, Tracey Horton, Dean University of Western Sydney and Jillian Broadbent, Member of the Board of the Reserve Bank.

The panellists for the 2008 awards noted the turbulent and difficult economic times facing leaders and agreed that leaders are leading in a period that 'demands realistic, not flamboyant, leadership'. According to the panel, 'unforeseen shocks are typical of what is central to leadership in these trying times'. Jillian Broadbent noted that 'You (the leader) are not really tested until you get to the bad times, then it is not just the intelligence but the courage that you need to display. In bad times, that is really when you (the leader) need a bit more strength'.

According to Peter Shergold, while courage is vital to effective leadership in testing times, 'troubled times also reinforce the role integrity plays in leadership'.

The focus of this chapter is on the qualities and traits of effective leaders. Throughout this chapter you will be given opportunities to identify your personality traits and to understand better who you are and why you do the things you do. As you read through the chapter and undertake the activities, keep in mind what this elite panel of leadership experts regard as the traits of effective leaders in turbulent times and compare these traits against what the theories suggest and what your self diagnosis tells you.

Some of the traits identified by the panellists as necessary in turbulent times are:

- Courage
- Strength
- Integrity
- Intelligence
- Conviction
- Clear sightedness.

Source: The Australian Financial Review *BOSS* magazine, August, 2008.

Chapter 5 on leadership development identifies a number of traits known to be key to leadership success. The traits listed above by the panel of experts for the *BOSS* True Leader awards closely resemble the traits identified in chapter 5 by leadership trait theory. In addition to traits, chapter 5 also details a theory known as 'servant leadership'. Many of the critical characteristics said to belong to servant leaders are also similar to the traits identified here. It appears, then, that there is a strong correlation between the theory of leadership as outlined in chapter 5 and the actual practice of leadership recognised in the *BOSS* True Leader awards. In this chapter you will be given an opportunity to discover some of your critical personality traits.

Introduction

In chapter 2 we outlined the significance of a person's values and how a person's values affect their leadership style and ethical behaviours. In the previous chapter we introduced the concept of self awareness and the need for leaders to be reflective if their leadership is to be improved and they are to reach their full potential. In this chapter we will continue the theme of assisting leaders to understand who they are and why they do the things they do, and provide you with further guidance on understanding yourself. By having a better understanding of yourself, you will begin to have a better understanding of others and therefore be in a better position to lead them.

First we will examine what are known as the 'big five' personality traits and give you an opportunity to assess yourself against these five personality traits. Then we will turn to the cognitive factors that are said to underpin effective leadership behaviour and are one of the building blocks of a person's self-concept. You will also be given the opportunity to discover your own cognitive style. We will then briefly examine other well known personality style indicators and the impact of gender on leadership. Lastly, we will provide you with a practical way of building on your own strengths as a leader and then take a pause to allow you to build your *individual leadership profile* at the end of the chapter.

The big five personality traits

Over many years, psychologists have developed theories to explain how and why people behave as they do. Psychological testing has been around for centuries and is also widespread among different cultures. It is used extensively in modern organisations for staff selection and development activities and for the development of leaders. One form of psychological testing is personality profiling. Personality is the combination of traits that classifies the behaviour of an individual and profiling is a way of classifying and measuring these traits. These tests measure what many psychologists consider to be fundamental dimensions of personality.

In our discussion of leadership theories in chapter 5 we briefly examine trait theory as the first and underpinning approach to the study of leadership. As explained in chapter 5, traits are personal characteristics that distinguish one person from another. Trait theory continues to have relevance in leadership research including the development of the five-factor model of personality also known as 'the big five', the subject of this section. There is widespread acceptance of the five-factor model among personality researchers and the big five have achieved an unusual scientific consensus amongst personality psychologists.

As a part of gaining self awareness, leaders need to understand their basic personality type. As stated in the introduction to this chapter, once a leader has good self awareness, they can extend this awareness to the understanding of others, particularly those who follow them. Knowing and understanding the personality types of others assists leaders to predict the likely behaviour and job performance of team members and take actions that are appropriate to the different personality types in a team. This leads to more effective communication and effective outcomes.

We know from psychological research that personality is developed by a combination of three significant factors — namely:

- *Genetics* — i.e. the genes you received from your parents,

- *Environmental factors* — e.g. peer groups, family, school experiences etc., and

- *The situation* — which influences the effects of genetics and environment on personality. In other words, an individual's personality which although stable and relatively consistent from the age of about seven years can change in different situations.

The big five model of personality commenced with the research of Fiske (1949) and allows us to reliably categorise most of the known traits into one of five dimensions. The five dimensions are (Judge, Heller & Mount 2002):

- *Surgency* (also known as self confidence, the need for power and extraversion),

- *Agreeableness* (also known as empathy and need for affiliation),

- *Adjustment* (also known as emotional stability or self control),

- *Conscientiousness* (also known as dependability or prudence), and

- *Openness to experience* (also known as curiosity, intellect and learning approach).

Before we review each of the five dimensions, undertake the activity that follows to categorise yourself and measure your strength on each of the five dimensions.

Activity 4.1 Undertake the personality profile exercise below

Personality Profile

There are no right or wrong answers, so be honest and you will really increase your self-awareness. We suggest doing this exercise in pencil or making a copy before you write on it. We will explain why later.

Using the scale below rate each of the 25 statements according to how accurately it describes you. Place a number from 1 to 7 on the line before each statement.

Somewhat like me			Like me		Not like me	
7	6	5	4	3	2	1

_____ 1. I step forward and take charge in leaderless situations.

_____ 2. I am concerned about getting along well with others.

_____ 3. I have good self-control; I don't get emotional or get angry and yell.

_____ 4. I'm dependable; when I say I will do something, it's done well and on time.

_____ 5. I try to do things differently to improve my performance.

_____ 6. I enjoy competing and winning; losing bothers me.

_____ 7. I enjoy having lots of friends and going to parties.

_____ 8. I perform well under pressure.

_____ 9. I work hard to be successful.

_____ 10. I go to new places and enjoy travelling.

_____ 11. I am outgoing and willing to confront people when in conflict.

_____ 12. I try to see things from other people's point of view.

_____ 13. I am an optimistic person who sees the positive side of situations (the cup is half full).

_____ 14. I am a well-organised person.

_____ 15. When I go to a new restaurant, I order foods I haven't tried.

_____ 16. I want to climb the corporate ladder to as high a level of management as I can.

_____ 17. I want other people to like me and to be viewed as friendly.

_____ 18. I give people lots of praise and encouragement; I don't put people down and criticise.

_____ 19. I conform by following the rules of an organisation.

_____ 20. I volunteer to be the first to learn and do new tasks at work.

_____ 21. I try to influence other people to get my way.

_____ 22. I enjoy working with others more than working alone.

_____ 23. I view myself as being relaxed and secure, rather than nervous and insecure.

_____ 24. I am considered to be credible because I do a good job and come through for people.

_____ 25. When people suggest doing things differently, I support them and help bring it about; I don't make statements like these: it won't work, we never did it before, no one else ever did it, or we can't do it.

Score

Surgency		Agree-ableness		Adjustment		Conscien-tiousness		Openness to experience	
___1.	35	___1.	35	___1.	35	___1.	35	___1.	35
___6.	30	___6.	30	___6.	30	___6.	30	___6.	30
___11.	25	___11.	25	___11.	25	___11.	25	___11.	25
___16.	20	___16.	20	___16.	20	___16.	20	___16.	20
___21.	15	___21.	15	___21.	15	___21.	15	___21.	15
_____	10	_____	10	_____	10	_____	10	_____	10
Total	5	Total	5	Total	5	Total	5	Total	5

To determine your personality profile:

1. In the blanks, place the number from 1 to 7 that represents your score for each statement.

2. Add up each column – your total should be a number from 5 to 35.

3. On the number scale, circle the number that is closest to your total score. Each column in the chart represents a specific personality dimension.

The higher the total number, the stronger is the personality dimension that describes your personality. What is your strongest and weakest dimension?

Continue reading the chapter for specifics about your personality in each of the five dimensions.

Source: Lussier, R & Achua, C 2004, *Leadership: Theory, Application, Skill Development*, 2nd edn, pp. 28-29, South-Western, a part of Cengage Learning/Nelson, Inc. Reproduced by permission <www.cengage.com/permissions>.

Dimensions of the personality profile

Surgency

This trait includes characteristics such as excitability, sociability, assertiveness, and high amounts of emotional expressiveness. The dimension captures how one feels about relationships and social interaction. Individuals high in surgency are outgoing, competitive and decisive. Individuals low in surgency tend to like to work by themselves and do not wish to compete with others. One therefore might expect that leaders will have higher surgency scores than followers.

Agreeableness

This personality dimension includes attributes such as trust, altruism, kindness, affection, and other pro-social behaviours. It therefore concerns how one gets along with others as opposed to leading others. Individuals higher in agreeableness tend to be approachable and sensitive while individuals lower in agreeableness tend to be insensitive and distant to others.

Adjustment

This dimension concerns how an individual reacts to stressful situations, failure and even personal criticism. Individuals high in this dimension tend to experience emotional stability, tend to be calm and not react to personal failure in a negative manner. Individuals low in adjustment tend to be subject to anxiety, moodiness, irritability, and sadness.

Conscientiousness

This dimension includes how one approaches work and life in general. Individuals with high conscientiousness have high levels of thoughtfulness, with good impulse control and goal-directed behaviours. Those high in conscientiousness tend to be also organised and mindful of details. Individuals lower in conscientiousness are less concerned with meeting commitments and may be more creative and spontaneous.

Openness to experience

How an individual approaches problems or learns from new experiences is related to the open-to-experience dimension. Individuals high on this dimension feature characteristics such as imagination and insight and also tend to have a broad range of interests. Individuals lower in this dimension tend to be practical people with a narrower range of interests.

The dimensions are not personality types as in some other forms of personality trait measurement (see Myers-Briggs Type Indicator later in this section), so people vary continuously on them, with most people falling in between the extremes. The dimensions provide a unifying personality framework and research has established relationships between the personality dimensions and job performance. After researching a broad range of occupations, Hurtz and Donovan (2000), for example, found there was evidence that surgency predicted performance in managerial and sales positions. This finding has face validity as both these occupations require high levels of social interaction. They also found that openness to experience was linked, as might be expected, to training proficiency.

Leader in action: Sue Gordon

Sue Gordon, AM, is a retired indigenous Australian magistrate from Western Australia. She was born at Belele sheep station in Western Australia in 1944, and removed from her mother as part of the government's assimilation polices for part-Aboriginal children. She was then taken to a Catholic Home in Perth where she was educated and sent out to work at the age of 16.

After leaving school, she joined the army as a full-time soldier and between 1961 and 1964 was a full-time member of the Women's Royal Australian Army Corps (WRAAC) based mostly in the eastern states. She considers her stint in the army to be one of her best jobs. The army environment and disciplined culture possibility served to assist her to develop some of her outstanding leadership qualities.

Following her army career she worked in various administrative positions around Australia and, in the early 1970s, started a long association with the Pilbara region, working mostly in Aboriginal Affairs. As a result of her work with Aboriginal people and community affairs, she received the Order of Australia in 1993. She undertook a law degree at age 50.

She was appointed as Commissioner for Aboriginal Planning in 1986, becoming the first Aboriginal person to head a government department in Western Australia. In 1988 was appointed as a magistrate in the Perth Children's Court, at which time she was the first full-time and first Aboriginal magistrate in the state's history. Her leadership skills and string of successful professional challenges led to Sue's appointment to a number of significant government inquiries and in June 2007 she responded to a call by the then Commonwealth Government and was appointed as Chair of the Taskforce of the Northern Territory Emergency Response (NTER), a politically sensitive and difficult project aimed to bring law and order to Aboriginal communities and to protect children from abuse.

When asked to comment on the leadership qualities needed to steer through such a controversial and politically charged project, Sue cites people skills at the top of the list. 'Some (leaders),' she said, 'lead by example, some are aggressive, some screech at people. But if you work with people, you get more out of people'.

Sue's leadership traits include an ability to listen rather than talk, she is skilled at gaining rapport and at understanding people issues, particularly in cross-cultural environments. Some of these traits come naturally to her and her skills would have been learned from the resilience of her family and during the significant leadership positions she has held over decades.

Two important traits that enabled her to succeed in difficult times include the ability to focus and discipline. She passes these qualities to others by using the terms as her favourite watchwords.

A panellist in the 2008 *BOSS* True Leaders Survey, Peter Shergold, said of Sue Gordon:

She is a very courageous Indigenous person...who saw first-hand the devastating effects of dysfunctional communities and took on that difficult job and won the confidence of her new minister. She led the Northern Territory intervention with distinction. She showed extraordinary courage, integrity and strength when she took that role and forged ahead with it whilst weathering the firestorm of criticism.

Source: The Australian Financial Review *BOSS* magazine, August 2008, p. 52.

Sue Gordon has had many firsts in her long career, demonstrating outstanding leadership qualities not just for herself, but more generally for indigenous people and for women. It may be that the discipline she displays is as a result of her early army experience. However, this discipline is contrasted with the two issues she values most for effective leadership – people skills and the ability to listen.

Cognitive factors underpinning leadership

A person's cognitive (or thinking) style is the natural strategy or preference they use to gather, process, interpret, evaluate and respond to data and information. There has been strong research linking a leader's thinking style to their behaviour and cognitive style is said to be one of the building blocks of a person's self-concept. In the modern organisation, leaders and their followers are faced with increasing amounts of data and information that must be processed and used as the basis for decision making. It is known that people have preferred styles to process this information and will approach problems and decisions using different decision-making strategies. In other words, people have different learning styles and will take different meanings from the same data or experience. If leaders are to get the most out of the people in their teams, they must learn the way in which they and their team members prefer to process information and relate and interact with them in accordance with their preferred styles.

Measuring cognitive style

There are literally dozens of ways of measuring cognitive style and researchers use many different dimensions to measure the concept. However, two major dimensions of thinking style dominate the research—namely:

- information gathering, and
- information analysing,

and we will adopt these dimensions for the purposes of this chapter. The theory underpinning these two dimensions is based on the work of Carl Jung (1923), a Swiss psychiatrist and influential thinker and the founder of Analytical Psychology. Many typology tests and personality indicators are based on his work.

Information gathering

The first core dimension for measuring information processing preferences is the 'information gathering' dimension. There are two strategies for gathering information. These are 'sensing' and 'intuiting'. Undertake Activity 4.2 to locate yourself on this dimension.

Activity 4.2 The information gathering dimension of cognitive style

Read the descriptors for each end of the scale. Then locate yourself on the scale by placing a mark on the line that best describes the degree to which your preference is described by the sensing strategy or the intuiting strategy. For example, if the descriptors for the sensing strategy seem to a fair description of how you gather information, then the mark on the scale should be more towards the sensing strategy box than toward the intuiting strategy box.

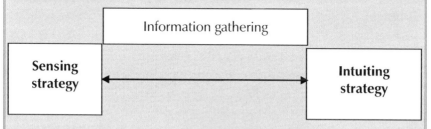

Information gathering

Sensing strategy ⟷ **Intuiting strategy**

Descriptors

- Dislikes new problems
- Likes established routines
- Works at a steady rate
- Likes to reach a conclusion
- Is patient
- Makes few errors of fact
- Likes precision in their work

Descriptors

- Likes new problems
- Dislikes routines
- Works in bursts
- Jumps to conclusions
- Is impatient
- Often makes errors of fact
- Often imprecise in their work

Sensing

As shown in the descriptors in the activity above, the sensing strategy focuses on detail and on individual parts of the data rather than on relationships between the parts. Those with a sensing strategy are rational thinkers who take time to thoroughly investigate and gather data and information in a meticulous way. Sensing types prefer concrete, factual and structured situations. They make few errors because of their careful gathering of data and good accuracy.

Intuiting

An intuiting strategy on the other hand is characteristic of those who look at problems or decisions holistically and tend to look for commonalities, patterns and relationships in the data or information rather than taking the time to focus on individual parts. The intuitive type prefers possibilities and theories and often become bored with detail.

Information evaluation

Now let's turn the second core dimension for measuring information processing preferences or the 'information evaluation' dimension. There are two strategies for evaluating information — namely:

- thinking, and
- feeling.

Undertake Activity 4.3 to locate yourself on this dimension.

Activity 4.3 The information evaluation dimension of cognitive style

As for Activity 4.2, read the descriptors for each end of the scale. Then locate yourself on the scale by placing a mark on the line that best describes the degree to which your preference is described by the thinking strategy or the feeling strategy. For example, if the descriptors for the thinking strategy seem to a fair description of how you evaluate information, then the mark on the scale should be more towards the thinking strategy box than toward the feeling strategy box.

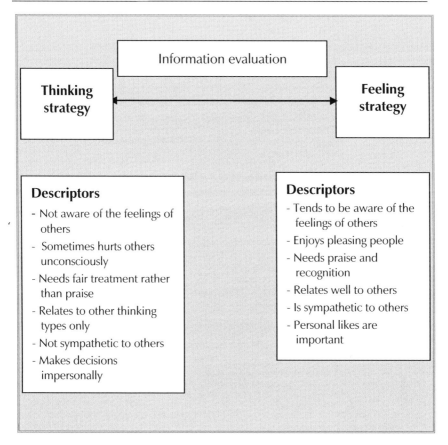

Thinking

As shown in the descriptors in the activity above, the thinking strategy evaluates data and information in a systematic, logical and unemotional way. Those with a thinking style tend to be able to remain more objective than others and are methodical. Thinking types avoid irrationality and making decisions based on feelings.

Feeling

Those with a feeling strategy tend to approach evaluation of data and information in a more subjective way and often can reach conclusions without being able to articulate the methods by which they reached the conclusion. Those of a feeling style rely heavily on their own personal values and are more interested in people than in impersonal logic.

Now let's put the two dimensions together and endeavour to locate your overall cognitive style on a two-dimensional model by undertaking Activity 4.4.

Activity 4.4 The two-dimensional cognitive style model

Transfer the mark you placed on the continuum in Activity 4.2 for the sensing and intuiting strategy and the mark you placed in Activity 4.3 for the thinking and feeling strategy onto the two-dimensional model below. Where your two lines intersect should locate you in one of the four quadrants of the model. This location is your preferred cognitive style.

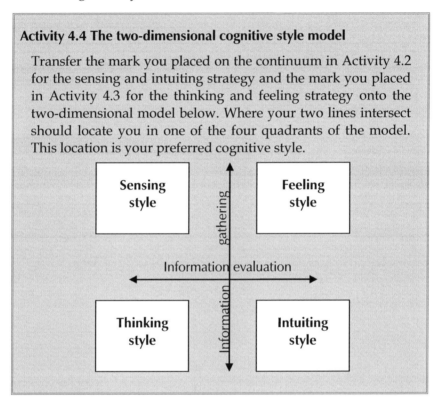

Most people have different degrees of intensity for each of the dimensions of sensing, intuiting, thinking and feeling. No strategy or style is inherently better or worse than another but in any team environment, it is better to have team members from all styles so that the team is well balanced. Knowing your own overall preferred cognitive style and the intensity of each of the dimensions, and that of the people in your work team, will assist you to demonstrate the leadership behaviours that are more likely to be effective.

For example, team members with a thinking style will prefer to have more time and a greater amount of detail when considering tasks and issues than other types. Leaders who are thinkers require similar elements and also do not do well in situations where the full information on an issue is not available or creative thinking is required.

Intuitive and sensing leaders and team members will thrive in these circumstances but have a tendency to make more errors because they will try new approaches that may not work.

When leaders and team members have self knowledge about their individual cognitive styles and the styles of those they work with, the team is more likely to achieve a more effective and balanced outcome. In other words, leaders need to behave in a way that meets the cognitive styles of all their team members and not to act as if everyone in the team has the same preferred style.

Activity 4.5 The cognitive style instrument

Undertake the cognitive style instrument below to determine your score for each of the four strategies of sensing, intuiting, thinking and feeling. Compare your scores with how you rated yourself in the preceding activities and with comparative data shown for males and females. You could use this activity for a team building exercise with your work team.

The cognitive style instrument

In this instrument you should put yourself in the position of someone who must gather and evaluate information. The purpose is to investigate the ways you think about information you encounter. There are no right or wrong answers and one alternative is just as good as another. Try to indicate the ways you do or would respond, not the ways you think you should respond.

For each scenario there are three pairs of alternatives. For each pair, select the alternative that comes closest to the way you would respond. Answer each item. If you are not sure, make your best guess. When you have finished answering all the questions, compare the scoring key as a basis for comparing your score with others.

Suppose you are the chief executive of a company and have asked division heads to make presentations at the end of the year. Which of the following would be more appealing to you?

_____ 1   a   A presentation analysing the details of the data
         b   A presentation focused on the overall perspective

_____ 2   a   A presentation showing how the division contributed to the company as a whole
         b   A presentation showing the unique contributions of the division

_____ 3   a   Details of how the division performed
         b   General summaries of performance data

Suppose you are a scientist with the CSIRO whose job it is to gather information about the moons of Saturn. Which of the following would you be more interested in investigating?

_____ 4   a   How the moons are similar to one another
         b   How the moons differ from one another

_____ 5   a   How the whole system of moons operates
         b   The characteristics of each moon

_____ 6   a   How Saturn and its moons differ from Earth and its moon
         b   How Saturn and its moons are similar to Earth and its moon

Suppose you are visiting an African country and you are writing home to tell about your trip. Which of the following would be most typical of the letter you would write?

_____ 7   a   A detailed description of people and events
         b   General impressions and feelings

_____ 8   a   A focus on similarities of our culture and theirs
         b   A focus on the uniqueness of their culture

_____ 9   a   Overall, general impressions of the experience
         b   Separate, unique impressions of parts of the experience

Suppose you are attending a concert featuring a famous symphony orchestra. Which of the following would you be most likely to do?

_____10 a   Listen for the parts of individual instruments
       b   Listen for the harmony of all the instruments together

_____11 a   Pay attention to the overall mood associated with the music
       b   Pay attention to the separate feelings associated with different parts of the music

_____12 a   Focus on the overall style of the conductor
       b   Focus on how the conductor interprets different parts of the score

Suppose you are considering taking a job with a certain organisation. Which of the following would you be more likely to do in deciding whether or not to take the job?

_____13 a   Systematically collect information on the organisation
       b   Rely on personal intuition or inspiration

_____14 a   Consider primarily the fit between you and the job
       b   Consider primarily the politics needed to succeed in the organisation

_____15 a   Be methodical in collecting data and making a choice
       b   Mainly consider personal instincts and gut feelings

Suppose you inherit some money and decide to invest it. You learn of a new high-technology firm that has just issued shares. Which of the following is most likely to be true of your decision to purchase the firm's shares?

_____16 a   You would invest on a hunch
       b   You would invest only after a systematic investigation of the firm

_____17 a   You would be somewhat impulsive in deciding to invest
       b   You would follow a pre-set pattern in making your decision

_____ 18 a You would rationally justify your decision to invest in this firm and not in another

b It would be difficult to rationally justify your decision to invest in this firm and not another

Suppose you are being interviewed on TV, and you are asked the following questions. Which alternative would you be most likely to select?

_____ 19 How are you more likely to cook?
a With a recipe
b Without a recipe

_____ 20 How would you predict the Rugby League winner next year?
a After systematically researching the personnel and records of the teams
b On a hunch or by intuition

_____ 21 Which games do you prefer?
a Games of chance (like Bingo)
b Chess, Chequers or Scrabble

Suppose you are a manager and need to hire an executive assistant. Which of the following would you be most likely to do in the process?

_____ 22 a Interview each applicant using a set outline of questions
b Concentrate on your personal feelings & instincts about each applicant

_____ 23 a Consider primarily the personality fit between yourself and the candidates
b Consider the match between the precise job requirements and the candidates' capabilities

_____ 24 a Rely on factual and historical data on each candidate in making a choice

b Rely on feelings and impressions in making a choice

Scoring key

To determine your score on the two dimensions of cognitive style, circle the items below that you checked on this instrument. Then count up the number of circled items and put your scores in the spaces below.

Gathering information		Evaluating information	
1b	1a	13a	13b
2a	2b	14b	14a
3b	3a	15a	15b
4a	4b	16b	16a
5a	5b	17b	17a
6b	6a	18a	18b
7b	7a	19a	19b
8a	8b	20a	20b
9a	9b	21b	21a
10b	10a	22a	22b
11a	11b	23b	23a
12a	12b	24a	24b
Intuitive score	Sensing score	Thinking score	Feeling score

Comparison data

Males	5.98	6.02	6.08	5.20
Females	6.04	5.96	6.94	5.06

Source: Whetten, David A & Cameron, Kim S 1995, *Developing Management Skills*, 3rd edn, pp. 47-49, reprinted by permission of Pearson Education Inc., Upper Saddle River, NJ.

Other personality style indicators

The Myers Briggs Personality Type Indicator

The most widely used and well known of all the personality frameworks is the Myers Briggs Personality Type Indicator (MBTI). This instrument is a 100 item personality test where an individual responds to how they feel or act in particular situations (Quenk 2000).

On the basis of the personality test, individuals are classified as:

- Extroverted (E) or Introverted (I)

- Sensing (S) or Intuitive (N)

- Thinking (T) or Feeling (F)

- Perceiving (P) or Judging (J)

These classifications are then combined into the 16 personality types that are possible from the combination of the eight types. For example, an individual may be classified as an ESFJ or INTP. There are strengths and weaknesses for each of the types and understanding your type and the types of others can assist in building upon your personality strengths and devising strategies to work on your weaknesses.

If you refer back to the 'Cognitive factors underpinning leadership' section in this chapter, you will see that the MBTI has built upon Jung's two-dimensional model. Research on the MBTI instrument over the last decade has demonstrated high levels of reliability and validity both within and across cultures (Bathurst & Cash 2001, Hoha 2001, Russinova & Pencheva 2001, Routamaa 2001, Shen 2003). To administer the instrument, the facilitator must be an accredited practitioner.

Gender and leadership

Research on brain activity has reliably shown what is often stated in popular books like John Gray's best selling *Men are from Mars, Women are from Venus* — i.e. that there are differences in the 'hard wiring' of male and female brains.

For example, research (Bell *et al.* 2006) from the University of Alberta showed that men and women utilise different parts of their brains while they perform the same tasks. The study involved volunteers who performed memory tasks, verbal tasks, visual spatial tasks and simple motor tasks while their brain activity was monitored with Magnetic Resonance Imaging (MRI) technology.

It is clear from our own experience in organisations that there are also common stereotypes about men and women leaders that sometimes seem to fit. Often men are characterised as leading in a 'masculine way' dominated by qualities such as competitiveness, hierarchy and analytic problem solving. Women are characterised in an alternative 'feminine way' usually dominated by qualities such as cooperativeness, collaboration and intuitive problem solving.

While scientists continue their search for these differences, social science research demonstrates that in the area of leadership, there are considerable complexities and that gender in leadership can be viewed from several different perspectives. Research evidence also shows that while there may be sex differences in leadership styles, the differences are typically either not large or are trivial, are not especially impactful and do not relate to any differences in the effectiveness of men and women leaders (Eagley & Johnson 2006).

Management roles and the culture of organisations that leaders work in also put constraints on the way leaders undertake their roles and there is a tendency for all leaders, irrespective of their gender, to conform to these cultures and therefore to display similar behaviours. Accordingly, there is little reason to believe that either women or men are more effective leaders. What is more likely, and consistent with the men and women highlighted in case studies throughout this book, is that within both sexes, there will be excellent leaders and leaders who are not so effective and that people can succeed as leaders by better understanding who they are and by developing the necessary qualities and skills known to be important in the leadership of modern organisations.

Strengths and limitations of the focus on the person

With all personality assessment attempts, one needs to keep in mind that situational factors can affect an individual's personality in different situations. It is also difficult to validly place human beings, because of their complexity, neatly into boxes or personality types as many people will not fit into one personality type or classification and may have attributes of two or more of the types.

Notwithstanding these difficulties, as a leader you can improve your leadership by leveraging your natural talents and skills and developing strategies to cope better with your weaknesses.

The Reflected Best Self (RBS) exercise

Roberts *et al.* (2005) provide a useful systematic way to discover your strengths and develop a strategy to build on them. The technique is called the Reflected Best Self (RBS) exercise to allow leaders to develop a sense of their personal best in order to improve their potential. The purpose of the exercise is to allow the leader to develop an action plan so that the leader can understand their strengths but also tap into unrecognised areas of potential. There are four steps to the exercise.

Step 1

Identify respondents and ask for feedback. This step requires that the leader identify a number of people both from within their workplace and outside it. Some authorities refer to this process as a 360 degree feedback process. However, the process can also include friends, family and teachers not connected to your workplace. Ask these people independently to provide you with feedback on your strengths with examples or instances of when or how you used these strengths in a way that was meaningful to them. Often leaders perceive that they have particular strengths or weaknesses but when they engage in an exercise of this type they are surprised to learn that what they thought were weaknesses are seen by others as strengths. Of course, the opposite is also sometimes true.

Step 2

Analyse the patterns in the feedback from step 1. In this step you search for common themes or patterns of behaviour, looking for uniformity or consistency in the feedback. For example, you might be able to identify high ethical standards, good team building skills or that you work well under pressure situations. Where the feedback is diverse and perhaps some comments are even competing, look for why this might be so. For example, do you act differently in different situations? Organise the feedback in a table with three columns. The first column heading could be 'common themes'; the second column, 'examples given'; and the third column 'possible interpretations'. Once the feedback is in table form, you can develop a picture of your capabilities and see yourself and how you behave in a broader context. For leaders who are not aware of their strengths the exercise can be very illuminating and can shed light on skills they may be taking for granted thus giving them more confidence in using them.

Step 3

Develop a self profile. In this step, your task is to write a description of yourself. It should commence with the phrase 'When I am at my best, I ...' and be about two to four paragraphs in length, without using bullet points. This technique will allow you to draw connections between the themes. The description should weave the themes you identified in the table from step 2. The profile of yourself is not meant to be a psychological profile like the activities undertaken in this chapter. Rather, it can be used as an insightful image of your previous behaviours and actions and a guide for future actions and interactions with other people.

Step 4

Redesign your personal role description. Having now identified your strengths (and probably also your weaknesses), the next step is to redesign your role to build upon what you are naturally good at. That is, to create a better fit between your work and your best self. You should be able to make small changes to the way you work, your behaviours, your team composition or how you spend your time to maximise your strengths.

Reflections

Completing the activities in this chapter will assist you to discover your personality profile and cognitive style. Now, undertake a reflective exercise following the Reflected Best Self technique. Develop the feedback table and then write a self profile. Put into action the strategies emerging from the exercise to reach your full potential.

Summary

This chapter and the chapters that preceded it are designed to allow you to develop a full self assessment of your leadership values, ethics, behaviours, and aspects of personality. Whatever you have determined to be your individual leadership style, remember that there is no one simple leadership style or formula that leaders can adopt to ensure effective leadership.

Leaders today who wish to lead more effectively and to reach their full potential must take time to stop and reflect on their own leadership style. Reflection does not mean musing on oneself but taking the time to analyse aspects of ourselves, what we do and why we do it. By synthesising and analysing ourselves, we can discover why things happen and look for ways of improving our leadership practice.

This chapter has provided you with insights into the big five personality traits. These traits include dimensions such as surgency (also known as self confidence, the need for power and extraversion), agreeableness (also known as empathy and need for affiliation), adjustment (also known as emotional stability or self control) and conscientiousness (also known as dependability or prudence). Research has established relationships between the personality dimensions, effective leadership and job performance.

Another important dimension for leaders to understand is that of cognitive style—said to be one of the building blocks of a person's self-concept. Carl Jung developed two major dimensions of thinking style. The first core dimension is the 'information gathering' dimension. The second core dimension is the 'information evaluation' dimension. The Myers Briggs Personality Type Indicator

(MBTI) has built upon Jung's two-dimensional model. The instrument is widely used and has demonstrated high levels of reliability and validity both within and across cultures.

Research evidence on gender differences in leadership shows that while there may be sex differences in leadership styles, the differences are typically not large or are trivial, not especially impactful and do not relate to any differences in the effectiveness of men and women leaders.

Finally, there are approaches that leaders can take to build upon their leadership strengths. The Reflected Best Self (RBS) exercise was outlined as method to allow leaders to improve leadership by leveraging on natural talents and skills. It was noted that leaders themselves spend very little time examining their own styles and performance and often believe that, as they have already achieved a leadership role or have been successful up to now, they are above improvement and have no need to develop their leadership effectiveness further. Such a belief could not be further from reality.

This chapter concludes the journey of self discovery and reflection. Having gained self awareness of your leadership attributes, the next chapter of this book explores the importance of leadership development and will allow you to articulate your own theory of leadership.

Reflection on your leadership practice

The reflection for this chapter is to pause your reading and complete the *individual leadership profile* at the end of this chapter.

References

Bathurst, J & Cash, M 2001, in Ginn, C edn 2001, *Leadership, type, and culture: Perspectives from across the globe*, Centre for Applications of Psychological Type, Gainesville, Florida.

Bell, E, Willson, M., Wilman, A., Dave, S & Silverstone, P 2006, 'Males and females differ in brain activation during cognitive tasks', vol. 30, No. 2, 1 April, pp.529-538.

Carlopio, J, Andrewartha, G & Armstrong, H 1997, *Developing Management Skills in Australia*, Longman, South Melbourne.

Eagley, A & Johnson, B 2006, 'Gender and Leadership Style: A Meta-Analysis', in Pierce, J & Newstrom, J, *Leaders and the leadership process*, 4th edn, McGraw-Hill, New York.

Fiske, D 1949, 'Consistency of the factorial structures of personality ratings from different sources', *Journal of Abnormal Social Psychology*, vol. 44, pp. 329-344.

Hoha, A 2001, in Ginn, C, edn 2001, *Leadership, type, and culture: Perspectives from across the globe*, Centre for Applications of Psychological Type, Gainesville, Florida.

Hurtz, G & Donovan, J 2000, 'Personality and Job Performance: The Big Five Revisited', *Journal of Applied Psychology*, vol. 85, no. 12, December.

Judge, T, Heller, D & Mount, M 2002, 'Five-Factor Model of Personality and Job Satisfaction: A Meta-Analysis', *Journal of Applied Psychology*, vol. 87, no. 12, June.

Jung, C 1923, *Psychological types*, Routledge and Kegan Paul, London.

Lussier, R & Achua, C 2004, *Leadership: Theory, Application, Skill Development*, 2nd edn, pp. 28-29 Thomson South-Western, USA.

Quenk, N 2000, *Essentials of Myers-Briggs Type Indicator Assessment*, Wiley, New York.

Roberts, L, Speitzer, G, Dutton, J, Quinn, R, Heaphy, E & Barker, B 2005, 'How to Play to your Strengths', *Harvard Business Review*, Online version, January.

Routamaa, V 2001, in Ginn, C, edn 2001, *Leadership, type, and culture: Perspectives from across the globe*, Centre for Applications of Psychological Type, Gainesville, Florida.

Russinova, V & Pencheva, E 2001, in Ginn, C, edn 2001, *Leadership, type, and culture: Perspectives from across the globe*, Centre for Applications of Psychological Type, Gainesville, Florida.

Shen, W 2003, An investigation of the differences in personality styles and leadership styles of selected women deans in American and Taiwanese institutions of higher education, Dissertation abstracts international.

Whetten, D & Cameron, K 1995, *Developing Management Skills*, 3rd edn, Harper Collins College Publishers, USA.

INDIVIDUAL LEADERSHIP PROFILE

Use a pause in your reading as a moment of reflection. Complete this leadership profile, taking a holistic view of your values, behaviours, personality and cognitive types.

The format for the profile is straightforward. Under each heading there is a brief explanation of what is required; it is up to you to fill in the details.

Your values (from Chapter 2)

My instrumental values are:

....
....
....
....
....
....

My terminal values are:

....
....
....
....
....
....
....

Your behaviours (from Chapter 3)

How would you characterise your leadership behaviours?

....
....
....
....
....
....
....

Your current reality (from Chapter 3)

List the positive elements of your current reality:

....
....
....
....
....
....
....

List the negative elements of your current reality:

....
....
....
....
....
....
....

Your personality profile (from Chapter 4)

Insert your scores from Activity 4.1 into the space in the table below:

Surgency	Agreeable-ness	Adjustment	Conscientiousness	Openness to experience

Each column in the table represents a specific personality dimension and your total should be a number from 5 to 35. The higher the total number, the stronger is the personality dimension that describes your personality. What are your strongest and weakest dimensions? What do your scores mean about your personality?

....
....
....
....
....
....
....

Now that you know your own personality style, you will recognise that other people might have a different personality style to you. Therefore, you may need to change your behaviours to suit the styles of others if you wish to work with them effectively.

Your cognitive style (from Chapter 4)

My preferred cognitive style is .... (from Activity 4.4).

Insert your scores from Activity 4.5 into the space in the table below:

Intuitive	Sensing	Thinking	Feeling

Compare your scores with the comparison data below:

Comparison data

Males	5.98	6.02	6.08	5.20
Females	6.04	5.96	6.94	5.06

What do your scores indicate about your cognitive style?

....
....
....
....
....
....
....

Now that you know your own cognitive style, you will recognise that other people might have a different cognitive style to you. Therefore, you may need to change your behaviours to suit the styles of others if you wish to work with them effectively.

Your strengths and weaknesses

Having now evaluated the outcomes of the activities above, and using the information you have gained from the activities, record below what you think are your leadership strengths and weaknesses.

My leadership strengths are:

....
....
....
....
....
....
....

My leadership weaknesses are:

....
....
....
....
....
....
....

Note: This profile is not meant to be a full self-assessment of your leadership values, behaviours or aspects of your personality. It is simply a tool to aid reflection. Reflection does not mean musing on oneself; rather it refers to taking the time to analyse aspects of ourselves, what we do and why we do it. By synthesising and analysing ourselves, we can discover why things happen and look for ways to improve our leadership practices.

Chapter 5

LEADERSHIP DEVELOPMENT

CHAPTER CONTENTS

Spotlight: Heather Ridout, Ai Group

Heather Ridout is Chief Executive of the Australian Industry Group (Ai Group). The Ai Group is a leading industry association in Australia. The 10,000 member businesses of the Ai Group employ around 750,000 staff in an expanding range of industry sectors including manufacturing, engineering, construction, defence, ICT, call centres, labour hire, transport, logistics, utilities, infrastructure, environmental products and services and business services.

It is an organisation committed to helping Australian industry meet the challenge of change. It focuses on building competitive industries through global integration, human capital development, productive and flexible workplace relations practices, infrastructure development and innovation.

Heather has responsibility for the overall development and implementation of the Ai Group's policies, strategies and services. Her policy interests embrace the whole range of industry and she has been particularly active in developing the Ai Group's public policy in relation to economic, industry, innovation, education and training.

Heather was named in the AFR *BOSS* Magazine twenty 'true leaders' in 2008, not just because of her leadership of the Ai Group but because of the perception that she embodies two of the qualities seen as critical for leaders in the current global environment — namely, ethics and integrity.

Heather has demonstrated that she can work with governments of different political persuasions with integrity. Since the election of the Rudd Labor Government, Heather has transformed the standing of the Ai Group, achieving a level of cabinet access that any business lobbyist might aspire to. Despite representing a declining manufacturing sector, Heather's leadership skills have seen her become the public face of the nation's employers. She is regarded as close to the Prime Minister and has been appointed to several government committees, including the Taxation Review

Committee, Infrastructure Australia, the Business Advisory Group and Skills Australia.

According the one of the judges for the true leader awards, Heather has 'been willing to go on the media and tell it like it is, as she sees industrial relations, and both sides have attacked her at various times. She is an independent thinker, is genuinely interested in public policy issues and is most effective because of her integrity'.

An example of her independence and integrity came in a moment she describes as 'defining' when the then Howard Government called on the Ai Group to join the campaign for its 'Work Choices' industrial relations policy, as other employer groups had supported the policy. 'I could have said we are not planning anything at this stage but I felt that would have been the wrong thing to have done — that we had to make a definite decision, make an early call, and stick to it'. The Ai Group did not support the policy and it enabled the then opposition to capitalise on the split of employer groups.

For Heather, leading an organisation representing a declining manufacturing sector, having to present a policy view different to the government's means to be effective it is a question of courage and integrity. To have any impact on the political agenda, she must be perceived by other leaders and her constituents as able to communicate effectively with the ethical standards that make people listen.

Source: AFR *BOSS* Magazine, vol. 9, July and vol. 10, August 2008.

The skill set and qualities of Heather Ridout demonstrated in this short profile did not come about by chance. While some personal qualities like ethics and integrity may be innate in some people, these qualities can be learned and developed. Communication skills in all their forms can all be learned and developed in leaders. In this chapter we will be reviewing a number of techniques and methods organisation's utilise to help their leaders learn and develop and in doing so, try to assist their leaders to develop the characteristics, qualities and competencies organisations need and value.

The leadership characteristics and qualities ascribed to Heather Ridout, like ethics, integrity and courage are stressed in contemporary leadership development programs. While leadership development programs come and go, it is clear that there are fundamental issues of character and personality that define leaders and that may be outside the capacity of any developmental program. This chapter will help you to identify and analyse these issues.

Introduction

How do leaders improve their leadership capacity and become more competent and successful? If we knew the answer to this question with certainty, this chapter would outline the simple steps you could follow to improve your leadership effectiveness.

However, leadership is a very personal phenomenon that is usually context specific and situational, so it is not easy to define one specific process for leadership development. Despite what is espoused in popular books and some theory, there is no one simple leadership style or formula that ensures effective leadership of others. Indeed, very little is known about the processes by which leadership is learned.

To add to this complexity, it is known that leaders spend very little time examining their own styles and performance. Reflection is often the least favourite activity of leaders and managers. Our experience shows that the busy work lives of leaders, together with intense pressures to perform, mean there is actually little opportunity available for reflection.

Leadership development processes like the one utilised in this book, together with formal educational programs, are a dominant focus for leadership development. But research has confirmed that leaders appear to learn best through informal life and on-the-job work experiences. Therefore, it could be said that to the extent that leadership can be learned, it is learned through the experiences of the leader. Consequently, on-the-job experience should be at the heart of any leadership development program. It may thus be useful to take an experiential approach to learning leadership, concentrating firstly on self-reflection and then on examining your own work and life experiences and those of notable other leaders. This is the approach taken in this book.

Key areas that might develop your leadership potential are:

- experiences, such as stretching work assignments;
- the influence of other leaders you regard as notable;
- learning through critical incidents (difficult organisational incidents and hardships) in your work life; and
- an examination of your own habits and behaviours in your current work context.

In this chapter, we will reflect on these and other more formal developmental processes to assist in understanding how individuals come to learn about leadership. However, we want to emphasise the critical importance of reflection. We only learn from experience if we think about that experience – otherwise we are destined to repeat our mistakes or successes without knowing why!

One of the key abilities of individuals is the ability to learn vicariously. That is, learning about leadership by observing others. Observation and reading about the lives of other leaders are good ways to improve your own leadership. The Australian Financial Review BOSS magazine publishes in August each year the BOSS True Leaders survey, which identifies those who are assessed to be the best leaders in Australia and New Zealand for the year. We highly recommend that you obtain this publication each year and, throughout the year, read case studies and articles about how other leaders practise their leadership.

A key issue for leadership development is the identification of the appropriate strategy or mix of strategies. They need to be relevant to the organisational context, the business needs, the personal journey of the leader, and the culture in which they lead.

There are also a plethora of leadership training programs in the market-place. However, research shows it is unlikely that attendance at a formal leadership development program will, in itself, send you back to the workplace a more effective leader. To achieve effective leadership, you must first understand how you lead now and why you lead the way you do – you must then improve your leadership ability and talents. In other words, improving your leadership is largely an exercise of self-reflection and self-development.

Numerous theories and models of leadership have been developed over the years, and new theories emerge frequently. In the general sense of the word, a 'theory' is a structure designed to explain a set of observations. A 'model' is a representation designed to show the main workings of a concept. Theories therefore usually explain why things happen while models attempt to be predictive and offer some procedures that leaders can follow or that can be repeated.

Before reviewing the approaches to leadership development, undertake Activity 5.1 to enable you to articulate your own theory of leadership.

Activity 5.1

Do not take a long period to think about the answer to this question. Write down what first comes into your mind.

Think of three people you know, or know of, who you consider to be effective leaders. The people may be parents, colleagues, work associates, politicians, sports stars or anyone else you choose.

In three words or short sentences describe what you think makes each person an effective leader.

What you have written in response to the activity is your own 'theory' of what constitutes an effective leader or effective leadership. Your theory is a result of the leaders you have observed (both effective and ineffective) or a result of your own experience. You use this theory either consciously or unconsciously to assess leaders you see in action each day and to judge their effectiveness. When you attend leadership development programs, you bring this lay theory with you consciously or unconsciously and it is difficult to alter it. At the end of this chapter when you have been exposed to some theories that underpin some leadership develop programs, we will return to your personal theory of leadership to see if you wish to revise it.

Approaches to leadership development

There are four distinct approaches to the study of leadership which are generally used to explain leadership theory and some that underpin formal leadership development programs — namely:

- trait approach,
- behaviour approach,
- contingency approach, and
- integrative approach.

Trait approach

Some of the first attempts by researchers to explain leadership during the period from the 1900s to the 1940s were by identifying the personal characteristics or traits of effective leaders. Traits are personal characteristics that distinguish one person from another. The underlying assumption of the research was that certain traits could predict who would emerge as effective leaders. This early view of leadership was based on the assumption that 'leaders were born and not made'.

To identify measurable traits, researchers applied two approaches. They compared:

- the traits of people who emerged as leaders against those who remained as followers, and
- the traits of effective leaders against those of ineffective leaders.

After hundreds of studies, no universal list of traits emerged but the following traits (Kirkpatrick & Locke 1991) are often found to be key to successful leadership:

- drive,
- desire to lead,
- honestly,
- integrity,
- self-confidence,

- cognitive ability, and

- knowledge of the business.

While some of the traits identified by the researchers correlated with leadership behaviour, these studies failed to isolate any traits that clearly and reliably separated leaders from followers or effective leaders from ineffective leaders—a welcome finding to teachers of leadership otherwise we would be inclined to think it was unproductive to attempt to increase our leadership potential.

While these studies supported the view that leadership could be learned, most of the studies found that effective leadership was, to some extent, dependent upon the match of the leader's traits with the requirements of the situation she or he was facing. As you will see later in this chapter, trait approaches to research continue to have relevance in leadership research.

Activity 5.2

Return to the 'lay model' of leadership that you recorded in response to activity 5.1. Examine the words you used to describe what you regard as effective leadership. Would any of these words be considered to be traits? Traits are considered to be personal characteristics of the person. If the words you have written are predominantly traits, then you are drawing heavily on trait theory as the basis for your understanding of leadership.

Behavioural approach

When trait theories of leadership failed to explain effective leadership, researchers in the 1950s focused their attention on the behaviours that effective leaders displayed, that is, what they did as leaders which made them different from followers.

It was thought by researchers that if behaviour could be learned then leaders could be easily trained to be effective in all situations. Unfortunately, most studies on behaviour showed that leadership behaviours effective in one set of circumstances were not necessarily appropriate in others.

However, the behavioural basis for the study of leadership did confirm that certain leadership behaviours are more effective than others in most situations.

This aspect of the behavioural school focused on two types of leadership behaviour — namely:

- task-centred behaviour (concern for task), and

- people-centred behaviour (concern for people).

A task-centred leader tended to stress concern for productivity and the task to be completed. Research findings generally conclude that this type of leader has a high productivity work group with low group satisfaction and cohesiveness. One might predict that high productivity would be a short-term phenomenon only.

A people-centred leader stresses concern for people. Research showed that people-centred leadership is not consistently related to productivity but does tend to enhance group satisfaction and cohesiveness. As we will see shortly when we examine leadership models, a balance between these two types is seen as most appropriate, dependent upon situational factors.

Like trait theory, the behavioural approach to leadership did not offer a comprehensive explanation for why people emerge as leaders and researchers turned their attention to situational factors.

Activity 5.3

Return to the 'lay model' of leadership that you recorded in response to activity 5.1. Examine the words you used to describe what you regard as effective leadership. Would any of these words be considered to be behaviours? If the words you have written are predominantly behaviours, then you are drawing heavily on behavioural theory as the basis for your understanding of leadership.

Situational/contingency approach

As researchers during the 1960s and 1970s became frustrated with the reality that a leader who is effective in one situation might be ineffective in another, they attempted to identify the situational factors (the context and environment) that determine how effective a particular style of leadership might be. This perspective on leadership gave rise to what was termed situational leadership or contingency theory. The situational models of leadership attempt to:

- identify which situational factors are most important in a given situation, and

- assist leaders to adopt the style of leadership that will be most effective in the situation.

In this approach to leadership and for most of the models developed, it is most important to note that leaders are said to be able to vary their leadership style to suit different circumstances. However, there is still debate about whether leaders can actually change their leadership style to suit a situation. What is known is that leaders who attempt to lead in a style that is inconsistent with their basic personality and values are unlikely to use that style effectively.

The theories developed during this time, while compelling and demonstrating that it is important for leaders to understand the situation, also did not have the predictive power necessary to adequately explain leadership effectiveness.

Activity 5.4

Return to the 'lay model' of leadership that you recorded in response to activity 5.1. Examine the words you used to describe what you regard as effective leadership. Would any of these words be considered to be related to situational factors? If the words you have written are predominantly related to situational factors, then you are drawing heavily on situational theory as the basis for your understanding of leadership.

Integrative approach

In the mid-to-late 1970s, the paradigm began to shift to integrative theory. As the name implies, integrative leadership theories attempt to combine trait, behavioural, and situational theories to explain successful, influencing, leader–follower relationships. Researchers try to explain why the followers of some leaders are willing to work so hard, making personal sacrifices to achieve the group and organisational objectives, or how effective leaders influence the behaviour of their followers. Theories identify behaviours and traits that facilitate the leader's effectiveness and explore why, depending on the situation, the same leadership behaviour may have a different effect on followers.

Activity 5.5

Return to the 'lay model' of leadership that you recorded in response to activity 5.1. Examine the words you used to describe what you regard as effective leadership. Are the words you used a mixture of traits, behaviours and situational factors? If the words you have written are a mixture of all approached, then you are drawing heavily on integrative theory as the basis for your understanding of leadership.

Leader in action: Ian Darling

Theories and models of leadership are diverse and sometimes contradictory, making it difficult to profile a leader in action that demonstrates the general thrust of the theories. The leader previewed here embodies the contemporary theories of leadership and in particular the 'worldly' theory of leadership. A 'worldly' theory of leadership emphasises concepts of ethics, sustainability and leadership for the common good.

Ian Darling is a successful fund manager who devotes his life to leading successful organisations. He is Chairman of the Sydney Theatre Company and the Sydney Theatre Company Foundation.

Simultaneously Ian is raising awareness of social issues like youth education and homelessness. He is the Chairman of the Caledonia Foundation, a private foundation focusing on the education, training and welfare of disadvantaged young Australians. He is Chairman of the Documentary Australia Foundation, a new philanthropic initiative for foundations, charitable organisations and documentary filmmakers. He is also the creator of the 'Australia's Homeless Youth' project. The project produced the documentary *The Oasis*, established the independent National Youth Commission and launched the report into youth homelessness in April 2008.

His leadership style, vision and values demonstrate that leaders of large organisations can not only attend to profit maximisation and shareholders return but can wear many hats, paying attention to higher order societal priorities or issues that relate to the common good.

In an interview with Louise Arkles from Australian Philanthropy, Ian talks about overlap between his diverse activities:

'Everything seems to be enmeshed, my films and my communities. The third film I made was 'In the Company of Actors' on the Sydney Theatre Company (STC). I'm a strong believer in the arts, not only as entertainment but what the arts can do for the community as an education tool, a tool for personal development, or for social change. For a healthy society it's really important to have a strong, vibrant and thriving arts community. Since making that film I've become Chairman for the STC, extending my interest in the arts. 'The Oasis', my latest documentary, came out of having spent ten years in a variety of voluntary roles, with Paul Moulds from the Salvation Army. I worked in Oasis as a volunteer, getting a sense of how big the whole problem is. So each of the films has been in a sense a personal journey, but over time I've been able to relate them to my philanthropic work—so I'm proud to say I eat my own cooking! Why has 'The Oasis' been so successful?'

In his investment activity, Ian supports leaders who 'carve their own path and do things really decently', supporting strong management teams with equity investment and, at the same time, using documentary films to make a difference by communicating the stories of selfless people dedicating their lives to worthy causes.

The combination of two powerful forces—the desire to succeed and humility—seem to sum up the leadership traits of Ian Darling. In respect to how he sees leadership, Ian says:

'It is very difficult to show leadership in the philanthropic space, because the last thing you want is to be seen as blowing your own

trumpet and saying 'Look I'm giving away money' or 'Look, I'm making a difference'.'

Nonetheless, Ian is making a big difference as a leader in his investment organisations and in the society generally.

Source: Australian Philanthropy, Issue 69, April 2008 & AFR *BOSS* Magazine, August 2008.

The profile above of Ian Darling shows that leadership can be and should be for the common good. Many leadership development programs today, take an essentially Harvard approach to leadership development, concentrating on finance and marketing skills. There are more important, higher order issues for leaders at all levels of an organisation. Issues like sustainability, ethics and decency in organisations need to take the same priority as finance and marketing skills if leaders, like Ian Darling, are to really make a difference that matters.

Leadership development programs

The development of leadership potential and capacity in organisations is seen by business in particular to be very important. Even in the political arena there are constant calls for improved leadership. So how do you develop the leadership you want, or have identified as being lacking in an organisation?

We have already discussed development through self awareness and the insightful processing of behaviour required. There are number of ways to use this self awareness to develop leadership skills. They include:

- development through self discipline,
- on-the-job experience, and
- education.

Over the years research examining leadership development has consistently shown that less than 10% of the experiences leaders reported as 'key events' and 'shaping events' come from traditional education or training programs. For instance, in the original study (Lindsey, Homes & McCall 1987), coursework was 6.2% of events and in the later study (McCall & Hollenbeck 2002) it was 9%, not the often cited 10% of the misleading so called 70, 20, 10 dictum where 70% represents experience on-the job, 20% for learning from peers and observations of other leaders and 10% classroom based.

Development through self discipline and EI

Self discipline plays an important part in the continuous monitoring of one's behaviour to ensure that needed self development occurs and that our actions have the desired results on followers. You may be aware of habitual behaviour on your own part — self discipline is required to stop yourself behaving in the 'normal' way and change to more productive behaviour. Once you are aware of how you behave in certain circumstances, for example how you habitually behave in meetings, you are then more likely to be able to adopt different and more productive behaviours when circumstances warrant it.

By purchasing this book and working your way through it, you are acting through self discipline and undertaking a leadership development program. There is no substitute for leaders taking responsibility for their own development and acting on their own initiative to self improve.

In chapter 3 we raised the concept of emotional intelligence (EI). Understanding one's feelings and self discipline are important components of EI. Leadership development programs based around the concept of EI are emerging and may be an important part of leader development in the future.

On-the-job experience

On-the-job experience is an obvious contributor to leadership development and effectiveness. However, reflection on experience is necessary if learning is to occur. You do not necessarily learn simply by doing something or experiencing something. In other words, there is a significant difference between ten years of experience and one year's experience ten times over. Peter Senge (1990, pp. 23, 24)) suggests caution in assuming that having had an experience automatically means you have learned from it:

> The most powerful learning comes from direct experience. Indeed we learn eating, crawling, walking and communicating through direct trial and error … But what happens when we can no longer observe the consequences of our actions? What happens if the primary

consequences of our actions are in the future or in a distant part of the larger system within which we operate? ... When our actions have consequences beyond our learning horizon, it becomes impossible to learn from direct experience.

Therefore, on-the-job experience when used as a developmental tool for leaders needs to be framed in wider learning processes like action learning, where significant organisational problems are tackled under senior executive sponsorship, succession planning, coaching and mentoring. Cultural issues must also be understood and addressed.

McCall (2010) lists seven conclusions about how on-the-job experience is useful in leadership development programs:

1. Leadership is learned from experience. Research shows that around 30% of leadership capacity is explained by heredity with the remaining 70% the result of experience.

2. Certain experiences matter more than others. Some on-the-job experiences that are known to be effective include:

    a. early work experiences and unfamiliar responsibilities

    b. short term assignments that stretch the leader

    c. major line assignments that stretch the leader

    d. observation of other leaders (including very good or very bad superiors)

    e. Hardships of various kinds (both at work and personal)

    f. some training programs like coaching and mentoring programs, especially leaders training leaders

    g. job rotations

    h. inheritance of problems that are in need of attention

    i. dealing with difficult people

    j. working in roles where there is a need to exert influence without formal power or authority

    k. working with a difficult or incompetent supervisor.

3. On-the-job experiences are powerful learning aids if they are challenging, include unexpected issues, have high stakes, are complex, include pressure and involve some novelty.

4. Different types of experiences teach different lessons. The trick for making an experience useful to the learning of the leader is to ensure that the experience goes to the heart of what drives the organisation and how organisational design helps to achieve it. Also, research on practice (DeRue and Ashford, 2010) demonstrates that the reflection on the experience is a key to gaining learning and insights. The reflection should

    a.   focus only on a few critical issues in the experience,

    b.   be in close temporal proximity to the action,

    c.   follow a structured process, for example like action learning,

    d.   lead back to more action and experience quickly, and

    e.   not be reserved only for failures but should be undertaken for successes as well.

5. All jobs and work assignments can be made more developmental. Work assignments to enhance experience can be done without forcing the leader to change roles. Early feedback, mentoring and coaching can also increase the probability that learning will occur.

6. People can get many of the experiences they need in spite of obstacles. Whoever controls who gets what job, also controls the developmental opportunities for leaders. It is a matter of knowing who needs what experience, having the appropriate experiences available and being willing to put developmental priorities ahead of other priorities in the organisation.

7. Learning takes place over time and is dynamic. The path of learning and experience is filled with serendipity, accidents, dead-ends and second attempts.

While it might appear intuitively obvious that on-the-job experience is one of the best methods of developing leadership talent, it is surprising how few organisations actually do it effectively. This is because organisations generally want results in the short term while development of people is a long term proposition. Often programs do not connect with business results and therefore senior leadership buy–in is not achieved.

Education

Most high-level leaders, particularly in today's world, are intelligent, well informed people who gather knowledge throughout their career. Formal education often forms part of this process. A broad general education is seen as important to effective leadership by most employers. Education gives you access to a wide range of knowledge and skills that may prove useful in the leadership role.

Educational programs for leaders, like the one that underpins the approach taken in this book, that focus primarily on self awareness, self understanding and double loop learning (see chapter 3) enable leaders to learn from their experiences and in doing so it multiplies the traditional benefits usually associated with the educational approach.

Leadership development programs

Leadership development programs have become big business all around the developed world, organised by a wide range of education and training institutions. These programs often use different approaches to leadership development. The next section will review some of these approaches. In practice, however, the various teaching and learning strategies often overlap, or a program will include more than one approach.

Approaches to leadership development include:

- feedback intensive programs,
- skill-based programs,
- conceptual knowledge programs, and
- personal growth programs.

Feedback intensive programs

These programs provide feedback that helps leaders see their patterns of behaviour more clearly. The 360 degree survey and executive coaching are particularly popular forms of this approach. They often take place in the workplace.

Skill-based programs

Skills training involves acquiring abilities and techniques that can be converted into action. Communication is often viewed as a skill and can be learned so to negotiation and conflict resolution skills. These are given as just some of the examples of skills-based programs.

Conceptual knowledge programs

A standard university approach to leadership development is to equip people with conceptual understanding of leadership. Conceptual knowledge is important because it alerts the leader to information that will make a difference to leadership understanding and behaviour.

Personal growth programs

Leadership development programs that focus on personal growth assume that leaders are deeply in touch with their personal dreams and talents and they will act to fulfil them. This approach assumes that leadership is almost a calling.

Activity 5.6

With your trusted peer managers, discuss what sort of leadership development activities you have undertaken so far in your career. Discuss the strengths and weaknesses of each method you have tried. Identify the activity/incident from which you learnt the most about leadership and which changed your attitude or behaviour. Among the group different methods may well have worked differently for different individuals.

Common theories used in leadership development

In this section we outline some of the seminal theories and models that are used by educators when they develop formal leadership development programs. We outline these to give you some understanding of the conceptual approaches taken by educators in developing the programs you will no doubt attend at some time in your career.

The Leadership Grid

The Leadership Grid© (formerly the Managerial Grid©) originally developed by Drs Robert R. Blake and Jane S. Mouton in 1964 depicted how two fundamental concerns (concern for people and concern for results) manifest seven distinct styles of relating. By studying each style and the resulting relationship skill behaviours, leaders can examine how behaviours help or hurt bottom line results in objective terms.

The current version of the Leadership Grid (shown in Figure 5.1) shows the possible combinations of concern for people and concern for results and the assumptions of the five different leadership styles. Two additional styles combine aspects of the other five styles. They include:

- 'paternalism' which is a linking of the production '9' and the people '9', and

- 'opportunism' which incorporates several of all of the other grid styles.

The leader's style on the grid is determined by a Grid Style self-assessment completed at the beginning and end of a Grid© seminar. The seminar delivers insight into what might be termed 'soundest' and 'actual' behaviours and how leaders should change behaviours to be more effective. Grid consultants worldwide use the seminars in organisational development activities and in assisting leaders to adopt a style closer to the 'team management' style (9,9), which Blake and Mouton suggest is the most effective style for most situations. The assumption is therefore that leaders can alter their leadership style to suit behavioural requirements.

The Grid technique assumes leaders are able to change their style and work towards an ideal style of leadership with the aid of Grid consultants and the developmental program. However, there is along standing debate amongst leadership authorities on whether a leader is able to successfully change their style to any significant degree.

Notwithstanding the grid's wide use and longevity, many critics argue that there is an inherent conflict between the push for productivity and the needs of people. A high score in both dimensions is therefore idealistic and has inadequate regard for the political and cultural elements in organisations.

Figure 5.1 The Leadership Grid©

 9,1 Grid Style: CONTROLLING
(Direct & Dominate)

I expect results and take control by clearly stating a course of action. I enforce rules that sustain high results and do not permit deviation.

 1,9 Grid Style: ACCOMMODATING
(Yield & Comply)

I support results that establish and reinforce harmony. I generate enthusiasm by focusing on positive and pleasing aspects of work.

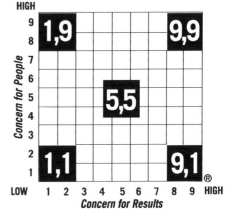

 5,5 Grid Style: STATUS QUO
(Balance & Compromise)

I endorse results that are popular but caution against taking unnecessary risk. I test my opinions with others involved to assure ongoing acceptability.

 1,1 Grid Style: INDIFFERENT
(Evade & Elude)

I distance myself from taking active responsibility for results to avoid getting entangled in problems. If forced, I take a passive or supportive position.

 PATERNALISTIC Grid Style
(Prescribe & Guide)

I provide leadership by defining initiatives for myself and others. I offer praise and appreciation for support, and discourage challenges to my thinking.

 OPPORTUNISTIC Grid Style
(Exploit & Manipulate)

I persuade others to support results that offer me private benefit. If they also benefit, that's even better in gaining support. I rely on whatever approach is needed to secure an advantage.

 9,9 Grid Style: SOUND
(Contribute & Commit)

I initiate team action in a way that invites involvement and commitment. I explore all facts and alternative views to reach a shared understanding of the best solution.

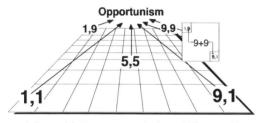

In Opportunistic Management, people adapt and shift to any Grid style needed to gain the maximum advantage. Performance occurs according to a system of selfish gain. Effort is given only for an advantage for personal gain.

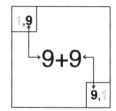

9+9: Paternalism/Maternalism
Reward and approval are bestowed to people in return for loyalty and obedience; failure to comply leads to punishment.

Sources: The Leadership Grid©. *The Power to Change* by Rachel K. McKee & Bruce Carlson, Austin: Grid International, Inc. 2009, p. 16. Copyright by Grid International, Inc. Reproduced by permission of the owners. The Leadership Grid© figure, Paternalism Figure and Opportunism from *Leadership Dilemmas-Grid Solutions*, by Robert R Blake & Anne Adams McCanse (formerly the Managerial Grid by Robert R Blake & Jane S Mouton), Houston: Gulf Publishing Company, (Grid Figure: p. 29, Paternalism Figure: p. 30, Opportunism Figure: p. 31). Copyright 1991 by Blake & Mouton, and Scientific Methods, Inc. Reproduced by permission of the owners.

Least preferred co-worker model (Fiedler's contingency model)

The contingency model of leadership is probably the most well known situational theory. It is used widely in business as a foundation to psychometric testing to select managers for specific positions. The basics of the model revolve around understanding the leader's critical behaviours (or leadership style) and then the critical aspects of the situation. The contingency model suggests that leader effectiveness is primarily determined by selecting the right kind of leader for specific situations or changing the situation to suit the leader's style. Leaders are assumed not to be able to change their leadership style.

In order to determine the leader's dominant style, Fiedler developed the least-preferred co-worker (LPC) scale. The scale requires the leader to think of a single team member with whom they have the most difficulty working (that is the least-preferred co-worker). The leader then describes that person by answering a series of questions on the scale. Undertake Activity 5.7 to determine your LPC score.

Activity 5.7

Least Preferred Co-worker (LPC)

Instructions: Think of the person with whom you can work least well. This may be someone you work with now or someone you knew in the past. It does not have to be the person you like least well, but it should be the person with whom you had the most difficulty in getting a job done. Describe this person as he or she appears to you, by circling a number for each scale.

Pleasant	8	7	6	5	4	3	2	1	Unpleasant
Friendly	8	7	6	5	4	3	2	1	Unfriendly
Rejecting	1	2	3	4	5	6	7	8	Accepting
Helpful	8	7	6	5	4	3	2	1	Frustrating
Un enthusiastic	1	2	3	4	5	6	6	8	Enthusiastic
Tense	1	2	3	4	5	6	6	8	Relaxed
Distant	1	2	3	4	5	6	6	8	Close
Cold	1	2	3	4	5	6	6	8	Warm
Cooperative	8	7	6	5	4	3	2	1	Uncooperative
Supportive	8	7	6	5	4	3	2	1	Hostile
Boring	1	2	3	4	5	6	7	8	Interesting
Quarrelsome	1	2	3	4	5	6	7	8	Harmonious
Self-assured	8	7	6	5	4	3	2	1	Hesitant
Efficient	8	7	6	5	4	3	2	1	Inefficient
Gloomy	1	2	3	4	5	6	7	8	Cheerful
Open	8	7	6	5	4	3	2	1	Guarded

Scoring

Your LPC score is the sum of the answers to these 16 questions. A high score (greater than 64) reflects a relationship-orientation, while a low score (less than 57) signals a task-orientation. A score of 58 to 63 places you in the intermediate range.

Source: Fiedler, F 1967, *A theory of leadership effectiveness*, McGraw-Hill, New York, p. 41. Reprinted with permission of the author.

The leader, having determined their LPC score, is categorised as a low-LPC leader or a high-LPC leader. Low-LPC leaders are primarily motivated by the task. Their dominant behaviours revolve around task accomplishment before they concern themselves with relationships with team members. High-LPC leaders, on the other hand, are primarily motivated by forming good relationships before concerning themselves with the task. Leaders whose LPC score falls in the intermediate range can not be easily categorised within the model.

The other critical variable in the model is 'situational favourability' — the degree of control the leader has over the team members. Three sub-elements were identified as determining situational favourability — namely:

- *Leader-member relations.* The extent to which relationships between the leader and team members are friendly and team members have respect for the leader. High leader–member relations would mean the leader has the support and trust of their work team. This is the most powerful determinant of overall situational favourableness.

- *Task structure.* An assessment of how structured or unstructured is the work being performed. Is the work repetitive or routine? Are there clear guidelines for the team members to follow or is the task ambiguous? Leaders in a structured situation are said to have more influence that leaders in unstructured situations. This element is the second in potency in the model.

- *Position power.* The ability of the manager to assign work, punish or reward team members. The leader with more positional power has more influence over the team members. This is the weakest sub-element in the model.

The relative weights of the above sub-elements, considered together, are used to create the overall degree of situational favourability. Undertake Activity 5.8 to apply the model to your work group or a work group you know of.

Activity 5.8

Use Figure 5.2 to describe the situational variables present in your work group or a workgroup you know of by following the steps:

1. Go to the scale at the foot of the figure.

2. For the *leader–member relations* variable choose either *good* or *poor* to describe a work situation you know of. Using the selected *good* or *poor* side of the scale as a continuum, estimate the degree to which leader–member relations are good or poor and mark the scale at this point.

3. Now consider the *task structure* variable. If you selected the good side of the scale for the leader–member relations variable, choose either the *structured* or *unstructured* category immediately below it on the scale. Similarly, if you selected the *poor* side of the scale for the leader–member relations variable, then position the task structure variable by selecting either the *structured* or *unstructured* category below it on the scale. Again, using the selected side as a continuum, estimate how structured or unstructured the task is and mark the scale at this point.

4. Select either *strong* or *weak* for the *leader position power* variable. This position will vertically align with the numbers one through eight between the scale and the diagram. It represents your *point of diagnosis* of the work situation.

5. Draw a vertical line into the diagram from the one-through-eight score you have selected. Where the vertical line crosses the line in the diagram it will predict the leader type suited for the position. For example, if the vertical line crosses the diagram line in the lower half of the diagram, a task-centred leader would be appropriate for the situation. If the vertical line crosses the diagram line in the upper half of the diagram, a people-centred leader would be more suited to the situation.

6. The model attempts to predict the best type of leader for each situation enabling the 'right' style of leader to be selected. Once the situational favourability has been determined for a specific situation, the model enables the situation to be 'matched' with a leader whose style is suited to lead in that situation.

Figure 5.2 The Fiedler least preferred co-worker model

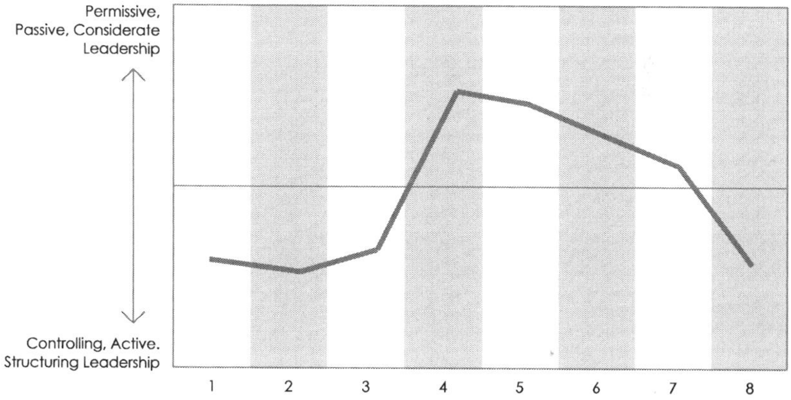

Leader-Member Relations	Good	Good	Good	Good	Poor	Poor	Poor	Poor
Task Structure	Structured		Unstructured		Structured		Unstructured	
Leader Position Power	Strong	Weak	Strong	Weak	Strong	Weak	Strong	Weak

Source: Reprinted by permission of Harvard Business Review, Exhibit 11, from Fiedler, F 1967, 'Engineer the job to fit the manager', Harvard Business Review, Sept-Oct 1965, p. 118. Copyright © 1967 by the Harvard Business School Publishing Corporation; all rights reserved.

This model may be interpreted to mean that both task-centred and people-centred leadership styles may be successful if applied in the correct situation. Therefore a leader could be selected on the basis of his/her preferred leadership style and matched to the three situational variables. A very favourable or unfavourable situation suggests that a task-centred leader would be most successful while in a moderately favourable situation, the people-centred leader would be most effective.

This model is not without its critics. Criticisms include:

- the unreliability of team members' ratings of their leader, and

- the absence of other situational variables such as the impact of technology.

Notwithstanding these criticisms, the model has been used as the basis for training leaders in how to alter the situational variables to match their leadership styles and in the selection of managers for known situations.

The assumption in the model is therefore that leaders are not able to change their style. Therefore either the situation must be changed to suit the leader's style or a leader with the desired style must be recruited for that situation. Recall however, there is a long standing debate amongst leadership authorities on whether a leader is able to successfully change their style to any significant degree.

Situational leadership theory

The following section was composed with assistance from Brandy Archambeault, Centre for Leadership Studies, Escondido, California.

Hersey and Blanchard (1989) first published their 'Life Cycle' theory of leadership in 1969. In this theory, the sole variable to be considered was termed the 'maturity' of the team members. Maturity was defined not as age or emotional stability but as:

- the ability of the team members to act in an independent manner,

- their desire for achievement,

- willingness to accept responsibility, and

- task-related ability and experience.

The focus was therefore on 'development'.

For example, in working with highly trained and educated research and development people, the most effective leader style might be low-task/low-relationship behaviour. But in the early stages of a project, the leader must impose a certain amount of structure as the project's requirements and limitations are established. The leader can move rapidly through the project cycle back to a mature low-task/low-relationship style.

Willingness

Willingness is a combination of the varying degrees of confidence, commitment, and motivation. Any one of these variables can be prepotent—that is, a person may be completely committed to the job, to quality, and to the organisation; the person may be motivated with a strong desire to do well but at the same time be insecure about their ability to do the job. Even though the person's commitment and motivation are strong, their insecurity will have to be addressed before they can move forward into *readiness*. Someone or something will have to help them over this hurdle. The primary error in diagnosing willingness is to view someone who is insecure or apprehensive as unmotivated.

Ability

Ability is determined by the amount of knowledge, experience, and demonstrated skill the follower brings to the task. A diagnosis is based on the actual display of ability. The caution here is not to diagnose *readiness* based on the leader's beliefs of what the follower should know. A frequent leadership error is to *assume* knowledge and to hold the follower accountable for skills he or she has not had an opportunity to demonstrate.

It was with these changes that Hersey's Situational Leadership® model was born in 1980. Prior to 1980 Situational Leadership® had been viewed as a theory. Since then the Situational Leadership® model has continually undergone refinements.

Blanchard retained many of the tenets of the early Situational Leadership® model but engaged in minor revisions in the 1990s. His version was renamed 'Situational Leadership 11' (SL11) to distinguish it from the earlier model and from Hersey's current one. Blanchard made minor changes to the titles of four leadership styles—from 'Telling, Selling, Participating and Delegating' to the more contemporary and acceptable terms of 'Directing, Coaching, Supporting and Delegating' respectively.

The model has been used extensively for several decades in leadership training worldwide and therefore has considerable face validity. Figure 5.3 outlines the model.

Figure 5.3 The Situational Leadership Model

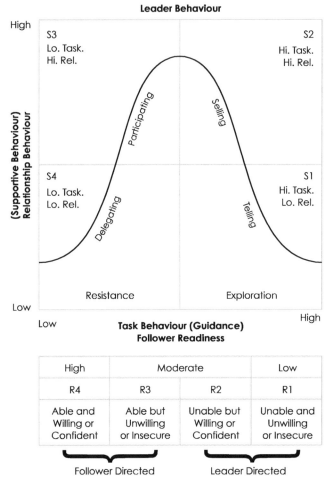

Source: Hersey, P, Blanchard, K & Johnson, D 1996, *Management of Organizational Behavior: Utilizing Human Resources*, 7th edn, Prentice Hall, p. 200. Used with permission.

The model requires the leader to assess the characteristics of the team members and the situation, and directs that leaders need to assess the 'readiness' of the team members and vary their leadership style as team members pass through the various stages.

In the initial phase an inexperienced person may enter the team or be new to the organisation. Initially this team member will require instruction in the tasks and familiarisation with the organisation's rules and policies. A non-directive manager may cause confusion and therefore a high task orientation by the manager is appropriate. As new team members become more experienced, the manager may apply a more people-centred style, while maintaining high task orientation until the team member can accept full responsibility for their tasks.

In the third phase, as experience and a sense of responsibility increases, close supervision may be resented so lower task orientation by the manager would be appropriate. The manager will continue to give support to build trust and confidence in the team member. In the final stage the team member reaches high readiness and becomes a respected colleague in the work team. The team member now works unsupervised and accepts full responsibility for their tasks.

This model has generated some interest because it is dynamic rather than static in nature. It recognises that while managers may adopt an overall style for their work teams, individuals within the team may require different approaches until each team member is equally mature. The model has been used extensively in leadership training worldwide for several decades and therefore has considerable face validity.

Activity 5.9

For effective and experienced leaders, situational leadership theory is often a statement of the obvious. But how might the theory be applied to an unwilling or incapable team member? Discuss briefly.

Summary

Leadership theory has developed over thousands of years and there have been many different approaches to the study of leadership. These different approaches lead to different approaches as to how leaders should be developed.

Very little is known about the processes by which leadership is learned. To add to this, it is known that leaders themselves spend very little time examining their own styles and performance. However, research has confirmed that leaders appear to learn best through informal life and on-the-job work experiences.

There are four distinct approaches for the study of leadership that generally underpin formal leadership development programs— namely:

- trait approach,
- behaviour approach,
- contingency approach, and
- integrative approach.

Leaders develop through self awareness and the insightful processing of behaviour required. There are number of ways to use this self awareness to develop leadership skills. They include:

- development through self discipline,
- experience, and
- education.

On-the-job experience is one of the best methods of developing leadership talent. But it is surprising how few organisations actually do it effectively. This is because organisations generally want results in the short term while development of people is a long term proposition. Often programs are also not connecting to business results and therefore do not get senior leadership buy in. Some on-the-job experiences that are known to be effective include:

- Early work experiences and unfamiliar responsibilities
- Short term assignments that stretch the leader
- Major line assignments that stretch the leader
- Observing other leaders (including very good or very bad superiors)
- Hardships of various kinds
- Some training programs like coaching and mentoring programs, especially leaders training leaders
- Job rotations

- Inheriting problems from others that are in need of attention
- Dealing with difficult people
- Working in roles where there is a need to exert influence without formal power or authority
- Working with a difficult or incompetent supervisor.

Common theories and models that are used by educators when they develop formal leadership development programs include the Leadership Grid, Fiedler's Contingency Model and Situational Leadership theory.

Reflection on your leadership practice

The theory and models presented in this chapter were developed by identifying diverse 'variables' said to affect the leader's style. For example, some of the variables identified in the various models include follower readiness, follower confidence, leader/member relations, task structure, positional power, environmental forces, and so on. These variables may be useful to consider in your own theory of leadership.

At the commencement of this chapter, you were invited to write down your own lay theory of leadership. Now that you have reviewed some of the theories and models of leadership, do you wish to alter your model to include other components — or has this chapter simply reinforced your own theory?

References

Blake, R & Mouton, J 1978, *The New Managerial Grid*, Houston, Gulf Publishing Co., New York.

Blake, RR & McCanse, AA 1991, *Leadership dilemmas-Grid solutions*, Houston, Gulf Publishing Company.

Blake, RR & Mouton, JS 1964, *The managerial grid*, Houston, Gulf Publishing Company.

DeRue, D & Ashford, S 2010, Power o the People: Where has personal agency gone in leadership development, *Industrial and Organizational Psychology*, vol. 3, pps. 24-27.

Fiedler, F 1967, *A theory of leadership effectiveness*, McGraw-Hill, New York.

Fiedler, F 1986, The contribution of cognitive resources to leadership performance, *Journal of Applied Social Psychology*, vol. 16, pp. 532-548.

Fiedler F & Garcia, J 1987, *New approaches to leadership: Cognitive resources and organizational performance*, John Wiley, New York.

Hersey, P & Blanchard, K 1989, *Lead - Leader Effectiveness and Adaptability Description*, Center for Leadership Studies, California.

Hersey, P, Blanchard, K & Johnson, D 1996, *Management of Organizational Behavior: Utilizing Human Resources*, Prentice Hall, NJ.

Kirkpatrick, S & Locke, E 1991, 'Leadership: Do traits matter?', *The Academy of Management Executive*, vol. 5, no. 2, pp. 48-60.

Lindsey, E, Homes, V and McCall, M 1987, Key Events in Executives' Lives, Technical Report 32, Centre for Creative Leadership.

McCall, M 2010, 'Recasting Leadership Development, *Industrial and Organizational Psychology*, vol. 3, pps. 3-19.

McCall, M and Hollenbeck, G 2002, *Developing Global Executives*, Harvard Business School Press, Boston.

Senge, PM 1990, *The Fifth Discipline*, Random House, Sydney.

Chapter 6

CHARISMATIC AND TRANSFORMATIONAL LEADERSHIP

CHAPTER CONTENTS

Spotlight: Natasha Stott Despoja

In 1996, at the age of 26, Natasha Stott Despoja became the youngest woman in Australia to enter Federal politics. By 2001 she was elected leader of the Democrats. She left parliament in 2004 after the birth of her son.

Although best known for her role as leader of the Democrats party, Natasha has occupied a variety of leadership positions throughout her student and political career. Born in Adelaide on 9 September 1969, she graduated from the University of Adelaide with a Bachelor of Arts degree. It was at the university that she first became active in student representation, becoming president of the Students' Association. Between 1991 and 1995 Natasha worked as a political adviser to various Democrats senators.

As an attractive young woman, Natasha received more than her fair share of publicity. Much of the publicity was trivial, displaying a discomfort with so young a person holding such a responsible position. So what was it that drew her to politics and enabled her to be so successful so early in her career?

Natasha was a passionate advocate of human rights and social justice at a time when the primary political narrative was economic. She was an agent for change at a time when government was looking backward to the security of the past rather than to the challenges of the future.

She has a commanding presence. Her communication style is one of clear, concise dialogue with heartfelt delivery and a keen sense of humour. She lives in a world of ideas that she believes can and should be turned into reality for the benefit of Australia. Natasha refers to her time as leader of the Democrats as 'heady days'. On the strength of her ability to attract attention to the Democrats, to connect with the Australian public and hard work, six Democrats were elected to parliament in six months, the greatest election success ever for the party.

Natasha has a vision for the nation. She is committed to the idea of a government and parliament that holds certain basic principles at its core.

I think we need a complete re-instatement of a human rights agenda in this country, which I think is achievable and one day will happen. (Burrows, p. 99)

Natasha is a born communicator. Her words are carefully chosen and her message is succinct with little ambiguity. She is great believer in the power of the spoken word. She motivates people by appealing to their core moral values, constantly questioning the status quo, and debating the efficacy of legislation by highlighting impacts on the rights and dignity of human beings. She appeals at both the emotive and the logical level.

Natasha believes that power can be used for good and bad. She believes that this is a result of the person wielding the power rather than the power itself. She is confident and unashamed to stand up for what she believes is right. Some of the issues that she supported led to her receiving death threats.

Natasha's development over the years as a strong, confident leader was achieved mainly through a combination of on-the-job training, long hours and learning the ropes of the formalised political system. Her speeches are pitched to her audience. She utilises a combination of razor-sharp facts and emotional appeal. Natasha puts great store in communicating clear values, working with others towards a worthwhile vision—a vision with the potential to transform.

Source: Burrows, N 'Natasha Stott Despoja' in Dalglish and Evans, 2007, *Leadership in the Australian Context*, Tilde University Press, Melbourne.

The description of Natasha touches on many aspects of charismatic and transformational leadership. Natasha demonstrates that leadership is possible at a very early age, but that trying to change the status quo can come at a high price. Charismatic leaders often have as many detractors as they do admirers and there are many in politics, as in other fields of endeavour, who wish to maintain the status quo.

Introduction

Charisma has long been associated with leadership. As previous chapters have demonstrated the study of personality has been an integral part of the development of leadership theory. Charismatic and transformational leadership models move beyond simply considering personality—they explore the impact of leadership characteristics and behaviour on followers. They explore the relationship between the leader and their situation, bringing together aspects of traits theory and contingency theories. Transformational leadership and breakthrough leadership, an Australian model, also explore the impact of the leader's behaviour on the followers' behaviour and development. So the models examined in this chapter address all aspects of the leadership process, the leader's characteristics and behaviours, the followers and the situation.

Charisma and charismatic leadership

Charisma has come to mean many things. It is used in general conversation relating to many celebrities and others who catch the public attention. To a great extent this has devalued the power of charisma and its potential as an effective leadership attribute.

Charisma is a Greek word meaning 'divinely inspired gift'. In the study of leadership, charisma is seen as a special quality of leaders whose purpose, powers and extraordinary determination differentiate them from others (Conger & Kanungo 1988, cited in Dubrin, Dalglish & Miller 2006).

The famous German sociologist, Max Weber, described the charismatic leader as one who reveals 'a transcendent mission or course of action that may not be in itself appealing to the potential followers, but which is acted on because the followers believe their leader is extraordinarily gifted' (Weber 1947, cited in Dubrin, Dalglish & Miller 2006). These leaders were so personally extra-ordinary that they had followers in their thrall. The relationship between leaders and followers in a charismatic relationship is so powerful because the relationship is symbiotic. The charismatic leader and his/her followers are mutually dependent (Kellerman 2009).

The locus of charismatic leadership

The biggest question to come out of Weber's theory concerns where the locus of charismatic leadership lies. What creates charisma? Is charisma primarily the result of the situation or social context facing the leader and followers, of the leader's extraordinary qualities, or of the strong relationship between charismatic leaders and their followers?

The relationship with followers is particularly important. Charismatic leaders work deliberately at cultivating a relationship with group members through *impression management*. They take steps to create a favourable, successful impression. This is more than superficial. According to Gardner and Avolio 1998, (cited in Dubrin, Dalglish & Miller 2006), charismatic leaders, to a greater extent than non-charismatic leaders, value and pursue an interrelated set of images: they are perceived as trustworthy, credible, morally worthy, innovative, esteemed, and powerful. An implication of the impression management analysis of charismatic leaders is that they are skilful actors, presenting a charismatic face to the world.

It also appears likely that certain situations encourage the followers' perception of the leader and encourages them to be emotionally involved both in the mission of the charismatic leader and in the pursuit of their own goals. The followers must have a strong desire to identify with the leader. This can often occur when the followers feel alienated or threatened. They feel helpless and put their faith in someone who claims to be able to protect them and solve the problem. Leaders can also appear charismatic to followers after they have achieved something extraordinary—their achievements give them an aura of charisma. This creates an aura of charisma around those who hold high office.

Reflections

Scholars continue to explore the issue of the locus of charisma. Think about Natasha Stott Despoja. Which of the three interpretations concerning the locus of charismatic leadership do you think is true in the case of this leader?

Robert J House developed a theory of charismatic leadership that defines charisma in terms of its effects. He identified nine charismatic effects (House 1977). Jane A. Halpert clustered these outcomes into three dimensions — namely:

- referent power,
- expert power, and
- job involvement.

This is a helpful way of defining charismatic leadership as these dimensions are clearly defined. It can also help you develop your own charismatic skills.

Referent power

Referent power is the ability to influence others that stems from the leader's traits and characteristics — i.e. people like and trust the leader.

Expert power

Expert power is the ability to influence others because of one's specialised knowledge, skills and abilities.

Job involvement

Job involvement is the ability of the follower to make a contribution to meaningful goals.

Put the two power attributes together with *job involvement* and you have a powerful combination leading to charismatic leadership. The leader in action described later in this chapter, Barack Obama, is an interesting example of these three dimensions coming together.

By developing some of the traits, characteristics and behaviours of charismatic people, you can increase your own charisma. Through practice of the following behaviours (and self discipline) you will increase your charisma:

- Create a vision for others—a vision that creates an exciting image of where the organisation is heading and how it will get there.

- Be enthusiastic, optimistic and energetic.

- Develop an inspirational communication style using metaphors and analogies and gearing the language specifically to different audiences.

- Be persistent.

- Remember the names of people; make your group members feel capable and that they are contributing.

- Make an impressive appearance. Be willing to self-promote. Being dramatic and unique contribute to charisma.

- Demonstrate emotional expressiveness and warmth.

(Howell & Avolio 1992; Sellers 1996; Waldman & Yammarino 1999; Kellerman 2009.)

Communication skills, particularly verbal communication skills are extremely important in appearing charismatic. Charismatic communication appeals to followers in terms that they understand, often making emotional appeals and painting a picture of the future. Chapter 9 will deal extensively with leadership communication but in Activity 6.1 we will help you reflect on how 'charismatic' your oral communication may be.

Activity 6.1 Self assessment

Answer yes or no to the following statements:

- I enjoy speaking in public.

- I appear confident and in control when I speak.

- When I speak I paint a visual picture of my subject giving examples that the audience can relate to.

- When I speak most people stop and listen.

- I make sure that I have all the facts before I make a presentation or speech.

- I use examples to illustrate the facts I present.

- People have used terms such as enthusiastic, powerful or passionate about the way I speak.

- I use inclusive language that makes the audience feel part of my vision.

- I use emotive language as well as facts.

Count the number of times you said yes to the above statements. The more yeses you have the more likely your oral communication will contribute to your charisma.

The last two decades of the twentieth century and the first decade of the twenty-first century have presented organisations with unparalleled levels of uncertainty, turbulence, rapid change, and intense competition. Many organisations are struggling with the need to manage chaos, to undergo internal cultural change, to reinvent their businesses, to restructure their organisations, to adopt or invent new technologies, and to empower organisational members. In the face of such challenges, the charismatic style of leadership has become of renewed interest.

Leader in action: President Obama

Barack Obama became the 44th president of the United States of America in 2008. America decided to place its fate in the hands of a man who was born of an idealistic white teenage mother and a charismatic African graduate student who abandoned them. He grew up without money on the fringes of society, talked his way into good schools, and chose to work as a community worker in a difficult and disillusioned area of Chicago where the myths of racial 'brotherhood' were apparent. He was neither white enough nor black enough. He entered politics to make a difference, fighting his way first to the Senate and then to the White House. In just about every respect he represents a radical departure from the norm. To an alienated and angry population he preached reconciliation. He engaged people who had lost faith in government and the political process or who had never had it. He was able to do this precisely because he was an outsider himself, had a thin political résumé and few cronies, and could sell himself as a solution.

Timing was important. His predecessor was, by most commentators, considered a failure. He had taken the US to war for what was increasingly being seen as an unjust cause and he had presided over the worst economic crisis since the depression. This provided an opportunity to bring about fundamental change, change that the conservatism and checks and balances of the normal political process would make impossible. The United States and its people knew they were in trouble and they were looking for someone to lead them out of this trouble.

Using extraordinary rhetoric, Obama changed the political debate, something he could do because he was not strongly tied to any particular political ideology.

... the question we ask today is not whether our government is too big or too small but whether it works – whether it helps families find jobs at a decent wage, care they can afford, a retirements that is dignified.

There can be no doubt that his strong rhetorical skills contributed much to his success, but so did the content of his message, his personal behaviour during the campaign and the fact that he appealed not to large vested interests but to ordinary people to support his campaign financially. He raised small sums of money from large numbers of people who filled his election coffers to overflowing. His charismatic appeal caused his followers to move mountains to get him elected. They were directly involved in making his success possible.

The tone of his speech was resolute, suffused with sobriety, reflecting a tough-minded realism at home and abroad. This suited the mood of the people. Whilst the core of his message was sombre, he foretold of hardship, of a need for change. He also painted a picture of what was possible and millions trekked to Washington for the inauguration. He called for ordinary Americans to become involved—to call community meetings to address local issues. Ten thousand meetings were held. This is a new kind of politics for the United States, with the potential to be the most powerful citizen army in US history.

Already the Obama ethos is slipping into the nation's bloodstream. He rarely used the word I. He addressed the nation as a community of mature adults:

... they understand that our power alone cannot protect us, nor does it entitle us to do as we please.

He denounced what he considered false choices, such as those between national safety and national ideals. He stated clearly and unequivocally his stance on many issues of great concern in the US:

... those who seek to advance their aims by inducing terror and slaughtering innocents ... You cannot outlast us, and we will defeat you.

He placed responsibility for US recovery, not on the shoulders of government but on the people themselves:

What is required is a new declaration of independence, not just in our nation but in our own lives—from ideology and small thinking, prejudice and bigotry—an appeal not to our easy instincts but to our better angels.

He remains composed. He radiates assurance. He stays on message and communicates with astounding verbal fluency. He appears to be a genuinely charismatic leader. Will he also turn out to be a transformational one?

Even sceptics called his acceptance speech one of the greatest political sermons of our time. Can he deliver on its promise?

... they said this day would never come. They said that this country was too divided, too disillusioned to ever come together around a common purpose. But on this January night—at this defining moment in history—you have done what the cynics said we couldn't do.

Sources: Klein, J 2009, 'A New Destiny', *Time Magazine*, p. 14-17, 20 January 2009; Baldon, J 'How to Communicate Like Barack Obama, <http://blogs.harvardbusiness.org/baldoni/2009/01d/the_many_communicaton_styles.ht> , accessed 17/8/09 ; Kellerman, B 2009, The Nature of Obama's Charismatic Leadership, <http://blogs Harvardbuisness.org/cs/2009/01/the nature_of_obamas_charismat.html>; Sloan, JW 2009, Obama's Opportunity to be a Transformational Leader, <http:www.hnn.us/aticle/60699.html>; Gibbs, N 2008, Election 2008, *Time*, 17 November 2008.

The profile of President Barack Obama shows how charisma can be used to good advantage by some leaders. However, let's face it, not many of us will ever have Obama's communication skills or presence. This does not mean however that we should not strive to be excellent communicators. All of us also have attributes that can be used to increase our personal appeal (charisma) to others. Sometimes a good sense of humour can be an asset or even what others might regard as a disadvantage can be turned into something to work for us.

Transactional leadership

In his book *Leadership,* Burns (1978), maintained that power and leadership were two distinct entities.

Power-wielders

Power-wielders were those individuals who used their power to influence followers to behave in such a way as to accomplish the leader's goals. Power-wielders often saw followers as a means to an end and treated them accordingly. According to Burns, leadership is inseparable from the follower's needs and goals. From his perspective, all leaders were power-wielders but not all power-wielders were leaders. Power and influence will be discussed in greater detail in chapter 8.

Burns also believed that leadership could take two forms — transactional leadership and transformational leadership.

An exchange relationship

Transactional leadership is characterised by leaders and followers being in an exchange relationship. Examples might include exchanging money for work, votes for votes, loyalty for consideration, and so on. Two important aspects of transactional leadership are that it is very common and that it tends to be transitory, as there may be no enduring purpose to keep the parties together once the transaction is complete. Even within the transactional form of leadership Burns identified an ethical element. Transactional leadership depended on the transaction between leader and follower to be acceptable to both, that there was a fair exchange. If the transaction no longer met this criterion the follower could withdraw. This again emphasises the voluntary nature of Burns's view of leadership.

Transformational leadership

According to Burns (1978) *transformational leadership* serves to change the *status quo* by:

- appealing to followers' values and their sense of higher purpose. Transformational leaders articulate the problems in the current system and have a compelling vision of what a new society or organisation could be. This new vision is linked to both the leader's and the followers' values.

- reframing issues so that they are aligned with the leader's vision and the followers' values.

- operating at a higher stage of moral development than their followers. Their vision often appeals to the followers' end values. End values are the ideals by which a society or organisation should strive to live, and include justice, freedom and equality.

Researchers over the years have not always distinguished between charismatic and transformational leadership. Leaders often encounter the need to transform organisations from low performance to acceptable performance or from acceptable performance to high performance. At other times, a leader is expected to move an organisation from a crisis mode to high ground. To accomplish this, the transformational leader attempts to overhaul or renew the organisational culture.

Qualities for bringing about transformations

Bass (1990) undertook a great deal of research into transformation leadership and moved some way from the moral imperative apparent in Burns's original definition. Bass identified four qualities that are particularly useful in enabling leaders to bring about transformations:

1. Above all, transformational leaders are *charismatic* — they have vision and a sense of mission. They also have the respect, confidence and loyalty of group members. It is within this framework that all the elements previously discussed about charismatic leaders would sit.

2. Closely linked to charisma, transformational leaders practice *inspirational leadership*. Part of the inspiration derives from communicating a vision with fluency and confidence. By giving emotional support and making emotional appeals, transformational leaders inspire group members to exceed their initial expectations. Here again we see the importance of the follower — the group member — as an integral part of the transformation.

3. Transformational leaders provide *intellectual stimulation* by encouraging group members to examine old problems or methods in new ways. The transformational leader creates an atmosphere that encourages creative thinking and problem solving. Here, bringing about change using innovative methods becomes important. Intellectual stimulation keeps the followers engaged.

4. Transformational leaders demonstrate *individualised consideration* by giving personal attention to group members.

Perhaps the important distinction between charismatic leadership and transformational leadership is that true transformational leadership brings about positive change — for the leader, the organisation and the followers.

The role of the leader in the transformation

Dubrin, Dalglish and Miller (2006) identify a number of ways in which transformation takes place, and the role of the leader in the transformation.

- *The leader raises people's awareness* of the challenges, the issues and the possibilities.

- *The leader helps people look beyond self-interest.* The leader encourages followers to look at the big picture—to see the contribution they can make to the well-being of others, the organisation or other people. They become part of something bigger than themselves.

- *The leader helps people search for self-fulfilment.* Here the focus is on how each individual can benefit from the achievement of the organisational goals.

- *The leader helps people understand need for change.* People often resist change. Understanding why the change must happen is a critical element of the leadership task. This will be dealt with in greater detail in chapter 11.

- *The leader invests managers with a sense of urgency.* If there is no urgency, little is likely to change. The daily routine of survival has the power to drown new initiatives unless the urgency of the issue is clear.

- *The leader is committed to greatness.* The leader represents the best that is possible—they challenge for people to be the best, for high ideals to be maintained. The leader raises the issues and challenges above the mundane.

- *The leader adopts a long range, broad perspective.* Particularly in uncertain times, leaders are expected by their followers to look into the future, to provide the broad framework within which their particular challenges lie.

For Burns, these behaviours have to take place within a specific value system. Transformational leadership is not simply about change, but about change that involves followers' participation in activities motivated by end values. Later research has played the value base down, though the research now is distinguishing between authentic and non-authentic transformational leadership; the former meeting all of Burns's requirements.

Issues in transformational and charismatic leadership

Four particular issues arise when looking at the practice of both transformational and charismatic leadership.

- The special relationships charismatic/transformational leaders have with their followers do not happen by accident; rather, they are often a result of interaction between the leader's qualities, leader-and-follower values, and the presence of certain situational factors.

- Charismatic/transformational leadership does not develop overnight. It takes time for the strong emotional bonds between leader and followers to develop. There needs to be time for trust to develop.

- Studies undertaken by Bass (1997) have identified that transformational leadership appears to be universal and is particularly prevalent in countries possessing collectivist rather than individualistic societies (Jung, Bass & Sosik 1995).

- Various researchers have reported that females are more likely to exhibit an 'interpersonal leadership style' than men. These attributes are very similar to those attributed to transformational leaders. Rosener's (1990) survey research identified several differences in how men and women described their leadership experience. Men describe themselves in somewhat transactional terms, viewing leadership as an exchange with subordinates for services rendered. The women, on the other hand, tended to describe themselves in transformational terms. They helped their subordinates develop commitment for broader goals than their own self-interest and described their influence more in terms of personal characteristics like charisma and interpersonal skills than mere organisational position.

Reflections

Do you consider yourself charismatic or transformational? If so consider the specific elements that make you so. If not, what could you do to become more transformational?

Breakthrough leadership

Another version of the charismatic/transformational conceptualisation is *breakthrough leadership*. It was developed by Sarros and Butchatsky (1996) within the different cultural context of Australia. In the study (p. 3) they say that breakthrough leadership

> ... *extends beyond leadership by inspiring individuals through behaviour that encourages continuous learning, builds confidence and competence and ultimately results in a committed, enlightened and inspired workforce.*

Like transformational leadership, breakthrough leadership focuses on change and identifies how the behaviour of leaders brings about outcomes that are largely based on the behaviour and attributes of followers. In this aspect it also resembles servant leadership where the growth of the followers is one of the indicators of servant leadership. The motivation of the leader, however, may not be that of a servant leader. Here breakthrough leadership was concerned with effective leadership of an organisation in a time of change.

Sarros and Butchatsky identified four specific leader behaviours that contributed to breakthrough leadership — namely:

- *Respect for others.* An attribute particularly important in Australian culture, but perhaps equally effective in other contexts.

- *Values clarification.* Why things are being done needs to be explained together with the values that inform both the process and the outcomes.

- *Willingness to look, listen and learn.* Knowledge sharing is a two-way process.

- *A systems approach.* Leaders had the ability to look at the whole system rather than focus on one area where change may be required.

They argue that this type of leader behaviour creates followers who are confident, competent, committed and open to continuous learning. Breakthrough leaders create a climate within their organisations that encourages individual and group learning. The changes in the organisation are brought about by the changes in the people.

Differences between Australian and American perceptions of leadership

The theory of breakthrough leadership sits within a body of writing about Australian leadership and its similarities and differences to the predominant North American models. A number of researchers have explored the impact of Australian culture on management and leadership practice (Casimir, Waldman, Batram & Young 2006; Carless, Man & Wearing 1996; Pillai, Scandura & Williams 1999).

According to Parry and Sarros (1996) there are significant differences between Australian and American perceptions of leadership. It is within these differing perceptions that the breakthrough model was developed. Australian leaders are expected to inspire high levels of performance but must do so in a culturally appropriate way (Ashkanasy & Falkus 1997).

Breakthrough leadership is a model of leadership behaviour that focuses on bringing about change, just as transformational leadership does, but reflects the characteristics Australians expect from their leaders. These include:

- the importance of establishing good relationships and feelings of self worth in the workplace;

- the use of communication to develop trust;

- the need for leaders to care for their followers and to share their pain—success is heavily dependent on a leader's capacity to be seen to identify with and respond to the emotional needs of their followers;

- values grounded in fundamental human values such as benevolence, honesty and the 'greater good';

- personal gratification and reward that is genuine and low key; and

- the provision of consistent principled direction and guidance (Dalglish & Evans 2007).

Summary

Charisma has long been associated with leadership. The biggest question to come out of Weber's theory of charismatic leadership, and one that continues to be debated, concerns where the locus of charismatic leadership rests. What creates charisma? Is charisma primarily the result of the situation, the social context facing the leader and followers, the leader's extraordinary qualities, or the strong relationship between charismatic leaders and their followers?

Jane A. Halpert clustered the outcomes of House's research into the elements of charismatic leadership into three dimensions — referent power, expert power and job involvement. This is a useful way of identifying the defining characteristics that make a leader appear charismatic.

Burns differentiated between power-wielders and leaders. From his perspective, all leaders were power-wielders but not all power-wielders were leaders. Burns also coined the terms *transactional* and *transformational* leadership to differentiate between two different ways of leading.

Transactional leadership is characterised by leaders and followers being in an exchange relationship. Transactional leadership is a common form of leadership but can be transitory as the followers may cease to follow when a particular task has been completed. Transformational leadership, on the other hand, takes longer to develop. It appeals to followers' values and their sense of higher purpose rather than self interest. Transformational leaders reframe issues so as to align the leader's vision with the followers' values. Burns also saw true transformational leaders operating at a higher stage of moral development than their followers.

Bass identified behaviours that cause leaders to be seen as transformational. Above all, transformational leaders are charismatic — they have vision and a sense of mission. Transformational leaders practice inspirational leadership, often through the use of exceptional rhetorical skills. Transformational leaders provide intellectual stimulation by encouraging group members to examine old problems or methods in new ways, getting their engagement in the process. Transformational leaders demonstrate individualised consideration by giving personal attention to group members, making them feel that they are making a special contribution.

Breakthrough leadership can perhaps be seen as Australia's transformational leadership model as it inspires individuals through behaviour that encourages continuous learning, builds confidence and competence and ultimately results in a committed, enlightened and inspired workforce. All these things are valued in Australian culture. Breakthrough leaders create a climate within their organisations that encourages individual and group learning. The changes in the organisation are then brought about by the changes in the people.

Reflection on your leadership practice

To have yourself perceived as a transformational leader by more senior leaders will certainly increase your career prospects. Transformational leaders are highly regarded and sought after in modern workplaces for their ability to implement successful change and in doing so, bring people with them. Given what you now know about transformational leadership, how will you attempt to improve your perception and skills in this area?

References

Ashkanasy, NM & Falkus, S 1997, *The Australian Enigma*, Chapter submitted for inclusion in the first 'globe Anthology', Brisbane.

Baldon, J 2009, *How to Communicate Like Barack Obama*, viewed 17 August 2009, <http://blogs. harvardbusiness.org/baldoni/2009/01d/the_many_communicaton_styles.ht>.

Bass, BM 1990, *Bass and Stogdill's Handbook of Leadership: Theory, Research and Managerial Applications*, 3rd edn., New York: The Free Press, A Division of Macmillan.

Bass, BM 1997, 'Does the transformational-transactional leadership paradigm transcend organisational and national boundaries? *American Psychologist*, February, p. 130.

Burns, JM 1978, *Leadership*, Harper & Row, New York.

Burrows, N 2007, 'Natasha Stott Despoja' in Dalglish and Evans 2007, *Leadership in the Australian Context*, Tilde University Press, Melbourne.

Carless, S, Mann, L & Waring, A 1996, 'Transformational leadership and teams: an examination of the Bass and Kouzes-Posner models, in K Parry ed *Leadership Research and Practice: Emerging Themes and New Challenges*, Melbourne Pitman/Woodsland.

Casimir, G, Waldman, DA, Bartram, T & Yang, 2006, 'Trust and the Relationship Between Leadership and Follower Performance: Opening the Black Box in Australia and China', *Journal of Leadership and Organisational Studies*, Leadership and Organisational Studies, Flint, 2006 vol. 12, no. 3.

Conger, JA, Kanungo, RN & Associates 1988, *Charismatic Leadership*, San Francisco: Jossey Bass.

Dalglish, C & Evans, P 2007, *Leadership in the Australian Context*, Tilde University Press, Melbourne, Australia.

Dubinsky, AJ, Yammarino, FJ & Jolson, MA 1995, 'An examination of linkages between personal characteristics and dimensions of transformational leadership', *Journal of Business and Psychology*, Spring.

Dubrin, A & Dalglish, C 2003, *Leadership and Australasian Focus*, John Wiley & Sons, Milton.

Dubrin, Dalglish & Miller 2006, *Leadership 2nd Asia Pacific Edition*, John Wiley & Sons, Milton.

Dubinsky, AJ, Yammarino, FJ & Jolson, MA 1995, An examination of linkages between personal characteristics and dimensions of transformational leadership, *Journal of Business and Psychology*, 9(3), pp. 315–335.

Gardner, WL & Avolio, BJ 1998, The charismatic relationship: a dramaturgical perspective. *Academy of Management Review*, January, pp. 32–58.

Gibbs, Nancy 2008, Election 2008. *Time*, 17 November 2008.

House, RJ 1977, A 1976 theory of charismatic leadership, in JG Hunt & LL Larson eds., *Leadership: The Cutting Edge. Carbondale*, IL: South Illinois University Press.

Rosener JB 1990, Ways women lead, *Harvard Business Review*, 68, pp. 119–160.

Howell, JM & Avolio, B 1992, 'The ethics of charismatic leadership: submission or liberation? *The Academy of Management Executive.* May pp. 43-52.

Jung, DI, Bass, MB & Sosik, J 1995, 'Collectivism and Transformational Leadership', *Journal of Management Inquiry*, 2.

Kellerman, B 2009, *The Nature of Obama's Charismatic Leadership*, <http://blogs Harvardbuisness.org/cs/2009/01/thenature_of_obamas_ charismat.html>.

Klein, J 2009, 'A New Destiny', *Time Magazine*, p. 14-17, 20 January 2009.

Media Man Australia, *Dick Smith*, viewed 3 August 2009, <www.mediaman.com.au/ profiles/smith.html>.

National Library of Australia 2001, *Dick Smith Australian of the Year 1986*, viewed 15 March 2001, <www.nla.gov.au/exhibitions/ aoy/awards/1986_aoy.html>.

Parry, KW & Sarros, JC 1996, 'An Australasian perspective on transformational leadership', in KW Parry ed., *Leadership Research and Practice, Emerging Themes and New Challenges*, South Melbourne, Pitman Publishing.

Pillai, R, Scandura, T & Williams, E 1999, 'Leadership and organizational Justice: similarities and differences across cultures', *Journal of international Business Studies*, 30.

Ramsey, A 2000, 'Evasive action on air safety', *Sydney Morning Herald*, 1 April, p. 49.

Rosener, JB 1990, Ways women lead, *Harvard Business Review*, 68, pp. 119–160.

Sarros, JC & Butchatsky, O 1996, *Leadership*, Sydney: Harper Business.

Sellers, P 1996, 'What exactly is charisma?' *Fortune*, January 15, pp. 72-75

Sloan, JW 2009, *Obama's opportunity to be a transformational leader*, <http:www.hnn.us/article/60699.html>.

Sunday profile, July 17 2005, viewed July 2009, <www.abc.net.au/sundayprofile /stories/s1416294.html>.

Talking Heads, 7 May 2007, viewed 3 August 2009, <www.abc.net.au/talking heads/txt/s1913699.htm>.

Walderman, DA & Yammarino FJ 1999, 'CEO charismatic leadership; levels of management and levels of analysis effects', *Academy of Management Review,* April, 1999 pp. 266-85.

Walker, D 2000, Interview with Dick Smith.

Weber, M 1947, *The Theory of Social and Economic Organisation*, Trans & Ed Henderson, AM & Parson, T, New York: Oxford University Press.

Chapter 7

CULTURE AND LEADERSHIP

Management as the word is presently used is an American invention. In other parts of the world not only the practices but the entire concept of management may differ, and the theories needed to understand it may deviate considerably from what is considered normal and desirable in the USA. (Hofstede 1999, p. 81)

CHAPTER CONTENTS

Spotlight: Dr Mohamad Abdalla

In 2007 Dr Mohamad Abdalla (at only 37) was appointed spokesman for the newly formed Australian National Council of Imams. This council has an executive committee of fifteen, two from each of the states and territories who will examine issues that affect the Australian Muslim community, particularly things that relate to legal aspects of Islamic and Australian law.

Dr Mohamad Abdalla was born in Libya on 11 May 1970. His parents are Palestinians who met in Jordan, where Mohamad lived until the age of 15 years. Growing up with a father who is a master chief instructor in a Japanese martial art has given Mohamad a quiet confidence that compliments the humility expected by his Islamic faith.

In 1985, shortly after arriving in Australia, Mohamad won the Alex Goodsell Award for leadership whilst a prefect at Miller High School in Sydney. Upon moving to Brisbane, Mohamad attended Griffith University and with the encouragement of his community became secretary of the Queensland Palestinian Association. At the age of 21, Mohamad was approached by his community to become the Arab spokesman for the Gulf Action Coalition (GAC) during the first Gulf War. In 1991 he was again approached by a group of spiritual Muslim men who invited him to visit the mosque and spend three to four days in quiet reflection. That was the beginning of a new spiritual journey that changed the direction of his life. After this 'retreat' Mohamad discovered a newfound detachment from material possessions, and traded the traditional University dress code for that of a Muslim. Mohamad says,

I traded the concept of importance because of who you are, to that of what you are.

Mohamad has faced a number of daunting challenges, among the most significant indicating to his father that he wished to marry an Irish Australian Muslim with blonde hair and blue eyes, and witnessing the destruction of his local mosque following the terrorist attacks in the United States on September 11, 2001.

Mohammad married his intended bride. The burning of the mosque presented a different type of challenge. It required leadership under the most difficult of circumstances.

When the mosque was burnt down I believed that forgiving was the right thing to do. Obviously a small number of people were not happy with this, but I convinced them that it was the right thing.

During these troubled times Dr Abdalla became the media spokesperson for the Brisbane Muslim community. He led a reconciliation strategy that was instrumental in building bridges between the Australian Muslim community and the wider community. The actions and beliefs of this young 'acting' Imam made a difference and he was able to prevent retribution for a mindless act that could have tempted more hatred, and only created more problems for Australians at large.

In 2004 the local Muslim community funded his proposal to establish a research unit at Griffith University. The primary objective of his research unit is the promotion of 'moderate' Islam in an Australian context. He is Director of the Griffith Islamic Research Unit (GIRU), which has gained international recognition with one of his eleven PhD students being former Deputy Prime Minister of Malaysia, Dato Sari Anwar Ibrahim.

Mohamad's influence over the general community comes from both his position and his personal characteristics. He offers the spiritual and intellectual leadership that are associated with an Imam. He champions the belief that communities need to become more open and integrated into their chosen nation. He has done this by visiting other communities, such as Gympie, north of Brisbane, and introducing open days at the mosque, known as Harmony Days. Importantly, he focuses on what brings people together rather than what separates them.

I like to talk about similarities of civilisations, not the clashes. There is a collision of understanding and not a clash of civilisations.

Mohamad is ambitious, not for material possessions or personal glory or fame, but rather wanting to achieve more at the personal spiritual level. He is driven to understand and achieve, and to pass this knowledge and insight onto those that need the guidance that he believes the teachings of Islam can offer.

Cross-cultural leadership is a daily reality for Dr Abdulla. He believes that the challenge of leading in such a complex environment requires leaders to be sincere, dedicated, steadfast and hopeful; willing to listen and share, encourage and motivate.

Sources: Personal interview: Mark Deuis in Dalglish C & Evans P 2007, *Leadership in the Australian Context*, Tilde University Press, Melbourne;
<www.griffith.edu.au>;
<www.abc.net.au/rn/religionreport/stories/2007/1883247.htm>.

The description of Mohamad touches on many aspects of cross-cultural leadership. Mohamad demonstrates that leadership is possible in the most difficult of circumstances, but requires commitment and an understanding of the challenges of bridging cultural differences. Issues of cultural diversity are increasingly a reality for all leaders. It therefore becomes increasingly important to have local understanding, sensitivity, and a willingness to be determined and consistent so that trust develops. Because of the acts of a minority, large sections of the world's population have been demonised. It can be very easy to scapegoat groups when problems appear insurmountable. It is the leader's responsibility to prevent scapegoating and to use diversity as a tool for harmony and productivity.

Introduction

Understanding culture is necessary for effective leadership everywhere. Every business now operates on an international stage. In addition, most nations have considerable diversity within their borders. Recognising the importance of culture is a vital aspect of being effective. Without it, political stability, business success, and fairness will be at risk.

Because of historical events, myths build up about different ethnic groups. It is important that these myths are replaced with a real understanding of culture and how it affects behaviour and leadership.

Cultural diversity is relevant to leadership because it has an enormous impact on the context within which leadership occurs and the relevance given to particular leadership behaviours. What is seen as appropriate in one context may be seen as inappropriate in another. Leaders can be seen as the creators of organisational culture (Schein 1985). This is not about the purpose of leadership or the particular functions that leaders fill, but rather how they go about leading; how they create an environment where cultural diversity is seen as strength rather than grounds for suspicion. Leaders need to understand the perspective of their followers if they are to be effective in influencing over a range of different cultural contexts. Not recognising the cultural influences at play may have a serious negative impact on the ability to lead effectively within organisations, countries or internationally.

Understanding culture

Where people are involved, culture is present. The word 'culture' is used in many contexts to mean different things. It can refer to symbols of culture such as food or dress. It can refer to the arts. Management scholar, Ed Schein (1985), defined culture as:

> ... a set of basic assumptions – shared solutions to universal problems of external adaptation (how to survive) and internal integration (how to stay together) – which have evolved over time and are handed down from one generation to another. (p. 9)

Whilst Schein used this definition as a definition of organisational culture, it can apply to countries, ethnic groups within countries, organisations, professions or a combination of all of these. For example, there may be different professional cultures within an organisation—e.g. legal and engineering—or the organisation may be within a particular regional context within a given country. Each of these levels will have a 'culture'.

Layers of culture

Culture is a very complex process. There can be layers of culture that play themselves out in particular situations — e.g. the national culture may provide the framework for the organisation but there may be regional variations and professional differences within the organisation. It is therefore important to find out the specifics of the context in which you are to operate rather than to rely on stereotypes that may be correct as far as they go, but may miss extremely valuable elements of the culture that are essential for success. This means that to be effective, the leader has to understand the 'language' of behaviour within any given context.

Where leadership is happening in a familiar context, when the leader is a member of the 'group', culture maintains an unspoken influence. It determines instinctively the priorities given and ways in which people undertake their tasks. Where there is a diversity of cultures, many of the assumptions made by the leader may not hold true. The process of influence will require an understanding of the underlying assumptions within the group and how these are manifest through values and behaviours.

A growing diversity of intercultural relations

In today's world, leaders not only relate to those with whom they share a culture. Migration has meant that many countries have very diverse cultures within them. Australia, for example, owing to waves of migration from a broad variety of countries such as Italy, Greece, Vietnam, Britain and South Africa, is one of the most culturally diverse societies in the world. These migrants joined the descendants of early British settlers, convicts, and indigenous Australians who have a presence in Australia dating back at least 40,000 years. According to the 2001 Census, around 22 per cent of the Australian population was born overseas. Because of the successive waves of migration, Australian workplaces also include many second- and third-generation Australians whose values and beliefs are influenced by a mixed cultural heritage (Dalglish 2008; Patrickson & O'Brien 2001).

Australians have significant business contact with their Asian neighbours, with Japan and China being their largest trading partners. Australians also welcome large numbers of tourists to their shores every year and have adapted many of their practices to their needs (Dalglish & Evans 2007).

A similar picture is true of many other nations. Technology and internet communications mean that most business and political leaders will have contact in some way with people who come from different cultures and who have very different assumptions about what is important and how to behave. In the business environment, leaders will increasingly be responsible for organisations operating in a number of different countries at the same time. Here similar results will be required for each business but the cultural conditions in each may be very different and therefore require different behaviour.

Debunking the myths

With increasing globalisation two myths have to be challenged if leadership is to be effective in a culturally diverse environment (Schneider & Barsoux 1997; Dubrin & Dalglish 2003). With the advent of symbols recognised across the world, and the increasing use of English as the language of business, the myth has arisen that cultures are converging, that we are all becoming more like each other. This is a myth. The advent of the European Union has not reduced the differences between the French, Irish and Germans. What it has meant is that they must learn better to work with each other taking difference into account. It seems almost as though the pressure for homogeneity, the process of globalisation, is creating a pressure for divergence rather than convergence. (Kuckhom & Strodbeck 1961; Triandis 1972).

There is also an assumption (Hofstede [1999], cited at the beginning of the chapter) that what works well as 'management' in one culture will work equally well elsewhere — that management is a science with a set of universal principles. This also is a myth. As Takeo Fujisawa, cofounder of Honda Motor Company, said:

Japanese and American management practices are 95% the same, and differ in all important respects (cited in Schneider & Barsoux 1997, p. 73).

It is therefore important for leaders to be very conscious of the 'relevant' 5%. All countries may not have the same concept of leadership. Most of the research undertaken into leadership has occurred in Western industrial contexts, particularly the USA. Can we make the assumption that what Americans expect from their leaders is what those from other parts of the world expect from theirs? As democracy, in its many forms, becomes more and more common as the political system of choice, so people have more choice about who their leaders are and whom they will follow. The relationship between leader and follower is no longer simply one of tradition.

Reflections

Consider your experience with people from different cultures. Did you treat them differently from colleagues from your own culture? How and why? What assumptions did you make about the other person?

Activity 7.1

Select a small group of peer managers from your organisation. Identify the inter-cultural aspects of that organisation's operations. Do they buy from a different country, do they sell to a different country, do they have offices in a different country? Do they employ people from a range of cultural backgrounds? How is this diversity acknowledged and managed in the organisation?

Dimensions of culture

So how different are cultures? When we look around the world, different groups have found very different ways of surviving, and have had different circumstances in which to develop their patterns of behaviour. Much of any culture owes its origins to the past. It includes strategies and behaviours that have been successful in assisting the group to survive and prosper. But culture is not static. It changes as circumstances change, as the challenges of the external environment and internal cohesion change. Often whole continents have a culture attributed to them which misrepresents the differences and can lead to misunderstanding.

To respond effectively to many different influences it is vital first to understand the various dimensions that can make up culture and how these are reflected in your own culture. Here we will look at two bodies of research—Trompenaars and Hampden-Turner, and Hofstede—who have worked over many years to develop an understanding of how cultures differ, particularly with respect to the working environment.

Trompenaars and Hampden-Turner (2002) in their work with international business have identified a number of very useful indicators to describe and explain different cultural behaviours. The dimensions they identify as separating different cultural expectations are very useful for exploring how to lead effectively across different cultural contexts. Their analysis identifies a range of ways in which people from different parts of the world view their world differently and have different expectations. Cultures change all the time—not at the behest of leaders, but in response to circumstance and the needs for survival—both physical and in terms of identity.

The dimensions identified by Trompenaars and Hampden-Turner for dealing with people (2002) include:

- universalism versus particularism,
- individualism versus communitarianism,
- neutral versus emotional,
- specific versus diffuse, and
- achievements versus ascription.

They also identified that different cultures have different attitudes to time and to the environment.

Universalism versus particularism

The universalist approach argues that what is good and right can be defined and always applies. Rules can be established that will be useful in all contexts. In a particularist culture greater attention is paid to obligations and relationships and less to abstract rules.

This has important implications for leadership and the relationship between the leader and follower. In some universalist contexts the leader may be expected to 'play by the rules' and be predictable irrespective of differing circumstances. Constant changing may be seen as a sign of weakness. In a more particularist culture it would be expected that the leader would make decisions based on the particular situation and would not necessarily feel a need to apply rules consistently. This can appear unfair in a universalist world.

Individualism and communitarianism

This dimension illustrates where the emphasis is placed when action is considered—on the group or the individual. With the individualist approach it is more important to focus on the individual so that they can contribute to the community as and if they wish. This is overtly expressed in the transformational leadership formula (Dubrinsky, Yammarino & Jolson 1995) with the concept of 'individualised consideration'.

The communitarian perspective considers the community first; places the needs of the group, however defined, as more important than the rights or needs of any single individual. One of the aspirations of transformational leadership as described by Burns (1978) was to encourage followers to put higher values and the needs of the group as a whole ahead of their individual needs. This would appear to indicate at desirability of at least some shift from the individualist to the communitarian perspective, though starting with former. It is important to recognise that 'nations' are seldom the 'group'. A nation often has different groupings within it where local loyalties will be stronger than they are to any nation state. This is particularly true if the nation state is made up of groups who historically have not been allies.

Individualistic cultures make frequent use of the 'I' form of communication. People achieve alone and assume personal responsibility. People prefer to undertake activities in pairs or on their own. This is often how Western leaders are seen—promoting the value of themselves as individuals. In communitarian cultures the use of 'we' is more frequent. People ideally achieve in groups and assume joint responsibility—so whatever the dynamics of a leadership group—it is the group that takes responsibility. The leader will, as a matter of course, refer to the group and gains status from the group.

Neutral versus emotional

Do leaders have to be objective and detached, or is expressing emotion acceptable? In neutral cultures relationships are largely instrumental and are about achieving objectives. Bureaucracies grew up in this context where *role* is the key factor, expectations are clearly expressed and emotions considered largely irrelevant. In more emotional cultures, the expression of emotion on the part of a leader is acceptable. Emotions are recognised as an integral part of how people respond to life and are therefore more easily accepted in any context, including business. (Dalglish 2008)

In neutral cultures leaders may express themselves calmly and behave with cool self possession. Personal feelings are often seen as inappropriate. In more culturally emotional contexts, thoughts and feelings are more likely to be revealed both verbally and non-verbally. Touching, gesturing, and strong facial expressions are common. Interestingly, emotional expressiveness is an integral part of being charismatic (Dubinsky, Yammarino & Jolson 1995; Dubrin, Dalglish & Miller 2007). Charismatic leadership is recognised as being effective even in the most neutral of cultures. (Kudisch *et al.* 1995)

Specific versus diffuse

In diffuse cultures the whole person is involved in relationships. There is an assumption of a complex and holistic relationship between the leader and followers. In a culture that values specificity, principles and consistent moral standards are independent of any particular relationship. Each relationship is specific and purposeful. So, for example, a business relationship is about business only. The names on any contract make no difference, and the relationship between parties is not likely to extend beyond that particular business interaction.

In diffuse cultures morality tends to be situational depending on the person and the context. Rules are not drawn up as to the specific nature of the relationship. So acceptance of extenuating circumstances is accepted as the norm. In the development of a business contract, for example, the diffuse viewpoint would be that a relationship between the two parties needs to be built up so that trust exists. The individuals involved in the deal get to know each other. The contract, such as it is, is about the end goal, what the partnership wishes to achieve. Details are not important as it is assumed that it is not possible to know what the future will hold, but that with a sound and trusting relationship any future problems can be worked out. The character of the whole individual is important, not just their role in the single negotiation. The personal character of those involved becomes very important (Dalglish 2008).

In cultures where more specific roles and relationships are outlined, the parties to a contract may not regard themselves as being in a personal relationship at all, but one that is specific to particular context. They represent the organisation and any other member of the organisation might just as easily fulfil the role of negotiator. As result, any contract is very specific in what it sets out, both in terms of objectives and means. It attempts to outline required actions in all imagined situations. This is considered vital, as the person dealing with the concerns may not be the same one who negotiated the contract — it is the role not the person that is important. What is acceptable is set down by referring to clearly identified rules and there is often difficulty modifying these rules to suit different contexts.

Achievement versus ascription

How status is attributed is very important to leadership effectiveness. Followers have expectations about the status and credibility of those they follow. In achievement-oriented cultures, credibility focuses on what the individual has achieved. *Ascription* means that status and credibility are attributed as the results of external factors such family of birth, age, educational level, connections and so on. These ascriptions vary from culture to culture. In one, much emphasis may be placed on family and class where in another, it may be the university attended.

In achievement-oriented cultures much weight is put on what the individual leader has achieved — i.e. what their 'qualifications' for the role are. This needs to be articulated to create credibility. In ascription-oriented cultures the context is important. There is extensive use of titles; the family a leader comes from, the region, the university they attended — all will create credibility rather than 'evidence' of competence.

Attitudes to time

In some societies what someone has achieved in the past is not important—what is important is what they plan to do in the future. In other societies you can make more of an impression with your past accomplishments.

Another dimension of this is whether time is seen to be sequential—a series of passing events or whether it is synchronic with past, present and future all interrelated.

The following example appears in Trompenaars and Hampden Turner (2002):

> ... Dutch manager ... was terribly frustrated by his unsuccessful efforts to organise a Management of Change seminar with Ethiopian managers. They all kept harking back to a distant and wealthy era in Ethiopian civilisation and would not incorporate any developmental principles that were not based in this past. After discussion with Ethiopian colleagues, we decided to study some Ethiopian history books, looking at them from the perspective of modern management. What had Ethiopia done right in that period to make its cities and trade so flourishing? ... the Dutch manager posed the challenge anew. The future was now seen as a way of recreating some of the greatest glories of the past; suddenly, the Management of Change seminar had captured everyone's enthusiastic support (p. 133).

Attitude to the environment

Societies which conduct business have developed two major orientations towards nature and the natural environment. Either they believe that they can, and should, control nature by imposing their will upon it—or that man is part of nature and must go along with its laws, direction and forces. The first of these orientations Trompenaars and Hampden-Turner call inner-directed. This kind of culture tends to focus on control and winning. Outer-directed cultures are more focused on harmony, on maintaining relationships and winning together.

Activity 7.2

Using Trompenaar's dimensions, assess where you think the culture to which you belong lies. Use generally accepted ways of thinking and behaviour as your guide.

Universalism... Particularism

Individualism....................................... Communitarianism

Neutral... Emotional

Specific .... Diffuse

Achievements...................................... Ascription

Look ahead .... Look back

Control environment.......................... Adapt to environment

Activity 7.3

With a group of colleagues from the same cultural/ethnic/national group compare your analysis of your culture using Trompenaar's dimensions. What are the implications of your cultural background for your leadership?

Compare your analysis with that done by groups from other cultural backgrounds.

Identify the areas of potential conflict or misunderstanding.

How cultural differences work

Geert Hofstede (1980; 1999) was one of the first researchers to try to understand how cultural difference worked. He identified five value dimensions in research spanning eighteen years and involving people from over sixty countries. These dimensions include:

- individualism versus collectivism,
- power distance,
- uncertainty avoidance,

- masculinity versus femininity, and

- long-term versus short-term orientation.

It is important to recognise that culture is not static and these studies provide generalisations about national cultures. Individuals within cultures may differ from the predominant values and behaviour.

Individualism versus collectivism

With this dimension the two bodies of research agree. At one end of the continuum is individualism, a mental set in which people see themselves first as individuals and believe their own interests take priority. Collectivism, at the other end of the continuum, the mental set is that the group and society should receive first priority. Individualistic cultures in this research include Australia, New Zealand and South Africa. Collectivist cultures included Japan, Korea and many South American and Middle Eastern countries.

Power distance

The extent to which employees accept the idea that members of an organisation have different levels of power dependent on their position is referred to as *power difference*. In a high power distance culture the boss has decision-making authority because of hierarchical position. In low power distance cultures, employees do not readily accept a power hierarchy. High power distance countries include France, Spain, Japan and Mexico. Low power distance cultures include Australia and the Scandinavian countries.

Uncertainty avoidance

A culture that accepts the unknown and tolerates risk and unconventional behaviour is said to have low uncertainty avoidance. A society ranked high in uncertainty avoidance seeks a predictable and certain future, valuing tradition and conventional behaviour. Low uncertainty avoidance cultures include the United States, New Zealand and Scandinavian countries. High uncertainty avoidance countries include Japan, Italy and Argentina.

Masculinity/femininity

In this context masculinity refers to a valuing within the culture of assertiveness, success and competition. Femininity refers to a culture where the emphasis is on personal relationships, caring for others and high quality of life. Masculine countries include India, the United States and Japan. Feminine countries include Denmark, France and Korea.

Long-term orientation/short-term orientation

Those within a culture with a long-term orientation have a long-range perspective, they are often thrifty, save, and do not demand a quick return on their investments. A short-term orientation is often characterised by a demand for immediate results and a propensity to live for the now and not save. Japan and China are noted for their long-term orientation while the cultures of the United States, France and West Africa are characterised by a more short-term orientation.

It can be argued that effective leadership is 'in the eyes of the beholder'. That is, what is deemed to be effective leadership by one person will not necessarily be deemed to be effective leadership by another. The leader–follower relationship has to be developed and maintained and is responsive to the context and the group within which that leadership is occurring.

Leader in action: Lady Carol Kidu

Dame Carol Kidu is Papua New Guinea's Minister for Community Development. That a woman should hold such a position in a very traditional political climate is itself a surprise, and that she was in fact born an Australian makes it even more astonishing.

Carol Kidu grew up in the suburbs of Brisbane. In grade 11 she attended a school fitness camp on the Gold Coast where she met Buri Kidu, a scholarship boy from Papua New Guinea. Carol married Buri, moved to Port Moresby, raised four children and supported her husband who rose to become Chief Justice of Papua New Guinea after independence.

Papua New Guinea also presented a challenge. She felt considerable stress learning to live in a completely different cultural space, and so did Buri. They were his people and he had not anticipated difficulties when returning after a long time in Australia. Like Carol the reality of living in two worlds took its toll. People respond to the challenges and stresses of operating across two cultures in different ways. Buri internalised his stress as his mind withdrew within itself. 'Carol,' he said, 'coped with the culture stress through tears and emotional outbursts in our bedroom. ' Of herself, Carol said,

I suddenly had to realise that I had not married a man, I'd married a whole family, a whole society. My children weren't my children, they belonged to the family ... By the time I had my fourth child I was happy to hand them over and I'd learnt the benefits of an extended family.

In spite of all her adjustment problems, Carol came to realise that the wantok (relative or friend) system of the extended family could have more to offer than the small nuclear family system of her childhood. It is the society's safety net and it is essential in a country like Papua New Guinea, which does and could not have a comprehensive welfare support system.

It was the death of her husband in 1993 that led Lady Kidu to consider entering politics. She became involved in the establishment of the Sir Buri Kidu Heart Institute with donations she had requested rather than flowers at the funeral. She was approached to stand for parliament as her husband had been approached to do just before his death. She remembered the words of her husband just before his death when he was being asked to stand for parliament:

Why don't you bloody well do it? (Kidu 2002, p. 143)

She was unsure whether it was something she could do. She had grown up in a working class Australian family, learnt to be a Motu wife, and spent her married life immersed in Motu society. She was a teacher with no experience in the public service and with no particular interest in politics. But she had a strong conviction that she had to stand for politics herself because her husband couldn't.

She voted for the first time when she voted for herself. She stood in the family and clan name, with their permission. Her colour and her sex were used against her. As a champion of grassroots urban communities, however, she won with a bigger margin than had ever before been achieved. In 2002, after being re-elected, she became a member of the cabinet.

Her son Basil's comment on her getting elected expressed the difficulties she would be facing.

Geez Mum, you've really got yourself into deep shit this time. (Kidu 2002, p. 161)

As Minister for Community Development she is very aware of cultural differences—not only between the culture of her upbringing and that of her adopted home, but the differences within the community. Why has she been so successful? In the words of Sir Moi Avei, Acting Prime Minister, 'She gives hope. She's a very good listener. She is accessible.'

In her own words, Carol Kidu expresses her concern about the consequences of cultures clashing:

But what concerns me deeply is how we maintain the balance when momentous change is being imposed from the outside rather than change gradually evolving from within a society. A state of harmony and balance is extremely hard to attain when these circumstances exist as they do in Papua New Guinea in the new millennium. (Kidu 2002, p. 48)

Sources: <www.abc.net.au/austory/content/2004>; <www.goasiapacific.com/focus/pacific/GoAsiaPacific202904.htm>; <www.rmit.edu.au>; <www.abc.net.au/cgi-bin/common>; <http://journalism.uts.edu.au/acij/old_acij/cafepacific%20old/resources/aspac/ women.html>; Kidu, C 2002, *A Remarkable Journey*, Pearson Education Australia Pty Ltd., <www.lowyinstitue.org/Publication.asp?pid=797>.

The above profile of Lady Carol Kidu demonstrates the importance of understanding cultural difference. If you do not already work and lead in a culturally diverse environment, you soon will be. Lady Carol Kidu is an example of how to meet the challenges of cultural difference and reap the reward in doing so.

Impact of culture on leadership

Leaders set an example to others that can become the model for an entire group or organisation, for good or bad; and whether they want to or not. People pay far more attention to what leaders do, both in the workplace and out, than they do to policy statements. Leader behaviours are based on a set of values, many of which reflect the culture within which they lead. In leadership, therefore, you have a mix of individual values and cultural values, both of which are important to understand for effective leadership. One behaviour common to many good leaders is that they tend to align the values of their followers with those of the organisations; they make the links between the two sets more explicit. This being the case, cultural values have a significant role to play.

Leadership and individual values

England and Lee (1974) identified that individual values can affect leaders in six different ways. Cultural values, and the dimensions of culture mentioned earlier in the chapter, will also impact on these behaviours.

1. Values affect a leader's perception of situations and the problems at hand.

2. Leaders' values affect the solutions generated and decisions reached about problems.

3. Values play an important role in interpersonal relationships; they influence how leaders perceive different individuals and groups.

4. Values often influence leaders' perceptions of individual and organisational successes as well as the manner in which these successes are to be achieved.

5. Values may affect the extent to which leaders accept or reject organisational pressure and goals.

6. Values provide a basis for leaders differentiating between right and wrong and between ethical and unethical behaviour.

Understanding these cultural dimensions and their impact on decision making does not offer easy answers about how to lead effectively a culturally diverse constituency. However, the culture of the followers, those required to achieve goals will impact on how the leader is perceived and how effective he/she can be.

Activity 7.4

In a group of peer mangers, take one of the cultural dimensions identified either by Hofstede or Trompenaars and explore how a leader's perception of this dimension might impact on the six areas identified by England and Lee.

Provide tangible examples of the differences the leader's cultural values would make.

Organisational culture

All organisations have a culture of their own which determines how they respond to external challenges and internal performance and cohesion. Leaders have a significant impact on the culture that develops within any organisation.

Goffee and Jones (2000) assert that the culture of an organisation can be understood by looking at two concepts—sociability and solidarity.

- *Sociability* is a measure of friendliness among members of the organisational community.

- *Solidarity* is based on common tasks, mutual interest and clearly understood shared goals.

The two dimensions of organisational culture create four different types of organisational culture:

- high sociability and low solidarity = networked culture;
- high sociability and high solidarity = communal culture;
- low sociability and low solidarity = fragmented culture; and
- low sociability and high solidarity = mercenary culture.

Factors to be considered in building culture include:

- the leader's beliefs and values;

- the societal norms of the organisation's native and/or host country;

- the problems of external adaptation and survival—the external factors that impact on what you do; and

- the problems of internal integration—how everyone can work together effectively.

Developing a multicultural organisation

One of the most important things a leader needs to do in today's society is establish a fully functioning multicultural organisation. Such an organisation values cultural diversity and is willing to encourage and capitalise on such diversity. Such an organisation avoids the problems stemming from cultural misunderstandings, prejudice and conflicting values, and builds an organisational culture that is most suited to today's global environment.

Cox (1991) argues that the multicultural organisation has six key characteristics, all requiring leadership for their achievement. The characteristics include:

- *Creating pluralism.* Valuing diversity training is a major technique for achieving pluralism.

- *Achieving leadership diversity.* There needs to be a culturally heterogeneous group of leaders.

- *Creating full structural integration.* There should be zero correlation between culture group identity and job status. Again training and career development can help achieve integration.

- *Creating full integration of informal networks.* Minorities are often excluded from informal networks. Company-wide informal activities can help join different cultural networks within the organisation—as can full structural integration.

- *Creating a bias-free organisation.* Bias and prejudice create discrimination. Are there practices in the organisation that might, perhaps unintentionally, exclude particular ethnic or religious groups?

- *Organisational identification.* There is a strong identification between all ethnic groups and the organisation.

- *Minimising intergroup conflict.* To achieve a multi-cultural organisation conflict must be kept to healthy levels. It can be important to collect and share information about sensitive issues—rather than to avoid them.

Summary

Understanding culture is necessary for effective leadership everywhere. Every business now operates on an international stage. In addition, most nations have considerable diversity within their borders. Recognising the importance of culture is vital aspect of being effective.

With increasing globalisation, two myths have to be challenged if leadership is to be effective in a culturally diverse environment. With the advent of symbols recognised across the world and the increasing use of English as the language of business, the myth has arisen that cultures are converging, that we are all becoming more like each other. This is a myth. It seems almost as though the pressure for homogeneity, the process of globalisation, is creating a pressure for divergence rather than convergence.

There is also an assumption that what works well as 'management' in one culture will work equally well elsewhere—that management is a science with a set of universal principles. This also is a myth. As Takeo Fujisawa, cofounder of Honda Motor Company said (cited in Schneider & Barsoux 1997, p. 73):

> *Japanese and American management practices are 95% the same, and differ in all important respects.*

Trompenaars and Hampden-Turner identified a range of dimension for helping understand culture. These dimensions include:

- universalism versus particularism,

- individualism versus communitarianism,

- neutral versus emotional,

- specific versus diffuse, and

- achievements versus ascription.

They also identified that different cultures have different attitudes to time and to the environment. Geert Hofstede identified five value dimensions including:

- individualism versus collectivism,
- power distance,
- uncertainty avoidance,
- masculinity versus femineity, and
- long-term versus short-term orientation.

It is important to recognise that culture is not static.

One behaviour common to many good leaders is that they tend to align the values of their followers with those of the organisations; they make the links between the two sets more explicit. This being the case, cultural values have a significant role to play.

Reflection on your leadership practice

One of the most important things a leader needs to do in today's society is establish a fully functioning multicultural organisation. Such an organisation values cultural diversity and is willing to encourage and capitalise on such diversity. Such an organisation avoids the problems stemming from cultural misunderstandings, prejudice and conflicting values, and builds an organisational culture that is most suited to today's global environment.

Make a list of how your organisation values cultural diversity. Then examine yourself to see how you add value to the organisation's efforts.

References

Burns, JM 1978, *Leadership*, Harper & Row, New York.

Cox, T Jnr. 1991, 'The Multi-cultural Organisation', *Academy of Management Executive*, May.

Dalglish, C 2008, 'The Impact of Culture of Leadership' in *Contemporary Perspectives on Leadership*, James Sarros ed., Tilde University Press, Melbourne.

Dalglish, C & Evans, P 2007, *Leadership in the Australian Context*, Tilde University Press, Melbourne.

Dubinsky, AJ, Yammarino, FJ & Jolson, MA 1995, 'An examination of linkages between personal characteristics and dimensions of transformational leadership', *Journal of Business and Psychology*, Spring.

Dubrin, A & Dalglish, C 2003, *Leadership and Australasian Focus*, John Wiley & Sons, Milton, Australia.

Dubrin, Dalglish & Miller 2007, *Leadership 2nd Asia Pacific Edition*, John Wiley & Sons, Milton, Australia.

England, GW & Lee, R 1974, 'The relationship between managerial values and managerial success in the United States, Japan, India and Australia', *Journal of Applied Psychology*, 59.

Hofstede, G 1999, *Culture's Consequences: International Differences in Work Related Values*, Sage, Beverly Hills, California.

Kluckholn, F & Strodtbeck, F 1961, *Variations in Value Orientations*, Greenwood Press, Westport, Connecticut.

Kudisch, JD, Poteet, ML, Dobbins, GH, Rush, MC & Russell, JE 1995, 'Expert power, referent power and charisma: toward the resolution of a theoretical debate', *Journal of Business and Psychology*, Winter.

Patrickson, M & O'Brien, P eds., 2001 *Managing Diversity*, John Wiley & Sons Australian Ltd. Milton.

Schein, EH 1985, *Organisational Culture and Leadership*, Jossey-Bass, San Francisco.

Schneider, SC & Barsoux, J 1997, *Managing Across Cultures*, Prentice Hall, London.

Triandis, HC 1972, *The Analysis of Subjective Culture'* Wiley, Interscience, New York.

Trompenaars, F & Hampden-Turner, C 2002, *Riding the Waves of Culture* Nicholas Brealey Publishing, London.

Chapter 8

POWER AND INFLUENCE

CHAPTER CONTENTS

- ☐ Spotlight: Jim Taggart
- ☐ Introduction
- ☐ Sources and types of power
- ☐ Power and transformational leadership
- ☐ Influence tactics
- ☐ Connecting power and influence tactics
- ☐ Leader in action: James Cowley
- ☐ Gentle Influence
- ☐ Empowerment
- ☐ Summary
- ☐ Reflection on your leadership practice

Spotlight: Jim Taggart, The Taggart Group

The Taggart Group Pty Ltd was formed in 1987 to meet personal and corporate needs for financial services advice including general insurance and personal insurance. In the early 1990s Taggart Nominees Pty Ltd was formed to operate the financial planning and life insurance business and the Taggart Group maintained operation of the general insurance business.

The Taggart Group was granted an Australian Financial Services Licence and is authorised to provide general insurance financial services. The Taggart Group commenced operating under their AFSL on 1 March 2004. Since commencement, the success of the business has been achieved through a high work rate and excellent support structure.

The managing director of the Taggart Group is Jim Taggart. Jim's career began as a teacher. Later he became deputy principal of a Catholic high school. Since entering the field of financial planning in 1987 he has successfully developed his businesses to service nearly 6,000 clients.

Jim has lived in the Hills District at Kellyville in Sydney for over 26 years where he has been actively involved in community activities. He is Chairman of the Salvation Army Red Shield Appeal (Western Sydney), past Chair and current member of the Hills Excellence in Business 355 Management Committee, and past Chairman of the Advisory Council for TAFE NSW Western Sydney Institute.

He is a highly sought-after speaker in the areas of financial planning and motivation in Australia and at offshore conferences in such countries as Switzerland, New Zealand and the USA.

In 2005 Jim was awarded the Zurich/AFA Financial Adviser of the Year award. In January 2006 he was awarded the 2006 Baulkham Hills Shire Australia Day Community Service Award.

Jim influences people predominantly by his personal characteristics and behaviour. His general philosophical point of view is that he has built his life around doing things which are fundamentally good. His personal beliefs therefore manifest in a very tangible way in his behaviour as he goes about doing good things for people. For example, he is actively involved in charities, education, and business-related areas that motivate and help other people to obtain positive outcomes.

'I believe that education is important,' he says, 'and I want to be around people who also see that education is important, because if they see what is important for me and I demonstrate that, then I will see that in their own lives, and then hopefully see what I can do for them which is not only just work-related matters.'

By influencing through consistent behaviour, people know that they can depend on Jim to be committed to help them achieve their goals.

Jim believes that in the main, he uses three types of power in order to influence others. These include *connection power, expert power* and *referent power*. He draws on these power sources at different times and during different periods of a relationship to obtain the desired outcome.

'I think that different types of power should be used at different times. For example, I may want to get an outcome where I am simultaneously in a relationship or a position using and oscillating between expert power and referent power, sliding in and out of each of these within that meeting, depending on how the other person or groups of persons are acting and reacting to my comments. This in turn has a flow-on effect in the way I conduct myself, and how I want to try to either win or bring about change.'

Different stages of a situation may also require a wide range of influential tactics. So depending on what Jim is trying to achieve, and the importance of obtaining that outcome, he will use various influence tactics.

'So, for example, I may in fact use pressure to some degree to get an outcome. But I may also have within that inspirational

appeal, personal appeal and collaboration. So, depending on the importance of the situation, it will be shaped by my own inadequacies, but also my desire to achieve a particular outcome and the reliance on that person and or group to bring about that particular outcome.'

Jim provides the following advice for leaders who wish to influence the people they work with better.

'My view is that in order to use power and influence, and everybody has to do this, is to take the situation and break it down into parts that are critical to the outcome. Then the overriding driver for me in understanding power and influence is that the leaders need to provide a very clear analysis and understanding of what the desired outcomes are for individuals and the group as a whole. By doing this, in my opinion, it allows leaders to use a variety of different techniques at different times in order to obtain the desired outcomes by all parties'.

Source: Interview with Jim Taggart 22 June 2009.

The description of Jim Taggart provides leaders with an alternative view of power and influence. It can be easy for leaders to fall into the trap of using their position power in order to influence others. However, effective leadership in a modern environment does not involve the use of position power. Effective influence involves a combination of humility and a fierce resolve to make a difference. There are many alternative power sources available to modern leaders in order to influence followers. This chapter will provide the means for leaders to identify and utilise these alternative sources.

Introduction

Power and influence are at the very heart of what leadership is all about. They are closely related concepts.

Power is the *potential* or *capacity* of the leader to influence followers. Because power is the potential to influence, leaders often do not actually have to use power to influence others. It is therefore the perception of power rather than its use that influences others.

Influence is the ability of the leader to gain acceptance of requests and ideas. If it is accepted that power is at the heart of leadership, then leaders need power to increase their ability to influence others. Leaders, by definition, influence other people. In order to apply that influence, they must have some form of power. How they go about influencing others and exercising power is the subject of this chapter.

The exercise of power and influence in a workplace context is a complex phenomenon dependent on many factors. One of these factors is, of course, the position that the leader holds. Due to the managerial positions they hold, the managers of organisations are usually also referred to as the 'leaders'. As we will see from this chapter, however, the position of the manager in modern organisations is the power source least likely to give the manager influence with team members.

Leaders therefore need to nurture their ability to acquire different types of power. It should be recognised that the types of power that effective leaders can draw upon to influence others have changed in recent years. Western societies, and their younger generations in particular, have little respect for the *position* someone might hold. They are looking for leaders that can inspire and motivate them without having to rely upon their position.

Power – A dirty word?

Most of us have heard someone refer to a person in a position of influence as 'power hungry'. In organisational contexts the word 'power' for many people in Western societies has negative connotations. Kanter (1983) was among the first to acknowledge how power can be seen negatively. Kanter described power as:

> *'... the last dirty word. It is easier to talk about money – and much easier to talk about sex – than it is to talk about power.'*

So what is it about the word 'power' that some people have so much difficulty with? If power is the ability to mobilise resources (human, financial and technological) to get things done and to influence people, should not then leaders be 'hungry for power'? Should they not try to build as many power bases that are available to them so that they can use them effectively? Is it not time, then, to change the way we view power in organisations? Some recent research, for example, suggests that power might free some leaders from the influence of external forces and situations and that it is time to 'look beyond the stereotype of power as corrupting' (Galinsky *et al.* 2008).

The techniques leaders use to influence others are many and varied. Effective leaders have a diverse repertoire of influence tactics to draw upon. However, research demonstrates that many leaders still use what are now inappropriate techniques to influence others. Occupational health and safety legislation, now widespread in Western countries, generally regards workplace bullying, abuse, bad language and yelling by leaders to be illegal—yet bullying and violence in workplaces continues to be widespread.

It is a sad report on Western leaders that our workplaces are rife with bullying caused by inappropriate influencing styles. Workplace bullying is defined generally as any behaviour that demeans, humiliates or intimidates employees as individuals or groups. It may include unjustified or unnecessary comments about an employee, their work or capacity for work; comments aimed to discredit or undermine an employee or their work; or the exclusion of an employee from normal workplace activities.

International surveys are finding that more than half of those who respond have been bullied in the workplace and that a third have been subject to abusive language. Of those who had been bullied, over 70% stated the source of the bullying was the manager. The surveys show very similar responses—they demonstrate that employees believe that workplace leaders are becoming more aggressive in their influencing styles. This is a serious issue for leaders and for organisations as there are now legal and financial consequences of bullying both for the source of the bullying (usually the leader) and for the organisation.

Is it any wonder, then, that recent research has shown that approximately 80% of managers who are terminated by organisations are terminated because of an inappropriate influencing style? Organisations cannot afford the risk of legal exposure to the retention of leaders whose influencing style might be interpreted by employees and courts as bullying.

There is therefore an urgent need for leaders to examine the ways they attempt to influence others and to avoid inappropriate behaviours that are no longer acceptable.

First, we will examine the sources and types of power available to organisational leaders. Then we will review influencing tactics and their effectiveness.

Sources and types of power

Whatever the workplace context in which a leader is expected to perform, there are some resources that a leader can draw upon in order to influence their team. These resources are sometimes referred to as power bases. Much has been written to describe these power bases and the 'correct' way to apply them.

Sources and types of power have been identified by a variety of writers over the last few decades. Almost all of the taxonomies that classify the sources of power for leaders relate in some way to the five types (reward, coercive, legitimate, expert and referent) identified in 1959 by French and Raven. Two additional types of power (information and connection) have been added to the taxonomy to make the types of power identified in this chapter contemporary. The seven types of power discussed are conceptualised as arising from two sources as shown in Table 8.1.

Table 8.1 Sources and types of power

Sources of power	Positional power	Personal power
Types of power	Coercive	Expert
	Connection*	Referent
	Information	
	Legitimate	
	Reward	

Connection power can sometimes arise as a result of personal characteristics of the leader rather than, or in addition to, the position held. It could also, therefore, be categorised as personal power.

In this section will we discuss each of these power bases. Later we will demonstrate how they are connected to influence tactics.

Types of power arising from positional sources

Coercive power

Coercive power is the power to punish for non-compliance. It is based on fear. Employees often accept the demands of managers because of fear of being reprimanded, receiving poor performance reports or being dismissed. A manager giving an employee a formal warning of dismissal because the employee has failed to follow a legitimate request is an example of coercive power.

Connection power

Connection power arises from the manager's relationship with influential people inside and outside the organisation. Powerful connections can assist people in organisations by sponsoring their projects or careers. All organisations have coalitions of people who often form sub-cultures within the organisation. These are people with like minds, values or objectives. Often these coalitions are needed to bring about change or reforms in organisations. Connection power, therefore, is a form of organisational politics. A manager using the name of a more senior manager in a conversation with peers when it is well known among the peers that the more senior manager and the manager are close allies is an example of connection power.

Information power

Information power is power that arises from the manager's ability to control information that people need to do their work or stay informed. Managers often have access to information before their team members, or have access to information not provided to their peers or team members. This gives the manager the opportunity to release the information when it best suits them—or distort the information by biasing the interpretation of it to meet their objectives. Information in organisations, however, flows up and down the hierarchy. Managers must also rely on employees for information. Employees, therefore, also have information power when trying to influence management decisions. A manager omitting productivity data to make monthly reports look more favourable is an example of the use of information power.

Legitimate power

Legitimate power is based on the managerial position held by the leader. Employees usually accept directions from managers if the directions are within the scope of their own position description. Managers at higher levels in organisations usually have more positional power than managers at the lower levels of the organisation. Research has shown that the younger generations (generations X and Y) find this type of power less influential than do baby boomers, and often question directions from managers based solely upon the manager's position (Yu & Miller 2005). A manager seeking a report from a team member on progress with a task is an example of the use of legitimate power.

Reward power

Reward power is based on the leader's ability to provide employees with something of value to them. This may be a promotion, a pay rise, time off, flexibility in work arrangements and so on. Of course, leaders can use reward power only when the organisation allows the leader discretion over these rewards. At lower levels of management it is often the case that managers have no discretion when it comes to granting incentives to employees. A manager publically praising a team member for their work and paying them a bonus is an example of the use of reward power.

Types of power arising from personal sources

The two power types that fall under the personal power source are expert power and referent power.

Expert power

Expert power is the ability to influence others due to the manager's recognised skill or specialised knowledge. A person who is an expert or has highly valued skills makes others in the organisation dependent on them. The fewer people in the organisation that have those skills or knowledge, the more expert power the person can acquire. In modern organisations that are primarily based on knowledge, all employees can, to some extent, be classified as 'knowledge workers' and therefore have this type of power. Often, knowledge workers have more knowledge about their role than do the managers, reversing the traditional role this type of power has exerted previously. People constantly coming to a person for advice about a particular issue is an example of expert power.

Referent power

Referent power is based on the person's relationship with others and their ability to influence through what others perceive to be desirable characteristics. It could be compared to the personal appeal or prestige that someone has developed; it can be measured by the respect, reputation and friendships people are able to maintain in their workplace. Expert power and referent power contribute to perceived 'charisma', which some leadership authorities believe is an important aspect of leadership. Given this definition, referent power is not confined to people who hold managerial positions. A person with good people skills, whom others at the workplace respect and value as a person, is an example of referent power.

Effective leaders understand the existence of the above types of power. They learn to cultivate the types of power that are consistent with the organisational culture and societal norms for their organisations and then use these power bases appropriately for the interest of the organisation and not for themselves.

Activity 8.1 Self assessment

Instructions

The list of statements in Table 8.2 describes behaviours and rewards that leaders in workplaces are able to use to influence team members. Read each statement and then circle the number that best represents *how you would prefer to influence.*

Rather than list the statements in random order as in the original instrument, statements have been classified according to the types of power listed in this chapter, with information power and connection power added to the original instrument categories.

Use the following key:

1 = Strongly disagree

2 = Disagree

---

3 = Slightly disagree

4 = Neither agree nor disagree

5 = Slightly agree

6 = Agree

7 = Strongly agree

Table 8.2 Self assessment

	Strongly disagree	Disagree	Slightly disagree	Neither agree nor disagree	Slightly agree	Agree	Strongly agree
In order to influence others, I would prefer to:							
Coercive power							
1. Give them undesirable job assignments	1	2	3	4	5	6	7
2. Make the work difficult for them	1	2	3	4	5	6	7
3. Make things unpleasant here	1	2	3	4	5	6	7
4. Make being at work distasteful	1	2	3	4	5	6	7
Connection power							
5. Talk about my association with superiors	1	2	3	4	5	6	7
6. Let them know about powerful friends	1	2	3	4	5	6	7
7. Let them know about the organisations I am a member of	1	2	3	4	5	6	7
8. Tell them I am a member of important internal coalitions	1	2	3	4	5	6	7
Information power							
9. Let them know I have access to significant information	1	2	3	4	5	6	7
10. Give them only the information they need to do their job and no more	1	2	3	4	5	6	7

	Strongly disagree	Disagree	Slightly disagree	Neither agree nor disagree	Slightly agree	Agree	Strongly agree
11. Make them feel I have access to information they are not privy to	1	2	3	4	5	6	7
12. Release information only when it suits me	1	2	3	4	5	6	7
Legitimate power							
13. Make them feel they have commitments to meet	1	2	3	4	5	6	7
14. Make them feel like they should satisfy their job requirements	1	2	3	4	5	6	7
15. Give them the feeling that they have responsibilities to fulfil	1	2	3	4	5	6	7
16. Make them recognise that they have tasks to accomplish	1	2	3	4	5	6	7
Reward power							
17. Increase their pay level	1	2	3	4	5	6	7
18. Influence them getting a pay increase	1	2	3	4	5	6	7
19. Provide them with specific benefits	1	2	3	4	5	6	7
20. Influence them getting a promotion	1	2	3	4	5	6	7
Expert power							
21. Give them good technical knowledge	1	2	3	4	5	6	7
22. Share my experience and training	1	2	3	4	5	6	7
23. Provide them with sound job related advice	1	2	3	4	5	6	7

	Strongly disagree	Disagree	Slightly disagree	Neither agree nor disagree	Slightly agree	Agree	Strongly agree
24. Provide them with needed technical knowledge	1	2	3	4	5	6	7
Referent power							
25. Make them feel valued	1	2	3	4	5	6	7
26. Make them feel personally accepted	1	2	3	4	5	6	7
27. Make them feel that I approve of them	1	2	3	4	5	6	7
28. Make them feel important	1	2	3	4	5	6	7

Activity 8.1 continued

Scoring

Using Table 8.3, insert your scores in the space provided next to the relevant question number as shown.

Interpretation

A high score of 6 or greater on any of the seven power types implies that you prefer to influence others by utilising that particular type of power. A low score of 2 or less implies that you prefer not to utilise this particular type of power to influence others.

Your overall power profile is not simply reflected by the sum of the power derived from each of the seven types of power in the profile. For example, some combinations of power types are more than the sum of their parts and are synergistic. Referent power for example tends to magnify the impact of other types of power as the person being influenced tends to recognise the influence attempts are coming from someone they respect. Alternatively, some combinations of power types tend to lessen the overall sum of the parts. The use of coercive power tends to dilute other power types.

Now that you have some understanding of the relative strengths and limitations of these power bases and have developed your own personal power profile, you need to make an assessment of how to make the best use of these power sources.

Source: Adapted from 'Development and application of new scales to measure French and Raven (1959) bases of social power', by Timothy R Hinkin and Chester A Schriesheim, *Journal of Applied Psychology*, August 1989, pp. 561-567. Copyright © 1989 American Psychological Association. Adapted with permission.

Table 8.3 Self assessment

Coercive	Connection	Information	Legitimate	Reward	Expert	Referent
1	5	9	13	17	21	25
2	6	10	14	18	22	26
3	7	11	15	19	23	27
4	8	12	16	20	24	28
Total score						
Divide by 4						

Power and transformational leadership

There has been some research on the relationship between the power bases described and the concept of transformational leadership outlined in chapter 6.

You will recall from chapter 6 that transformational leaders are said to have the ability to implement successful change in organisations and that this ability is highly regarded in modern complex organisations.

The message for leaders who wish to be perceived as effective and transformational is that the use of personal power (both referent and expert) is related to the perception of transformational leadership. In other words, leaders who draw upon their personal power rather than their positional power are perceived as more able to implement change. In a modern workplace, a leader needs to be perceived in this way. Punitive and autocratic leaders are rarely perceived as transformational and therefore are often perceived as having a poor or inappropriate influencing style.

Reflections

Think about your own experience with the perception of power. In your experience in your organisation, are leaders who predominantly use positional power to influence others perceived positively or negatively?

Influence

The relationship between power and influence has already been stated. While conceptualisations of power have been recorded by scholars for some decades, it is only in recent years that the specific behaviours that leaders use to influence others have been empirically studied. Researchers have, in the main, identified various behaviours of leaders and titled them 'influence tactics'. Gary Yukl (Yukl, Lepsinger & Lucia 1992) and his colleagues have developed the Influence Behavior Questionnaire (IBQ) and their subsequent work (Yukl & Tracey 1992) has validated eleven influence tactics that are appropriate for influencing team members, peers and superiors in organisations.

It should be noted that the tactics outlined below are proactive. They are aimed at energising the person to be influenced. Reactive techniques and other behaviours that aim to guide team members are not included. The tactics include:

- rational persuasion,
- apprising,
- inspirational appeals,

- consultation,

- exchange,

- collaboration,

- personal appeals,

- ingratiation,

- legitimating tactics,

- pressure, and

- coalition tactics.

Influence tactics

Rational persuasion

Rational persuasion occurs when the leader uses logical arguments and factual evidence to support a request for action. There are varying degrees of rational persuasion; it may vary from a brief explanation of the reason for a request to detailed and sophisticated documentation and evidence to demonstrate that a course of action is feasible or appropriate. To use this tactic successfully, the leader must be deemed by the target of the request to be credible and trustworthy, and the target must be willing to be influenced. Research has shown that this tactic is likely to be highly effective if used skilfully and in the appropriate situation.

Apprising

Apprising occurs when the leader explains how a positive response to a request will benefit the target of the request personally or will assist the target person's career. A request to undertake an assignment or task will give the person an opportunity to learn new skills or gain new networks is an example of apprising. The tactic is differentiated from rational persuasion in that the benefits of a positive response are for the individual rather than for the organisation. Research has shown that this tactic is likely to be moderately effective if used skilfully and in the appropriate situation.

Inspirational appeals

Inspirational appeals involve an appeal to the values, ideals and emotions of the target person to gain their commitment to a request or proposal. Inspirational appeals are in contrast with logical arguments used in rational persuasion and apprising. The tactic is an attempt to arouse emotional responses from the target based on ideals such as fairness, equity, excellence and so on. Some of the bases used to appeal to a person are their desire to be important and to be recognised, to be a member of a high productive team or to be involved in continuous improvement. To use this tactic successfully, the leader must have some knowledge of the values, goals and hopes of the people to be influenced. Research has shown that this tactic is likely to be highly effective if used skilfully and in the appropriate situation.

Consultation

Consultation is a technique where the leader invites and encourages the target to develop suggestions to assist in planning a task or proposal that will occur in the future. The primary reason for using this tactic is to get support from the target for a decision that has already been made. It can take many forms — for example, from allowing input to a specific proposal, or presenting a general proposal and inviting specific comments on it. Research has shown that this tactic is likely to be highly effective if used skilfully and in the appropriate situation.

Exchange

Exchange occurs when the leader offers an incentive or suggests an exchange of favours if a request receives positive support. It is a useful tactic when the request offers no specific benefits for the target or is inconvenient or time consuming for the target person. The exchange of favours need not be explicit and the leader may offer to reciprocate at a future time in an unspecified manner. Research has shown that this tactic is likely to be moderately effective if used skilfully and in the appropriate situation.

Collaboration

Collaboration involves offering the target resources and assistance if they are willing to support a request or proposal. This tactic is similar to the exchange tactic but differs as collaboration involves reducing the difficulty or costs of carrying out a request while acting jointly, whereas exchange involves increasing a benefit to the target which may be unrelated to the task proposed. Research has shown that this tactic is likely to be highly effective if used skilfully and in the appropriate situation.

Personal appeals

Personal appeals occur when the leader seeks the assistance or support of the target out of friendship—essentially requesting a personal favour. This tactic can only be implemented if the target is on a friendly basis with the leader. If referent power is very strong, a personal appeal should not be necessary. Research has shown that this tactic is likely to be moderately effective if used skilfully and in the appropriate situation.

Ingratiation

Ingratiation is behaviour like praise or flattery that makes the target feel positively disposed toward the leader, either before or during the influence attempt. It is important that the ingratiation is perceived by the target to be sincere. If it is perceived to be insincere, it is likely to be received as manipulative. Ingratiation has been shown to be more useful as a long-term strategy for influence to improve relationships with the target than for short-term or immediate influencing attempts. Research has shown that this tactic is likely to be moderately effective if used skilfully and in the appropriate situation.

Legitimating tactics

Legitimating tactics occur when the leader uses formal policies or rules to verify the authority of a request. The philosophy is that the target will be more likely to comply with a request if it is viewed by the target as legitimate and proper. This tactic is useful when the request is unusual or falls outside the boundaries established by previous requests. Examples include showing that the request conforms to organisational policies, professional expectations, or was approved by some higher authority. Research has shown that this tactic is likely to be low in effectiveness.

Pressure

Pressure uses demands, threats, close supervision or repeated reminders to influence the target person. It is a useful tactic for team members who are difficult employees or malingerers, and who may not generally be willing to be influenced. The tactic will not result in any long-term commitment. It may, as has been alluded to earlier in this chapter, be perceived as bullying. As such, it might have serious consequences for the leader. There are hard pressure tactics — such as threats and warnings — and soft tactics like reminders and persistent requests. Research has shown that this tactic is likely to be low in effectiveness.

Coalition tactics

Coalition tactics involve obtaining assistance from other people to influence the target person. The leader seeks the support of others to persuade the target to respond positively to a request or proposal and uses that support as a reason for the target to comply. The tactic works more effectively if the support comes from people the target respects, and is usually used to complement other tactics. Research has shown that this tactic is likely to be low in effectiveness.

Choosing the right tactic

It is generally accepted that most influence attempts involve either a simple request or a lower-end use of the rational persuasion tactic. As a general rule, leaders should select an influencing tactic that will accomplish the objective with the least effort. Leaders, however, should be skilled at all tactics to be prepared for all situations.

Some of the tactics are more complex and sophisticated to use than others, and some work better under different conditions and situations. The point is that effective leaders use a range of influence tactics and do not rely on a limited repertoire. If you are a leader who overuses inappropriate tactics or who uses Machiavellian or manipulative techniques extensively, prepare to join the queue of leaders exiting workplaces due to inappropriate and socially unacceptable leadership styles.

Activity 8.2 Self assessment

Use the scale in Table 8.4 to rate how often you use each of the 11 influence tactics listed.

To determine your overall use of influence tactics, add the numbers you selected for each tactic. Your score will range from 11 to 55. The higher your score, the more influence tactics you use. The more influence tactics you use often, the more influential you probably are.

Table 8.4 Influence tactics

Influence tactic	Never	Not often	Sometimes	Often	Frequently
Rational persuasion	1	2	3	4	5
Apprising	1	2	3	4	5
Inspirational appeals	1	2	3	4	5
Consultation	1	2	3	4	5
Exchange	1	2	3	4	5
Collaboration	1	2	3	4	5
Personal appeals	1	2	3	4	5
Ingratiation	1	2	3	4	5
Legitimating tactics	1	2	3	4	5
Pressure	1	2	3	4	5
Ingratiation	1	2	3	4	5
Coalition tactics	1	2	3	4	5

> **Reflections**
>
> Review the eleven influence tactics outlined in this section and activity 8.2. Do you tend to use the influence tactics equally to achieve organisational objectives? Do you overuse any tactic or not take advantage of the variety of tactics available?

Connecting power and influence

There are some correlations between the influencing style of the leader and the types of power the leader predominantly draws upon to influence. While the correlations are less than perfect, the model developed below might be useful to you if you have determined in the self assessment that your predominant influencing style is overused (see Figure 8.1). Its main use, however, is in determining the appropriate influencing tactic and corresponding power bases to practice influence with team members of varying degrees of willingness to be influenced.

Figure 8.1 The relationship between power, influencing style and willingness of team members to be influenced

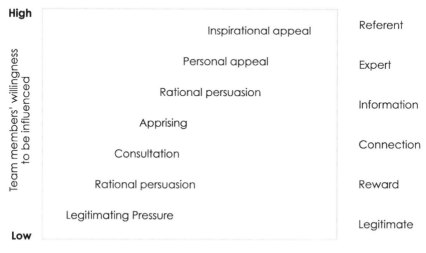

Appropriate influencing tactic

The model is intended to represent how influencing tactics might be used when considering available power bases. It should not be adopted as a prescriptive model. The variable on the left-hand axis, 'team members' willingness to be influenced' is a variable identified in the Situational Leadership model mentioned in chapter 5. The right-hand axis consists of the seven types of power identified earlier in this chapter. Leadership tactics comprise the horizontal axis.

A legitimating and pressure-influencing tactic using coercive and legitimate power bases would tend to be appropriate when team members are unwilling to be influenced to perform a task, are perceived as malingerers, or are known to be difficult people. It would be sensible, however, to ascertain the reason for the unwillingness before using the indicated tactics.

In contrast, inspirational and personal appeal or rational persuasion using referent and expert power bases would be appropriate where team members are very willing to be influenced.

Dis-connecting power and influence

The model in figure 8.1 is a useful theoretical tool for aligning power bases with influencing techniques. However, as was stated earlier in this chapter, in practice, a reliance on inappropriate sources of power in order to influence others will not lead to the sustained support or respect of others. The June, 2010 spectacular fall by former Prime Minister Kevin Rudd is a classic example of the dis-connection between **power** and **influence**. While being an example at its ultimate heights, is it a useful illustration that all leaders can benefit from as there are lessons to be learned. Mr Rudd held what must be acknowledged as the most powerful position in Australia – the Prime Ministership. While he held this **power**, he was not able to **influence** his followers to maintain support for him. Without followers, then by definition and as Mr Rudd discovered on 24 June, you are no longer a leader.

A leader can have **positional power** (and in the case of Mr Rudd, lots of it) but may have little or no **influence** over their followers. Mr Rudd did not cultivate his sources of personal power and his skill set as a diplomat was irrelevant to his then leadership role. The example of Mr Rudd's dramatic fall demonstrates that autocratic, non-consultative leadership styles will always be eventually unacceptable to others - even at the highest levels of leadership. This is why new Prime Minister Gillard has gone to great lengths in her first few days in office to use language to emphasise her 'consultative' style and her intention to 'collaborate' with her cabinet colleagues (and indirectly with the union opinion leaders). Ms Gillard wishes to distance herself and distinguish her leadership style clearly from the leadership style of Mr Rudd, relying on her personal power (expert politician and communicator) to influence rather than her position.

To bring this high level political example down to a workplace level, all managers (at every organisational level) in today's workplaces have positional power. However, many of these managers make the same mistakes as Mr Rudd when it comes to having power and using this power to influence others. These managers are not able to make the necessary changes in the organisation or bring about their vision for the workplace because they have no real **influence** over the people in the workplace. They are managers and not leaders. Of course they can use rewards and performance management to drive employees in the short term but only true leadership based on **personal power** sources will truly influence and motivate people to follow them in any sustained way.

Mr Rudd not only did not have the leadership style and skill set to succeed as Prime Minister, he never understood how leadership is connected with influence of his followers. While he lamented during his last night in office that he was 'elected by the people' to the position of Prime Minister, he failed to understand that Prime Ministers in Australia are elected by the members of parliament (and in the case of the Labor Party, also by union officials). These groups are the important followers for the purposes of the Prime Minister's leadership tenure, not the general public.

What are the lessons? Leaders have to understand who are their stakeholders (that is their followers). Without the support of your followers, while you might remain a manager or keep your position for a short time, you are no longer the leader! Personal power sources (expert and referent) are the only power sources that are sustainable in the longer run. These are the power bases that need to be developed by effective leaders.

Leader in action: Dr James Cowley

Throughout his career in building new organisations and in the disciplines of marketing research and strategy, trends, business innovation and education, Dr James Cowley has innovated. He has built highly profitable organisations from scratch with teams up to 150 people. These organisations have been in Australia and overseas. He has aimed for the organisations to be sustainable even after he left as CEO — with one of them now in existence for 38 years. He has consulted at the highest levels to corporations and government ('chief' or board levels; secretary or minister). He is sought-after as a keynote speaker at conferences, as a writer, and is often in the media. Years ago, in his spare time, he set up a counselling centre with volunteers at a time when counselling was not even a discipline. The centre later became a residential centre for people in difficulty. It still exists. He continues to innovate.

When asked how the concept of power and influence fits with creating sustainable organisations, James's response was:

'The first thing a leader has to do is train himself to reject power as a leadership or management approach. Once you believe you have power, you will lose the plot. Lasting influence does not come through power. You have to work on your own ego constantly to remind yourself that the day you move on, you are no-one again, and this applies to leaders at any level. It keeps you human. Of course, if you don't you will never adapt to future stages of your own life, because your jobs will be your only identity. And if you use power to make people do things, it does not build a sustainable organisation. You have to build organisations where people choose to do the things they do. So if we can get power and ego under control, we can then really make things happen. These are some of the practices I tried. Sometimes I was reasonably successful in putting them into practice, sometimes not, so you keep trying a bit harder.

You look for the potential in people and try to help them fulfil what they want from the work part of their lives. If you can listen to them, you find 99% will not let you down. And if they do, it's often because you as leader have not really understood where they needed more training. Often, quite small issues trip them up.

You mentor your team; you choose leaders who will mentor their teams. You do everything possible to teach people the skills they need to do the job brilliantly, so they can feel great about their achievements. And as people grow, you must back off and set them free to grow further. But you keep your network alive so that they can help you, and you can help them well into the future.

You keep your feet on the ground, and however large your organisation grows, you stay out there in contact with your customers or clients, and with your team. How can any executive 'feel' the pulse of consumers or see what trips their teams up, unless for some of their time they are at the 'coal face.' You show you are prepared to work as hard and at tasks as difficult as any of your team have to face.

You demonstrate innovation in every area of the organisation, internally and externally. By doing that, you give people the message to innovate and do things better. They are motivated by the fact that we do it better than competitors, and we all feel good about the successes. You show people that if they don't accept the status quo, they will find ways to do things better.

If you have a business partner, you have one like the one I have had in many ventures – Graham Bean – who you trust implicitly and where you respect each other's different skills.

You talk and articulate important things to everyone. You explain what is happening so people feel included and they trust, instead of being 'technically correctly communicated to' or 'technically and correctly engaged'.

Your modus operandi is to listen. By Listening you understand how others see the world. It's the only reality that there is that you are working with. Once you stop listening, you are lost in your own ego.

You set quality aims and then involve your team in working out how to get there. Then you celebrate quality with them. And you make sure they are the ones who get recognition.

If you are me, you don't have an office for yourself. When the MD has to balance his or her briefcase on one of their colleagues' filing cabinets in order to find a file and ask to borrow a workstation, it sends a message about power, status, silos and all those things that get in the way of performance.

You trust your team implicitly. You let them work when they want to, where they want to, and how they want, as long as they get the results for their job. Hardly anyone lets you down. The few failures cost a lot less than the draconian ways and systems we often introduce to prove to ourselves that people are working.

If clients or customers have a problem, then you empower your team to have a mentality to fix problems. If, however, they treat a team member badly or unfairly as a human being, then you defend your team member even to the extent of losing the client. You do everything possible to teach people that any form of prejudice, age, gender, handicap or ethnicity is a prison that they set for themselves, cutting themselves off from the richness in the diversity of people. Respect and kindness are values we often forget in business.

*And in any work for customers or clients you train yourself to be totally committed to their success, and **them** feeling good as a result of your work, products or services. But part of this is being **absolutely truthful and candid** with the advice or information you give, even if you risk losing them as a client. Paradoxically, this approach means you end up servicing the most senior people – executives leading corporations, government ministers, heads of departments and their executives – because the higher you go, the more difficult it gets to get people to tell you clearly what is needed and how to do it, even if it's contrary to what you think.*

And, of course, you tightly manage the finance and accounting of the organisation so that it runs so well that the team feels the security of a company built to last, even if some may never have experienced the opposite and don't realise how good a stable company feels. You have the responsibility as a leader to create a profitable business which can therefore give stability of employment to people. Even more importantly, in a world where many people turn up daily to jobs they find monotonous, colleagues who may not treat them correctly, organisations where power to achieve is centred away from individuals, games and politics are played rather than the best in people brought out and people attend in order to go through the motions – a leader must try to facilitate what he knows can be different.

When you lose it, as I do many times, and as we all do, and don't manage people as well as we should, you apologise if possible, try to improve things and spend time reflecting on how you can improve your leadership style. After many years you are still reflecting on how you could have done it better for so-and-so and you regret the harm you may have caused them.

And for those who say 'that's all OK, but businesses still have to make money!' I can confirm that it produces organisations that are both more profitable and achieve more of their goals than their competitors over sustained periods of time.

That's the leadership style I have tried to practice to some degree of success and I think it has facilitated the brilliant people I have had the privilege to work with. It's based on the refusal to use power. It's the commitment to influence by how you work with your team. It's also the style I have seen in some leaders, CEOs, government department executives and others who create great organisations that will last. It probably sounds soft. It's actually very hard.'

Sources: Interview with Dr Cowley on 6 May 2009.

The profile of James Cowley above shows a use of 'power' as not commonly accepted in organisations. James uses referent power to influence others in his organisation. He understands the relationship between the use of power and lasting, sustainable influence. He shares information as a way of building and increasing the shared power in his organisation. Leaders who abuse power and use it incorrectly never build relationships that lead to sustainable outcomes for the organisation.

Gentle influence

Many authorities believe that the 2008 global financial crisis was caused by widespread aggressive and inappropriate influencing (selling) tactics of sub-prime mortgages in the United States. There are also general trends in society and in workplaces around the world of aggressive direct forms of influence that might be regarded as bullying. Workplace bullying is a major issue for employers. A Productivity Commission report released in 2010 found the effects of workplace stress including bullying, cost employers $10 billion a year through absenteeism and loss of workplace productivity. Perhaps it is time for leaders to replace direct and aggressive forms of influence that represent a workplace risk, with techniques that might be regarded as more 'gentle'.

Leaders who try to influence others through intimidation, aggression and arguing can never have the sustained respect of others. Only through gentle, kindly, soft-selling influence can organisations and society as a whole evolve into places that command respect and treat others with kindness. All leaders can use more considerate and honourable ways to influence other people.

Eight techniques for applying gentle influence

Outlined below are eight techniques (Pace, Miller & Stephan 2008) that are gentler and more subtle than the influencing tactics identified previously, techniques that will increase the influence potential of effective leaders.

Technique 1: Mutual perspective

A mutual perspective occurs when two or more people see an object or view a thought from the same particular standpoint. *Mutuality* means having a common or joint relation to something; a *perspective* has to do with how you think about something. Thus a mutual perspective is achieved when two parties view things in a similar way.

There are two kinds of mutual perspectives: natural ones and acquired ones. *Natural* mutual perspectives occur when we see things the same way because we use the same assumptions to think about something. *Acquired* mutual perspectives occur when we are encouraged to see things in the same way, although our assumptions or values may differ. In exercising gentle influence, we should seek to locate natural mutual perspectives, but we should also work to create acquired mutual perspectives.

Technique 2: Sustaining agreement

Gentle influence evolves most effectively from a solid foundation of agreement. Once another person agrees with you, the process of gentle influence has begun. Securing sustained agreement begins with the other person's willingness to agree. This requires expressing yourself kindly, so as to develop the sense that you are gracious, pleasant, of goodwill, and benevolent. In addition, you must articulate acceptable ideas, or those ideas to which the other will consent, approve, assent to, and receive as true. Acceptability comes from the feeling that you have achieved a consistency of belief with the other person. Consistency is normally achieved at the level of basic beliefs where fewer differences exist.

Technique 3: Reciprocal act

This technique is a natural extension of a widely regarded principle called reciprocity. The principle holds that if you give people what they would like to have, they will, in return, reciprocate by bestowing upon you a similar gift. The duty to return deed-for-deed, measure-for-measure, kind-for-kind, and like value-for-like value is strongly ingrained in most cultures. Friendships are governed by the agreements implied by reciprocity. Thus, it is clear that if you want to get others to act on your behalf, you must first act on their behalf.

For influence to be implemented effectively, it is essential that you subordinate your own desires, interests, wants, needs, likes and preferences to those of others. Give people what they would like to have first and they will, in return, give you what you would like to have. Thus, you exercise reciprocity by acting in ways that allow and encourage others to reciprocate. You engage in acts that warrant and support acts in return.

Technique 4: Great expectations

For gentle influence to have its most enduring effect, those whom you are attempting to influence must feel that you believe in them, and that you are confident that they can do well, especially in doing what you would like them to do. People perform better when you expect the best from them. Supporting people in achieving high expectations endears them to you in a very positive way. In fact, they feel exhilarated in devoting considerable energy to achieving the goals and doing their best.

The great expectations technique exercises a subtle form of gentle influence. To achieve the expectations of others is an exhilarating experience. The first part of the great expectations technique involves helping others set goals that lead them to meet expectations. The second part of the great expectations technique involves building the confidence of others so that they can achieve goals and meet higher expectations.

Technique 5: Just noticeable difference

The just noticeable difference technique (JND) holds that people are most apt to change their thinking and behaving in a series of small, slight, casual adjustments rather than in large, dramatic, abrupt, extreme movements. The JND technique encourages, supports, and clears the way for others to take tiny steps, for them to make small, simple decisions that lead to accomplishing goals. It avoids jerking, jolting, and shoving people into something completely new. The philosophy of the JND technique is expressed in the adage that says 'by the inch it's a cinch, by the yard it's hard'. The JND technique moves people's thinking and decisions in slight increments while giving them support and encouragement.

A just noticeable difference is one that is barely apparent or capable of being observed. When change is only slightly noticeable, it tends to attract polite, favourable, and civil attention. Just noticeable differences reveal small, incremental steps in thinking and deciding about things that achieve goals. The movements in attitude and feeling they involve are small but conspicuous.

Technique 6: Positive social value

Nothing is more effective in achieving gentle influence than working with people to make them shine and to increase their positive social value. When people feel that they have value, they work with others more positively and with greater enthusiasm.

Social value is the feeling people have that they have worth and merit. They feel cherished, prized, uncommon and, in some cases, extraordinary. When they feel valued, they shine and act confidently on your behalf. People who challenge, rebuff and attack others are irritating. They respond to others with disdain and scorn, indicating that the other is unworthy of notice, undeserving of attention, and beneath them. People who are irritating and challenging do not respond well to influence.

Usually, when people deal with an irritating person, they become piqued — they take offence at the slight and the condescension. They may experience momentary impatience and seek ways to attack the irritant; they may become agitated, vexed, and exasperated — if not just annoyed. The irritant evokes conflicting passions, confusion over direction, and inserts disorder into one's otherwise orderly pursuits. The usual source of 'irritant' behaviour is low self-esteem, jealousy, intolerance of rivalry, suspicion and distrust, grudging envy, and discontentment with the success of others. This requires of gentle influence that it minimise intolerance, reduce suspicions, increase trust and contentment, and increase self-esteem.

Technique 7: Courtesy and consolation

The practice of gentle influence requires not only agreement and a comforting touch but words of courtesy and consolation; it requires a demonstration of visible goodwill. The goal is to make agreement as effortless and pleasing as possible. Interacting with others in a polite, even-tempered, poised, calm manner assures their attentiveness and respect.

Technique 8: Congeniality

If there were a single concept to exemplify gentle influence, it would be that people go along with you when they feel that what they want is in harmony with what you want. They will be eager to accept your influence if your silent actions indicate that you like them and appreciate them.

Tension, conflict, anxiety and vexation are signs that things are not going well. Harmony, accord, unity, and tranquillity signal the onset of positive progress. Gentle influence seeks to create as much harmony as possible so that positive feelings bring the other person along because that is where they want to go. The congeniality technique seeks to create real harmony rather than contrived harmony.

> **Activity 8.3**
>
> Observe the leaders in your organisation, the leaders you might have worked for previously or ones you know of. What methods do they use predominantly to influence others? Are they mostly direct or indirect? Which methods work best in the organisational culture you work in? Why? Can you learn anything from your observations?

Empowerment

The term 'empowerment' emerged in the 1990s. Over many decades previously, similar theoretical and practical attempts to 'empower employees' were discussed under the themes of employee participation, the human relations approach to management and shared leadership practices. The term is useful in a discussion of leadership and power and influence, and therefore is further discussed in this section.

There are many definitions of what empowerment means but in practice, empowerment occurs when the leader ensures that team members have the delegated authority to make judgments on how issues are to be solved and have the capacity to work independently. Empowerment does not mean abrogation of leader responsibility or merely delegation. Empowerment is not a gift bestowed on team members by a leader. Leaders don't *give* power. As was explained earlier in this chapter, power already exists in the team members. The job of the leader is to develop an organisational environment that unleashes power in their work teams—that is, to remove the barriers that keep team members from acting with power. When a leader shares power with others, the leader's own power and influence increase.

There are two fundamentally different approaches to the study of empowerment—psychological and environmental. Each of them provides some guidance to leaders on how to empower their team members.

214

Psychological empowerment

Spreitzer (1995) advanced a 'psychological' theory of empowerment whereby team members feel empowered when four related components are enabled:

- *Meaning* The value of the work or goal. A person is likely to feel empowered when they perceive they are doing meaningful work that is congruent with their personal values or beliefs.

- *Competence* The individual's belief that they have the capability and can undertake the work assigned to them within the expected performance standards.

- *Self-determination* The team member has some choice over the method or pace of the work or its initiation.

- *Impact* The degree of influence an individual has over strategic or operational outcomes in their work.

According to this theory, it is the psychological state of the team member(s) as measured by these four components that determines whether team members feel that they are fully empowered. When these psychological states are reached, team members feel more satisfied with their work, are more effective and committed to the organisation, have lower intentions to resign and demonstrate more positive work performance that those with lower levels of empowerment (Meyerson & Kline 2008).

Environmental empowerment

Lee and Koh (2001) researched an 'environmental' approach whereby empowerment arises because of the behaviour of the leader rather than the psychological state of team members. Environmental empowerment is therefore the actions by leaders that provide the tools or freedom for team members to decide how their work should be done.

According to this theory, when leaders display the appropriate behaviours and leadership style, team members feel more satisfied with their work, are more effective and committed to the organisation, have lower intentions to resign and demonstrate more positive work performance than those with lower levels of empowerment (Meyerson & Kline 2008).

Environmental empowerment is therefore closely related to the concept of transformational leadership discussed earlier in this chapter. Transformational leaders are more likely to provide the conditions for team members to feel empowered because of their leadership style. This style is characterised by behaviours aimed at inspiring and motivating team members, making work meaningful, and providing more autonomy.

Therefore, it might be said that a leader's behaviour profoundly affects the degree to which team members perceive whether they are empowered. This environmental form of empowerment may then, in turn, affect the level of psychological empowerment able to be reached by the team members.

When endeavouring to empower others, leaders need to note that there can be no empowerment of others unless there is first self-awareness. It is self-awareness that provides a basis for understanding others. That is, it is difficult to be conscious of another's need for empowerment without first having awareness of one's own motivation and needs.

Summary

Influence is what leadership is all about. If leaders cannot appropriately influence their followers, then perhaps they are not leaders at all. This chapter described a number of sources and types of power and a variety of influence tactics available to leaders. Effective leaders use a wide variety of influence tactics but some are not appropriate to be used often.

The exercise of power and politics by leaders in organisations is a necessity of organisational life that should not be viewed by leaders as negative. Leaders need power to increase their ability to influence others. They must play some politics in order to gain power, build relationships and avoid political blunders.

Whatever the workplace context in which a leader is expected to perform, there is a trend away from direct and aggressive forms of influence to more gentle and indirect forms of influence. The chapter outlined eight techniques that leaders can use to influence people more indirectly.

Reflection on your leadership practice

Examine your leadership style and in particular your use of the various power bases outlined in this chapter. Then re-read the section in this chapter on empowerment. Does your leadership style empower others? If the answer is 'yes', write a few lines on how your leadership style empowers others. If you feel your leadership style does not empower others, what changes might you make to it to ensure that in the future, your actions are empowering?

References

Galinsky, J, Magee, J, Gruenfeld, D, Whitson, J & Liljenquist, K 2008, 'Power Reduces the Press of the Situation: Implications for Creativity, Conformity, and Dissonance', *Journal of Personality and Social Psychology*. Washington: Dec 2008. vol. 95, no. 6; p. 1450.

French, JRP & Raven, B 1959, 'The bases of social power,' in D Cartwright ed., *Studies in Social Power*, Ann Arbor, MI: University of Michigan Press.

Kanter, R 1983, *The Change Masters*, Simon & Schuster, New York.

Lee, M & Koh, J 2001, 'Is empowerment really a new concept?', *International Journal of Human Resource Management*, vol. 12, no. 4. pp. 684-95.

Meyerson, S & Kline, T 2008, 'Psychological and environmental empowerment: antecedents and consequences', *Leadership and Organizational Development Journal*, vol. 29, no. 5, pp. 444-460.

Pace, W, Miller, P & Stephan, E 2008, *Gentle Juggernaut, The Amazing Power of Leaning in Influencing Others*, Eloquent Books, New York.

Productivity Commission, 2010, Performance Benchmarking of Australian Business Regulation: Occupational Health and Safety - Productivity Commission Research Report, April, Canberra.

Spreitzer, G 1995, 'Individual empowerment in the workplace: dimensions, measurement, validation', *Academy of Management Journal*, vol. 38, no. 5, pp. 1442-65.

Yu, HC & Miller, P 2005, 'Leadership style—The X Generation and Baby Boomers compared in different cultural contexts', *Leadership and Organization Development Journal,* vol. 26, no.1, pp.35-50.

Yukl, G, Lepsinger, R & Lucia, T 1992, 'Preliminary Report on the Development and Validation of the Influence Behaviour

Questionnaire', in K Clark, M Clark & D Campbell, 1992, *Impact of Leadership, Centre for Creative Leadership*, Greensboro, NC.

Yukl, G & Tracey, B 1992, 'Consequences of Influence Tactics used with Subordinates, Peers and the Boss, *Journal of Applied Psychology*, vol. 77, pp. 525-535.

Chapter 9

LEADERSHIP COMMUNICATION

CHAPTER CONTENTS

Spotlight: Brian Cook, OBS Technology Group

Brian Cook is the Chief Executive Officer of OBS Technology Group, an Australian information technology company that specialises in helping organisations to improve productivity through the use of Microsoft technologies.

OBS was formed in 1999 by a group of corporate IT professionals who shared a love of technology and a passion for helping people work smarter and more efficiently. OBS has grown from a small Melbourne services company focused on Microsoft Exchange, to Australia's largest Microsoft SharePoint Consulting Practice with offices in Melbourne, Sydney, Adelaide, Brisbane and Canberra. OBS is focused on attracting talented passionate people and giving them the environment, resources, and tools to create great outcomes for their customers. Over time, the organisation has created a high performance culture of people who excel, are balanced, love what they do and have a desire to change the world. The way the organisation communicates with their staff is a key factor to its success.

Based on the most extensive employee survey undertaken in corporate Australia, *Business Review Weekly* has recognised OBS as a top-ten place of employment in the 2009 'Best Places to Work' awards.

The communication process with staff commences on their first day when the organisation recognises the importance of keeping staff for the long term and ensuring that they gain a good understanding of the organisation's mission, vision and values. For example, on day one for the employee they are given an OBS gift box that includes OBS shirts, a guide to the company, sweets and material relating to their specific role. A broadcast email is sent to all staff to welcome them and encourage other staff to introduce themselves to the new staff member. Then the new employee participates in the development of a three-month plan with their manager. OBS likes the new employees to 'feel like part of the family from day one'.

Feedback and communication are essential parts of the company's culture. Long-term goals, principles and strategies are regularly communicated and discussed with all staff so that the staff can see the long-term future for the company. An online feedback tool allows staff at any time to provide feedback about a colleague, their team or the company generally. Strategies like this are in addition to a general open-door policy from all leaders that encourages open and honest communication. Communication is part of an overall continuous improvement philosophy in the company.

The company has also ensured that its communications systems are a priority. Breaking down barriers between the leaders and the teams is a constant challenge. Hierarchical levels in the organisation are kept very flat and efforts are concentrated on creating a team environment. For example, an open office floor plan encourages the leaders to 'manage while walking around'. The use of one-on-one casual conversations with people in the company, regardless of their role, is a technique adopted by all leaders.

The communication strategies adopted by the company are part of building a creative and flexible organisational culture. The culture of OBS is non-bureaucratic, fun, empowering and social. It encourages people to be curious and to question. According to the OBS human resources manager, Bianca Pickett, 'We all come to work to do a job—whether you're a manager or a receptionist makes absolutely no difference. We're all in it together, so a team culture is really important to us and we develop that fiercely'.

Active listening skills and empathy towards how employees see things is also an important skill for leaders in the company. Cook says. 'I think that it's really important as a leader that you are able to associate with them (employees) and put yourself in the shoes of employees that you lead. That's been key for me'.

Source: OBS website <http://www.obs.com.au>; Donaldson, C 2009, 'Putting yourself into their shoes', *Human Resources Leader Magazine*, no. 179, June.

The description of OBS and the leadership philosophy of its CEO, Brian Cook, provides a good summary of how communication skills for leaders and sound communication systems in organisations establish the foundation for organisational effectiveness and the building of attractive organisational cultures. The culture at OBS is demonstrated by an open-door policy of the senior leaders, effective active listening skills, structured feedback, and organisational systems that promote and encourage open and honest communication. The skills and techniques identified in this spotlight can be learnt. This chapter will assist leaders to think about and develop these skills.

Introduction

The possession of effective communication skills is critical for leaders. Communication has many definitions, but the one we will use in this chapter is the 'transfer of understanding and meaning to others'. This definition makes sense when we think about communication in a leadership context. The leader's main role is to attempt to influence others towards the organisation's vision and to assist others in understanding their role within the organisation. This gives followers meaning for their work. Everything a leader does when influencing others involves communicating. Good communication skills, when compared with other leadership skills, are foundational to effective leadership. Good communication skills alone, however, do not make an effective leader.

Complete books have been written to describe the communication skills and issues leaders need to be concerned with. We are not able to outline the full range of communication issues for leaders in one chapter so we have elected to concentrate on three levels of communication skills for leaders, then structure the chapter around these three levels, selecting what we think are the critical communication skills at each level. The three levels are:

- core communication skills,
- team communication skills, and
- strategic and external communication skills.

As a leader gains more responsibility in an organisation and undertakes more complex and demanding roles, the leader will need to improve core skills and become more effective in the broader team and strategic skills.

Communication can flow:

- downward from the leader to inform or inspire team members,

- upward to more senior leaders in the form of performance and status reports,

- laterally between other leaders at the same level in the organisation to aid in cross-functional co-ordination, or

- diagonally across both functional departments and organisational levels on specific issues.

In this chapter we take a broad view of communication — it does not just mean talking. It can be oral, written, non-verbal behaviour, or the facilitation of meetings. The mastery of some simple techniques outlined in this chapter can assist leaders to be more effective.

The importance of communication for leaders

Winston Churchill once said, 'the difference between mere management and leadership is communication' (Humes 1991). Effective leaders will attest to the critical importance for leaders to be able to communicate effectively. Research on managers and leaders over many years has demonstrated that leaders spend from around 75% to 90% of their time on communication activities. Effective communication skills enable leaders to provide their team members with greater access to information relevant to understanding and undertaking their roles.

Therefore, it is most unlikely that leaders can be effective without having attained at least some core communication competencies. The competencies necessary will depend upon the nature and culture of the organisation and the organisational level at which the leader has responsibility.

Core communication skills for leaders

Sometimes communication skills are categorised under a broader term known as *interpersonal skills*. Interpersonal skills are the skills needed to develop relationships with other people. Sometimes these skills are also referred to as *people skills*. Whatever term is used, research over decades has shown that these skills are most important for leaders.

Within the interpersonal skills framework, the following key skills are known to be essential — they are part of the core communication skills that leaders need:

- oral and written communication,

- non-verbal communication,

- active listening,

- giving and receiving feedback,

- emotional intelligence, and

- negotiation and conflict resolution.

The first five skills will be addressed in this section as core communication skills. Negotiation and conflict resolution are addressed separately later in the chapter.

Oral and written communication

It is not our intention here to detail the basic standards and techniques for oral and written communication. There are many good books available in these areas. However, what needs to be said is that leaders are expected to have reached at least an accepted standard in these areas and the standard will be dependent upon the organisational context in which the leader works and its usual communication practices.

All leaders, no matter the level at which they operate, are required regularly to write performance and status reports, letters and memorandums, and to engage in oral communications on one-on-one, small group and large group bases. When engaging in oral and written communication, Barrett (2006) advises that leaders need to:

- Establish a clear purpose for the communication and be very clear in the communication about its purpose. Usually, a communication will have the purpose to inform, persuade or instruct.

- Analyse their audience. The characteristics of the audience will determine the approach and the shape the message is to take. Every audience should be regarded as unique. Questions to ask are—what is the most effective way to begin the document or presentation for this audience; how should I organise the content to ensure the audience understands the main ideas; what is the most effective way to conclude?

- Pay attention to their language as a tool of influence and the inspiration others. They need to use the right words in the right way to achieve their intended purpose and outcome.

- Keep writing clear and concise. They need to avoid sexist and racist language.

Every communication, oral or written, builds a picture and creates an impression about the leader and their leadership. A leader's skills will be most visible when speaking informally, one-on-one, with groups, and when giving formal presentations. Effective leaders use these occasions to connect with people, so techniques like posture and eye contact are important to learn. Practice is often the best way to be good at formal presentations and public speaking. Leaders should take every opportunity to develop these skills.

Non-verbal communication

Facial expressions, body language, the way a person dresses, the way a person moves their hands when talking, the distance between them and the other person when talking, and their general demeanour—all send messages to others. Understanding their own body language and ensuring that oral and non-verbal communication is coherent is important to leaders who wish to improve their communications with others. Some research indicates that up to 90 per cent of the meaning of a communication is captured in the non-verbal clues.

As for the oral and written communication skills, we are not able to make a thorough analysis of non-verbal communication here. What is important is that leaders understand the significance of non-verbal communication as a communication technique and as part of their interpersonal skills in need of constant attention and development.

Active listening

Genuinely listening to others requires intellectual and physical effort. It is a skill that many leaders find demanding. Some leaders *hear* when others talk, but far too often they do not *listen* to what is being transmitted, either verbally or non-verbally. Active listening is listening for the full meaning of what is being transmitted and observing. It includes 'listening' to the non-verbal clues contained with the message without making premature judgements or interpretations.

According to Caputo, Hazel and McMahon (1994), there are four essential dimensions if the listener is to be active:

- The listener must concentrate with intensity on what the speaker is saying— summarising and synthesising the information in the communication and sorting it into the context of what has preceded it.

- The listener must empathise with the speaker by putting themselves in the speaker's shoes. Empathy requires the listener to understand what the speaker wants to communicate rather than the listener's interpretation or understanding of it, suspending their own thoughts and feelings on the issue.

- Active listeners listen objectively without judging the communication or interrupting it, demonstrating an acceptance of the communication or person even when they disagree with what is being said.

- Active listeners take responsibility for the full intended meaning of the communication and seek completeness of the interaction.

There are eight specific behaviours that leaders should endeavour to practise to build active listening skills (Robbins, Bergman, Stagg & Coulter 2003). These are:

- Make eye contact with the speaker so that they know you have focused your attention on them, that you are not distracted and that you can see their facial expressions and other non-verbal clues.

- Make affirmative nods and other appropriate facial expressions to show interest in what is being said. Appropriate movements and non-verbal listening responses on your part let the speaker know you are listening.

- Avoid distracting gestures that might make the speaker think you are bored or tired of what is being said. It is important that the speaker thinks they have your full and undivided attention.

- Ask questions to seek clarification and to ensure your own understanding—but leave it till the end so as not to be interruptive.

- Use the paraphrasing technique by restating and rephrasing the communication in your own words by commencing with, 'Do you mean …' or 'As I understand it, what you are saying is …'. This technique checks for accuracy and verifies you have listened correctly.

- Avoid interrupting the speaker until the end of the communication.

- Avoid talking over the top of the speaker. You cannot listen and speak at the same time!

- Make smooth transitions between the roles of speaker and listener—try not to think what you might say as you listen to the other person.

The behaviours can be learned, even though they may seem awkward and insincere at first try. The behaviours will become more natural if practised and will bring about attitudes of tolerance and empathy if persevered with.

Activity 9.1 Self assessment

Use the scale below to rate how often you use each of the eight active listening behaviours.

To determine your overall use of the correct active listening behaviours, add the numbers you selected for each behaviour. Your score will range from 8 to 40. The higher your score, the more effective you are as an active listener.

Active listening behaviour	Never	Not often	Sometimes	Often	Frequently
Making eye contact	1	2	3	4	5
Affirmative nods	1	2	3	4	5
No distracting gestures	1	2	3	4	5
Asking questions	1	2	3	4	5
Paraphrasing	1	2	3	4	5
No interrupting	1	2	3	4	5
No talking over the top	1	2	3	4	5
Smooth transitions	1	2	3	4	5

Giving feedback

Giving feedback on performance (both praise and criticism) is an integral part of effective leadership. It is also an activity which makes many leaders uncomfortable. It should, however, be daily activity in a team that is working effectively.

Feedback from leaders can be very diverse in nature. It can range from feedback on team member work performance to feedback on a team member's interpersonal behaviour. It can be both positive and negative. Research demonstrates that leaders like to give positive feedback and usually do so promptly and enthusiastically. Negative feedback, however, is often avoided by leaders, is inappropriately delayed, and often distorted by the leader to make it more acceptable to the receiver.

Getting effective feedback is essential to team members if they are to improve their performance, to develop, and to have clear expectations on work outputs and quality. Positive feedback assists team members to keep doing what they are doing well and to improve. Negative feedback assists team members with ways to change their attitude or behaviour to improve their performance. Feedback skills are related both to other communication skills listed in this chapter and to active listening, but often leaders who are good communicators are not good with feedback skills.

Hughes, Ginnett and Curphy (2006) provide the following guidelines for leaders who wish to improve their feedback skills.

Separate the behaviour from your *interpretation* of the behaviour. Focusing on behaviour when giving feedback is the key to giving good feedback, but many leaders find this much easier in theory than in practice. Take, for example, a leader responsible for assisting team members to improve their customer service who observes a team member speaking inappropriately to a customer. Interpretative feedback from this leader might be:

- You were rude and unhelpful.

- You do not seem to care.

The problem with interpretative feedback is that it often triggers a defensive reaction from the team member. The team member takes the feedback as a personal issue rather than a work issue. When people are defensive they put all their energy into counter-attacks and excuses, rather than listening with an open mind to ways in which they could improve. Therefore, when giving feedback, leaders need to focus on behaviour. Focusing on behaviour makes the feedback easier to accept by the team member. Focusing on behaviour, the leader might have said:

Do you remember when you were talking to that customer? I noticed that:

1. You didn't look at the customer when you spoke to them.

2. You interrupted the customer in mid-sentence.

3. You walked away to talk to a colleague before the customer was finished.

1, 2 and 3 are examples of specific behaviours. A specific description of behaviour is more neutral. Team members are generally more receptive to feedback which is presented in this way. In other words, negative feedback that is supported by evidence rather than interpretive is more meaningful to team members. When giving feedback, select examples of behaviour which will best help the team member to improve. Don't flood the person with criticism — choose about three examples to work on. Make sure you have a reasonable balance of criticism and praise.

Check whether the team member was aware of the required standards before he or she did the work and choose an opportunity to talk to the person in private, without interruption. Aim to give the feedback as soon after the event as possible so that the details of the task are still fresh in the team member's mind.

Finally, ensure that your feedback is clearly and fully understood. Ask the team member to rephrase the content of your feedback to ensure they fully capture the meaning that was intended.

Feedback is also more effective when it is designed specifically for the type of person receiving it. Below is a specific feedback model for giving positive and negative feedback. The effectiveness of the model is based on the assumption that team members will prefer to receive feedback based on their cognitive style (see chapter 4). You may recall from chapter 4 that cognitive style refers to the way a person gathers and evaluates information. The four cognitive styles include:

- sensing,
- intuiting,
- thinking, and
- feeling.

Feedback is, of course, a form of information. To operationalise the model and determine the appropriate feedback for a person, it is necessary that the leader identify the cognitive style of the person who will receive the feedback.

Experienced leaders who are aware of their own cognitive style can much easier judge the potential style of others. Instruments to measure cognitive style (like the one in chapter 4) are also useful for team-building activities and as an aid for leaders to diagnose the cognitive style of their team members.

Once the cognitive style of the recipient of the feedback has been determined (for example by asking them to complete the cognitive style instrument in a team-building activity) the specific form of feedback suggested below may be applied.

In general, in relation to positive feedback:

- look for others' accomplishments and contributions;

- ensure that the feedback is sincere, specific, immediate and personal;

- if your own cognitive style is the 'thinking' type, you may find that you need to work hard to remember to give positive feedback to others.

Use the specific style of feedback shown below for each type of receiver cognitive style.

Recipient's cognitive style	Positive feedback
Sensing	Describe the actual and specific positive behaviour or accomplishment you have observed.
Intuiting	Relate the actual behaviour to the big picture (e.g. team productivity) and mention any implications for the future.
Thinking	Determine and express the pleasant outcomes which occurred for you, for others, for your relationship, or for the team/organisation.
Feeling	Discuss the value of the person's action/accomplishment. Express what their behaviour has meant to you personally.

Activity 9.2 Self assessment for giving positive feedback

Use this guide to record how well you are delivering positive feedback to your team members. Do you:

- use 'I' statements to take ownership of the feedback message?

- describe fully the actual accomplishment or action? (sensing-style recipient)?

- reveal the meanings the contribution has on the present and future effectiveness of the work or employee? (intuiting-style recipient)?

- give logical reasons for continuing the desired behaviour or accomplishment (thinking-style recipient)?

- disclose how the behaviour impacted on others or on you personally (feeling-style recipient)?

In general, in relation to negative feedback:

- keep your own cognitive style preferences in mind;

- choose a time and place for giving feedback that is comfortable for the receiver;

- speak directly, clearly, and honestly; and

- use 'I' messages (e.g. 'I feel that you could be more assertive in meetings,' rather than 'You should be more assertive in meetings').

Use the specific style of feedback shown below for each type of receiver cognitive style.

Recipient's cognitive style	Negative feedback
Sensing	Describe the actual and specific unwanted behaviour or unfulfilled responsibilities you have observed. Be concrete. Use factual data.
Intuiting	Relate the actual behaviour to the big picture (e.g. team productivity) and give your impressions about how this behaviour or unfulfilled expectation has affected outcomes.

Recipient's cognitive style	Negative feedback
Thinking	Determine and express the logical outcomes of the behaviour. Discuss the consequences of the behaviour on you and others in the work unit.
Feeling	Disclose your values and feelings. Explain why this responsibility is important to you and why it matters.

Activity 9.3 Self assessment for giving negative feedback

Do you:

- use 'I' statements to take ownership of the feedback message?

- describe fully the actual unwanted behaviour or unfulfilled responsibilities (sensing-style recipient)?

- reveal the meanings the behaviour has for present and future performance (intuiting-style recipient)?

- disclose how the behaviour impacted on others or on you personally (feeling-style recipient)?

- give logical reasons for expected behaviour; state clearly the desired behaviour(s) or accomplishment(s) (thinking-style recipient)?

Receiving feedback from others

Leaders often receive criticism from team members, colleagues or their supervisor. It can be a stressful experience. An important thing for a leader to remember when receiving criticism is that the criticism should not be taken personally. People mostly criticise the leader's *position* rather than the *person* of the leader. Once you accept this basic tenet of leadership, receiving criticism is much easier.

Here are some suggestions for receiving negative feedback.

1. Listen until the end of the feedback. All feedback contains information, even personal attacks. You may find it helpful in some circumstances to take notes. Taking notes sometimes helps slow down emotional situations.

2. When the feedback from others is completed, summarise what has been said to demonstrate that you have actively listened to it. Your summary is not necessarily an indication of agreement—it is an indication of your professionalism and your ability to take criticism without reacting defensively.

3. Then ask for specific behavioural examples. For example:

- Can you give me a specific example of what I have done wrong?

- What would be a more helpful behaviour in these circumstances?

- Can you give me an example of circumstances when I get it right?

A calm, professional approach will often lead to a more reasonable response in the person who is criticising you. Then, after the feedback is completed, take time to reflect on it. How much of the criticism do you agree with? Which issues are valid? Often sleeping on it sheds a different light on the issues raised.

Your next step is to sort out options, trying out some suggestions yourself, and perhaps asking for constructive ideas from the other person. When you agree on a possible way forward, summarise action points and follow up with the person at an appropriate time later.

Emotional intelligence

Goleman (2004) introduced the concept of emotional intelligence (EI). EI refers to the capacity of a leader to deal effectively with their own and others' emotions. EI is a core communication skill for leaders. When applied to the workplace, emotional intelligence is about thinking intelligently with emotions—perceiving, expressing, understanding and managing emotions in a professional and effective manner at work.

A number of recent research studies have demonstrated a positive relationship between the ability to manage emotions and the quality of social interactions—and therefore leadership potential. EI is a combination of self-management and social skills that can transform and optimise individual or team performance. Chapter 3 details a key component of EI—the need for self-awareness.

Leader in action: Pat Grier, former CEO of Ramsay Health

Pat Grier is recognised as one of Australia's leading CEOs for his outstanding record of delivery to investors and his stewardship in growing Ramsay Health Care. He retired late in 2008 after 13 years in the position.

Under his leadership, Ramsay Health Care grew in profitably from a relatively small, privately-owned operation to the country's largest provider of private hospital services, with more than 25,000 employees and over 100 hospitals and 8,000 beds across Australia, the United Kingdom and Indonesia.

During his time as CEO the company passed a number of milestones, including the acquisition of the Department of Veteran Affairs hospitals, the launching of Ramsay as a public company, the acquisition of Alpha, Benchmark, Affinity and Capio UK and the reforming of the private hospital sector to a be a part of the balanced health care sector in Australia.

Pat was the architect of the company's special culture known as 'The Ramsay Way' which was central to the success of the organisation. Under his stewardship and guidance, Ramsay Health Care has become a well-respected leader in the private hospital industry in Australia.

When asked about the importance of communication to effective leadership, Pat responded:

'...absolutely ... effective communication is the key to unleashing effective leadership on both a personal and corporate basis. There are four main ingredients to a successful organisation and good leadership, and communication binds these four elements together:

- *a product that is of value to the consumer;*

- *a vision and a strategy which is the basis for growth of the organisation;*

> - *a strong and effective management with systems and procedures that maximises profits and other outcomes;*
>
> - *a special entrepreneurial culture which is values-based and motivates its people to do their very best for themselves and the organisation.*
>
> *And the good news for leaders is that, like effective leadership, effective communication can be learnt and developed.'*
>
> Pat says that in order to be a good communicator, you must clearly define the outcome you want, clarify what you want to communicate, and then design it to be understandable and acceptable to the receiver.
>
> 'Put yourself in the receiver's position,' says Pat. 'What's in it for them? How do you flavour it so it triggers the desired action? Then how do you add that something extra which will make the receiver want to go the extra mile? That is the true leadership ingredient — the human touch!'
>
> Pat will remain on the Board of Ramsay Health Care as a nonexecutive director assisting the company with its aim to expand its offshore business in the coming years.
>
> *Source*: Interview with Pat Grier 19 May 2009.

Pat Grier is an excellent example of a leader who understands the importance of organisational culture and the significance of communication in building an open and values based culture in an organisation. He is world renown for establishing the 'Ramsay Way' organisational culture that was a centre piece in his efforts to rebuild what was a failing organisation into an outstanding success. Like many other authorities on the matter, Pat makes it clear to leaders at all levels that these skills can be learned and developed.

Team communication skills

Chapter 10 details how teams develop and what leaders should do to ensure teams remain productive. In addition to these critical skills, leaders of teams must also have a number of other team communication skills. These skills may include ensuring that there is regular performance reporting for individuals in the team. Having an 'open door' policy (i.e. always being available for team members during the working day and allowing team members to meet with you informally at any time) is a good method of opening communication channels.

MBWA

'Managing by walking around' (MBWA) is another skill that leaders can learn in order to be more available for communication with team members. It enables the leader to find out what's happening in the work team and gives team members the opportunity to make informal contributions. Leaders who get out of touch with the individuals in their work team are also out of touch with their customers. Two important channels of communication are therefore opened using the MBWA technique. To open up these channels of communication in an informal way a good habit to develop is to wander around your area of responsibility on a regular basis. On these regular wanderings a leader is able to:

- use informal conversations to teach and reinforce organisational values to individuals in the team;

- listen and pay close attention to team members in their own work space where they feel most comfortable and confident;

- discover and acknowledge innovation and systems improvements not formally reported and spread them across other areas; and

- coach and mentor individuals in their own surroundings.

Some leaders are often uncomfortable with the concept of MBWA. If this informal communication practice makes you feel obviously uncomfortable, the work team will perceive it as spying or intensive supervision. To avoid this, leaders need to use MBWA as an active listening experience or as a way of exchanging information rather than for making on-the-spot decisions or immediately correcting team members for mistakes. Gradually team members will accept your presence on their turf as a genuine attempt to informally get closer to what's happening and to better communicate with them.

> ### Activity 9.4
>
> If you do not get out of your office and talk informally with your team members often, try the MBWA technique over a 30-day period. Initially, use it for informal information exchange with team members. Over time, fully embrace it as a way of leading your team.

Facilitating meetings

While the skills listed above are important, research shows that about 15% of the salary cost of large organisations is spent on employee meeting time. An improvement in meeting skills by the leader can have a significant effect on leadership effectiveness and productivity of work teams. Our main objective here, therefore, is to outline how to bring about effective communication at meetings as the primary team communication skill needed by leaders.

Carlopio, Andrewartha and Armstrong (2005) and Dubrin, Dalglish and Miller (2006) suggest that leaders need to acquire the communication skills to manage productive meetings and to use the 'four Ps' of effective meetings—namely:

- purpose,
- participants,
- planning, and
- process.

Purpose

The purpose is the reason the meeting is being held. There are generally a number of reasons why meetings are conducted, and the leader should ensure that team members are aware of the purpose of a meeting. Usually, meetings are called for:

- *information sharing*—when it is not clear what information is needed or available for an issue and some brainstorming is required to stimulate thought;

- *commitment building* — to engender action or to get team members involved in the planning or implementation of a task;

- *information dissemination* — when not all team members are aware of information important to the team or feedback and discussion is required;

- *problem solving* and decision making — when decisions need to be made or complex problems need to be resolved.

A single meeting might be held for all the above reasons. Leaders should ensure that team members are aware of the mode of the meeting at any point in time.

Participants

It is important for the leader to ensure that the right people are at the appropriate meetings. It is also important that the size of the meeting be appropriate to the task being undertaken. For example, if a meeting is too large, people might not be able to participate properly. If the meeting is too small, insufficient information will be shared or the decisions will not be adequately supported. The 3M company developed some guidelines for relating meeting size to the purpose of the meeting. 3M recommends that:

- decision-making and problem-solving meetings have about five participants,

- interactive seminars and training sessions have around 15 participants, and

- information meetings have no more than 30 participants.

Planning

The third 'P', planning, relates to the preparation for the meeting agenda. Meetings should not be held unless the purpose of the meeting is clear. If the purpose of the meeting is clear, it follows that an agenda for the meeting should be prepared well before the meeting so that participants can come to the meeting prepared to discuss the agenda items. Well-planned meetings do not cram the agenda with too much business. Tropman (2003) proposes the following guidelines when planning meetings:

- *The rule of halves.* Agenda items should be given to the meeting planner by the halfway mark between the last meeting and the upcoming meeting.

- *The rule of three-fourths.* The minutes of the previous meeting and the agenda for the upcoming meeting should be sent to participants at the three-quarter mark between the last meeting and the upcoming meeting.

- *The agenda rule.* Agenda items should be written with action verbs. For example, 'Minutes' as an agenda item should be expressed as 'Approve minutes of previous meeting'.

- *The rule of sixths.* About four-sixths of the meeting should be focused on current agenda items. One-sixth should be spent on past agenda items and one-sixth on future agenda items.

- *The reports rule.* Reports given at meetings should always include an executive summary.

- *The agenda integrity rule.* Only items that are on the agenda should be discussed.

- *The temporal integrity rule.* The meeting should start and finish on time.

- *The minutes rule.* Information recorded should relate to the agenda item and be decision-focused with actions agreed upon.

Process

The last 'P' relates to the actual conduct of the meeting. Huber (1980) suggested a seven-stage process to ensure the conduct of an effective meeting:

1. *Review.* At the commencement of the meeting, review the agenda and the tasks to be accomplished.

2. *Introductions.* Ensure that all participants are properly introduced.

3. *Ground rules.* The time allocation for the meeting, the kind of participation expected of participants, how decisions will be reached, the variations from the agenda that will be

allowed, and other important matters should be made clear.

4. *Reports.* Early in the meeting, those responsible for giving reports should be allowed to do so.

5. *Displays.* Participants should be encouraged to use a range of media to present information.

6. *Participation.* The chair of the meeting should ensure that each member is encouraged to participate in the meeting and that no one person is allowed to dominate discussion. Many leaders now rotate the chair of regular meetings to allow each team member the opportunity to experience the role and to ensure equitable participation from all team members.

7. *Summarise.* The chair should close the meeting by summarising the key points discussed at the meeting and the decisions reached. He or she should identify the date of the next meeting.

Activity 9.5

Apply the four P's to your next team meeting. After applying it, evaluate whether the meeting was more effective as a communication exercise.

Strategic and external communication skills

Strategic and external communication skills are needed by leaders at every level. As leaders rise towards the top of the organisation, however, these skills become critical. Communication becomes more complex as leaders need to address both internal and external stakeholders.

Statements of vision, mission and values

Leaders of organisations have long recognised the importance of clear vision and mission statements to articulate the future aspirations of the organisation's leaders to its stakeholders. Most large organisations have formal vision and mission statements in place.

In general, *vision statements* articulate a broad conceptualisation concerning the ultimate destination of the organisation. *Mission statements*, on the other hand, are about the more immediate future. They usually outline the organisation's reason for existing. To operationalise the reason for existing, mission statements often include statements about the organisation's purpose, objectives and goals.

Values statements are a recent addition to the corporate statements issued by organisations to inform people outside the organisation (such as investors and potential employees) about the organisation and where it might be heading. They are designed to complement vision and mission statements.

Values statements are the fundamental beliefs of the leaders and members of the organisation. That is, they represent underlying reasons for the actions and behaviours of organisational members. The organisational values statement is often expressed as 'individual values' and 'corporate values'. Individual values are those which staff within the organisation are expected to observe. Corporate values are the values staff are expected to observe collectively when representing the organisation.

Leaders must ensure that all forms of internal communication align with and reinforce the organisation's mission, vision and values, and that internal communications connect to them and are integrated into operational processes. Research has demonstrated that many organisations and their leaders do not communicate their vision as well as they might, leaving employees and external stakeholders confused about the direction of the organisation and where they fit in to it.

Regularity of communication is also important. Senior leaders must ensure that the people in the organisations they lead are regularly informed about progress towards the vision, long-term goals, principles and strategies of the organisation. They must reinforce the values of the organisation. Regularity can be achieved by techniques like regular (monthly) newsletters to staff or in broadcast emails.

Communication systems

Organisations that have effective communications systems are known to be more effective than organisations with poor communications systems. Communication systems include such things as manual and paper-based reporting systems, information technology systems (intranets and email) and statements of policy and procedures.

Leaders need to ensure that these internal communication systems are working to align with and reinforce the organisation's mission, vision and values statements. Polices are particularly important as part of the communication system. They provide the guidance and direction that the staff of the organisation need in order to communicate effectively with each other and express expected standards and norms.

Leaders as communication role models

While policies are important, what leaders actually do and say have a greater impact on staff behaviour in the organisation. Leaders, therefore, need set the standards for communication. They need to be role models for the types and tone of the communication they expect in the organisation. When leaders interact with others on a one-to-one basis, in groups, by email, by internal correspondence or any other form of communication, staff observe and then generally adopt what the leaders do. Leaders set the climate for communications in the organisation by the way they communicate with team members and other leaders, the transparency of their decision making, how often they are seen around the organisation and how often they address staff in person.

Knowledge management

Knowledge in all its forms is the new basis of competition in the global economy. As such, it is an organisational asset that should be closely managed as part of the communication system. Knowledge is not only data or information—it is a mix of organisational experience that provides a framework for evaluating and incorporating new experience and information. It originates in the minds of staff in the organisation and is captured in documents or filing systems, organisational routines, processes, practices, and norms. If we accept this broad definition of what constitutes knowledge, then the generation, documentation, transfer and creation of knowledge (known as knowledge management) is an important communication function for senior leaders. Senior leaders need the skills to design and monitor the management of knowledge and the management information systems that transmit it.

Ccommunication systems should be a regular item at senior planning meetings when discussion on the way staff in the organisation can be educated in the organisation's vision, mission and values sets the agenda.

External relations

Developing and maintaining a positive public image is a high priority task for all leaders in an organisation. An organisation's reputation is a significant resource to be protected. Any communication from an organisation that goes outside the organisation's internal boundaries (such as sales promotions, advertising and public relations initiatives) is a component of the organisation's external relations. Such matters must be managed very carefully. Leaders need skills in media and public relations if they are to be successful and effective at the top levels.

Activity 9.6

Collect a good sample of your organisation's public communication documents. These might include annual reports, sales promotions, advertising, public relations documents and letters to external stakeholders. Review each document and evaluate it to see whether it aligns with and reinforces the organisation's mission, vision and values statements.

Communication across cultures

There are many barriers preventing a leader from being an effective communicator. The different cultural backgrounds of people can be one of them. Cultural differences can affect the way a leader chooses to communicate. If these barriers are not recognised and acted upon they can stand in the way of achieving shared experience and mutual understanding. There are many good books giving guidance on communication across cultures—they cover topics such as gift-giving, greetings, gestures to avoid, exchanging business cards, and business dinners. Here we will provide a framework leaders may apply when communicating with different cultural groups.

A framework for understanding cultural differences

A number of frameworks exist to assist leaders to define and understand the most important cultural differences. Those of Hofstede (2001) and Trompenaars *et al.* (1998) are very popular but the one most applicable to business communication was developed by O'Hara-Devereaux and Johansen (1994). Understanding the variables in this framework will assist you to communicate more effectively with people from other cultures. According to O'Hara-Devereaux and Johansen (1994), the five cultural variables important across all cultures are:

- context,
- language,
- power,
- information flow, and
- time.

Context

Context is anything that gives meaning to a communication. Contextual issues may surround the communication or accompany it. They include history, relationships, status and events. Context is usually measured on a scale from low-context cultures to high-context cultures. Low-context cultures do not depend on existing relationships for meaning in communication; they rely more on explicit verbal messages. Australia and the United States would be classified as low-context cultures. High-context cultures rely extensively on relationships to understand the meaning of a communication; they place less emphasis on verbal messages. Japan, China and some other Asian countries would be classified as high-context cultures. In some cultures, context is more important than the spoken word while in other cultures, being *to the point* in communication is what matters.

Language

Language is often thought of as the most symbolic form of a culture. It transmits the thoughts and feelings of people and helps to shape thoughts and feelings. It is the most obvious form of cultural difference when people communicate. The same words can also have different meanings in different cultures. While it is often thought of as respectful to speak someone else's language when conducting business, the language is actually part of a context— without immersing oneself in the cultural context of the language, the nuances of it are difficult to understand and apply.

Power

Power concerns the way people in a culture view equality. In some cultures, the organisational and societal hierarchy are very important. There are clear distinctions between levels. 'Power distance'—a concept from Hofstede (2001)—defines the extent to which people in any particular country accept that power is unequally distributed. In a major research undertaking, Hofstede measured the power distance for many countries. His work is often cited when analysing cultural differences. Asian countries generally (and some European countries) are high power-distance countries. Australia and the United States are low power-distance countries. As outlined in the discussion of power and influence in chapter 8, the way that cultures view power is very significant to leadership. Leaders who undertake overseas assignments are often confused if they are not aware of the power-distance expectations of the staff in the overseas location. Barrett (2006) provides the following questions for leaders to assist in determining and appreciating differences in power:

- What is the attitude of people to titles and positions?
- Do individuals openly challenge authority?
- Is the organisation bureaucratic or flat in structure?
- How are decisions made in the organisation?
- Are team members consulted or told what to do?
- How is status displayed?

- What is the attitude of men towards women?

- What is the attitude towards age in the society?

Information flow

Information flow refers to how and how fast information is exchanged between people and levels in an organisation. Information flow also controls:

- who initiates information,

- what kinds of channels are used for it,

- what kind of messages are sent, and

- how formal or informal the exchange of information will be.

Australian and United States business people are known to be direct—they want the bottom line—while people from some Asian countries are less direct, often expressing agreement even when they have a negative opinion or do not agree.

Time

Time concerns whether cultures view time as a commodity or a state of being. Cultures that consider time as a commodity like to measure it and manage it. In these cultures people have diaries to record appointments and events; they schedule tasks and regard promptness as a virtue. These cultures are said to be monochronic. Polychronic cultures are more open-ended and flexible about time. They regard relationships and people as more important than meeting timeframes. These two types of cultures also view the past, present and future differently. Some cultures value the past and the lessons from it whereas other cultures value only what is happening now and look towards the future.

Globalisation results in leaders operating in multicultural environments with cross-cultural work forces. Analysis of cultural issues is made more easy by frameworks like that of O'Hara-Devereaux and Johansen, but leaders should remember that the characteristics described are generalised and typical of the groups identified—they do not necessarily apply to each member of the group.

Negotiation and conflict resolution skills

Leaders devote around 20% of their time to negotiating outcomes or resolving conflict. This is a low estimate, however, and in many organisational cultures the percentage is much higher. The 80/20 rule often also applies—i.e. that 80% of one's time as a leader will be spent on conflict involving 20% of the team members.

Negotiating and resolving conflict is a difficult but necessary role for leaders. Leaders need to have these skills; they need to use all the techniques at their disposal appropriate to the circumstance. Our experience is that many leaders are not only poorly skilled at negotiation and conflict resolution but also avoid conflict, allowing it to fester and to build into situations that are much more difficult to handle than if they were dealt with quickly at the first surface of the conflict or potential conflict.

No leader likes conflicts or having to intervene in them. As a rule of thumb, however, leaders must be the initiators of conflict resolution. They should handle any conflict situations when they arise. This frees the leader from having to think about the conflict and makes the leader, and those involved, much more productive.

While negotiation and conflict-resolution skills are related, they do have different theoretical underpinnings. When reading this section, keep in mind the discussion of power and influence in chapter 8—as power, influence, tactics and politics all play a role in the processes of negotiation and conflict resolution.

Negotiation

Negotiation is a process whereby two or more parties attempt to come to an agreement. Senior leaders often negotiate with trade unions or with suppliers and the various forms of negotiations require different approaches. It is generally accepted that there are two general approaches—namely:

- distributed bargaining, and
- integrative bargaining.

Distributive bargaining

Distributive bargaining involves negotiation over a fixed amount or sum— e.g. when trade unions and senior leaders negotiate over wage and salary increases. The resources are fixed and one side or the other will feel that they obtained a better outcome.

Integrative bargaining

Leaders at all levels are much more likely to be involved in *integrative bargaining* where negotiation is over solutions to problems or issues — i.e. where there is some flexibility and win-win solutions are possible. Negotiating using this approach is more concerned with maintaining or building good relationships for the long term so that the participants can continue to work together in the future.

Key skills for effective negotiation

There are a number of key skills that leaders can learn to be more effective negotiators. The following advice is based on the work of Fisher and Ury (1981).

Research the other party

Acquire as much information as you can about the goals and interests of the other party. Identify the key players; find what you can about their personalities, their cognitive and negotiation styles. The more you understand about the other party before you commence negotiations the better will be your chances of reaching an agreement. If you have worked with the other party before, you will know what their preferences are and what worked in the previous negotiation.

Set objectives for the negotiation

When you have researched the other party, ask yourself what you can expect in terms of outcomes. Set upper and lower limits on the possible outcomes and an objective that you think is fair to both parties. The other party will be undertaking the same game so do not accept opening offers. Be prepared to develop options and trade-offs and be flexible with your expectations. Often negotiations need to progress down a path that might at first seem irrational.

Anticipate questions

Prepare responses to the questions you anticipate. There are always issues to be resolved in any negotiation. By asking yourself the likely questions, and preparing for them, your confidence will increase.

Commence with positive overtures

It is best to enter into negotiations in a positive environment. So smile and be pleasant. Use the active listening skills outlined earlier in this chapter. It is often good to open with talk unrelated to the negotiation and to progress to the business of the negotiation once things are warmed up.

Address problems, not personalities

Leave the personal characteristics of the other party alone. Concentrate on the issues, even if the other party engages in personal attacks on you. Remember, the process is about long-term relationships rather than short-term wins.

Let the other party make the first offer

Treat initial offers as a starting point. Remember that both you and the other party have upper and lower limits on the possible outcomes, so it is foolish to offer other than the lower limit as the first negotiating position. Listen to what the other party has to say and ask questions like, 'Is this your final offer?' to seek information and clarification on positions.

Emphasise win-win solutions

Endeavour to frame outcomes in terms of the other party's interests. Look for solutions where you both can leave with dignity, ready for the next negotiation.

Be open to assistance

Often a third or neutral party can assist when a stalemate is reached. If progress is not being made, seek a postponement so that you have the opportunity to undertake further research.

Conflict situations

A conflict situation exists when there are perceived incompatible differences resulting in interference or opposition. Conflict should be viewed by leaders as a natural part of teams and team work and if resolved appropriately, can lead to improving team performance. It is generally accepted that conflict can arise in three forms:

- task conflict,

- relationship conflict, and

- process conflict.

Task conflict

Task conflict relates to the content and goals of the team. A low level of task conflict can have a positive effect on the team if it stimulates new ideas or discussion concerning tasks.

Relationship conflict

Relationship conflict relates to interpersonal relationships within the team. Relationship conflicts are the conflicts where most leaders spend most of their time and energy. A leader will accept this responsibility and understand – given the knowledge of how people have different values, behaviours and personality types. It is a natural part of teams and organisations.

Process conflict

Process conflict concerns how the team's work gets done. In an environment where continuous improvement is accepted, low levels of process conflict can have a positive effect on team performance.

Relationship conflict

In this section we will concentrate on relationship conflict, outlining the skills and techniques leaders can adopt for conflict resolution. It is the responsibility of the leaders to be the initiators of conflict resolution. That is, leaders are the ones responsible for confronting conflict and dealing with it because of their positions. If conflicts are ignored or avoided, they will fester, affect team performance and require greater attention than if they were handled when they first emerged. By avoiding conflict rather than dealing with it, leaders are abrogating their responsibility as leaders in the organisation.

Having the ability to handle conflict situations constructively also has a direct influence on how the leader is perceived by others. According to Lussier and Achua (2004), there are five conflict management styles that leaders may choose from. Every leader has a preferred style based on their personality and other leadership traits. No single conflict management style works best in all situations, so leaders should be skilled in each of the styles, selecting the one best-suited to the conflict situation. The five styles include:

- avoidance,
- accommodation,
- force,
- negotiation, and
- collaboration.

Conflict avoidance

In this style the leader attempts to ignore or avoid the conflict situation rather than resolve it. This style is not an option for effective leaders, either for conflicts in which they are involved or conflicts between team members. Leaders receive their position and a higher remuneration than others and should accept the responsibilities that go with the position and the greater remuneration. To avoid conflicts would be considered by more senior leaders, and team members generally, to be an abrogation of their position and responsibility to the organisation. The individuals who are having the conflict will suffer the effects of the conflict longer than they should and the longer it takes to address it, the more difficult it will be to confront the conflict.

Accommodation

People who accommodate to conflict attempt to resolve conflicts by passively giving in to the other party. Leaders should not use this style when it comes to their own personal conflicts because it creates an impression of being unassertive and lacking in leadership and courage. In most circumstances when team members are in conflict, this style is also not appropriate — it satisfies only one of the parties and not does resolve the nature of the issue. It is therefore counterproductive. Team members with strong personalities tend to take advantage of leaders who overuse this style.

Force

Leaders using this style attempt to resolve conflict by using aggressive behaviour to get their own way. As we discussed in chapter 8 on power and influence, this style is inappropriate in the modern organisational context. It may be viewed as 'bullying'. Using this style will also generate resentment towards the leader. It may, however, be appropriate in circumstances where an unpopular action must be taken.

Negotiation

Also known as the *compromising* style, the user of this style attempts to resolve conflict by making give-and-take concessions. It can be a useful style to solve conflicts quickly but may be counterproductive as the best outcomes are often not achieved. Overuse of this style by leaders can result in the leader being categorised as 'playing games', and may not lead to effective long-term relationships.

Collaboration

Also known as the *problem-solving* style, the user of it attempts to resolve the conflict jointly with the other parties in an effort to attain the best solution. Leaders who use this style are both collaborative and assertive and concerned about the needs of all the parties to the conflict. The style is based on open and honest communication. It requires leaders to have the core communications skills outlined earlier in this chapter.

The BCF model

The collaborative style is the one recommended for most conflict situations. It is very useful when the leader initiates the conflict resolution process. Lussier and Achua (2004) recommend that, when using this style to resolve conflict, the leader use the Behaviour, Consequences, and Feelings (BCF) model. The model has four steps:

Step 1

Plan a BCF statement that maintains ownership of the problem. Create a problem-solving atmosphere for the process by requesting the parties to assist in solving the problem. Describe the conflict in terms of behaviour, consequences and feelings using an 'I' statement similar to that described earlier in this chapter in the section on giving feedback. For example, a leader might plan to say to the conflicting team members: 'When you argue in front of the other team members (behaviour), it causes embarrassment and tension in the team (consequences) and I feel obligated to act on it (feelings).' Practise the statement before presenting it to the other parties.

Step 2

Present your BCF statement and agree on the definition of the conflict. Let the other parties respond to your statement and look for agreement from the parties that the conflict exists. If you cannot get agreement, restate the conflict in other terms and then try other conflict management styles if necessary.

Step 3

Ask for and give alternative conflict resolutions. Start by asking the conflicting parties for solutions to the conflict. If they have a resolution and it seems appropriate, that will result in a smooth transition to the next step. If they cannot suggest appropriate solutions, then appeal to common goals and work with the parties to find a solutions acceptable to them and the organisation.

Step 4

Make an agreement for change. Agree on specific actions for the parties. When necessary, write to the parties detailing the agreement so that there is a record if it is needed later.

Activity 9.7 Self assessment

Use the scale below to rate how often you use each of the five conflict management styles.

Conflict management style	Never	Not often	Some- times	Often	Frequently
Avoidance	1	2	3	4	5
Accommodation	1	2	3	4	5
Force	1	2	3	4	5
Negotiation	1	2	3	4	5
Collaboration	1	2	3	4	5

It is recommended that leaders use the first four styles infrequently. The collaborative style is the conflict style recommended for most conflict situations and is very useful when the leader initiates the conflict resolution process.

Summary

Everything a leader does to influence others involves communicating. Good communication skills are the foundation of effective leadership. Good communication skills alone, however, do not make an effective leader.

Communication skills for leaders can be categorised in three levels — namely:

- core communication skills,

- team communication skills, and

- strategic and external communication skills.

Within an interpersonal skills framework, the core communication skills that leaders need include:

- oral and written communication,

- non-verbal communication,

- active listening,

- giving and receiving feedback, and

- emotional intelligence.

Of these elements, active listening and giving and receiving feedback are people skills known to be most critical for effective leadership.

The team communication skills for leaders include:

- having an 'open door' policy,

- management by walking around, and

- facilitating meetings.

An improvement in meeting skills by the leader can have a significant effect on leadership effectiveness and productivity of work teams.

Strategic and external communication skills become critical as leaders rise towards the top of the organisation. Leaders must be able to:

- formulate and articulate clear vision, mission and values statements to organisational stakeholders,

- develop and manage sound communications systems, and

- maintain a positive public image to protect the reputation of the organisation.

There are many barriers that prevent a leader from being an effective communicator. The different cultural backgrounds of people can be one of them. Cultural differences between people can affect the way a leader chooses to communicate. If these differences are not recognised and acted upon they can stand in the way of achieving a shared experience and mutual understanding.

Leaders devote around 20% of their time to negotiating outcomes or resolving conflict. Negotiation and conflict resolution is a difficult but necessary role for leaders. Leaders need to have these skills and be able to use all the techniques appropriate to the circumstance.

There are five conflict management styles that leaders may choose from. These include:

- avoidance,

- accommodation,

- force,

- negotiation, and

- collaboration.

Reflection on your leadership practice

Go back through this chapter on communication skills for leaders. Review each of the elements under core communication skills, team communication skills and strategic and external communication skills. Given the level of your current leadership position, what are the skill areas where you need the most development? Write these areas down and use this data later when you develop your leadership development plan (at the end of chapter 12).

References

Barrett, D 2006, *Leadership communication*, McGraw Hill, Boston.

Caputo, J, Hazel, H & McMahon, C 1994, *Interpersonal communication: Competency through critical thinking*, Allyn and Bacon, Boston.

Carlopio, J, Andrewartha, G & Armstrong, H 2005, *Developing management skills: A comprehensive guide for leaders*, 3rd edn, Pearson Education Australia, Frenchs Forest.

Dubrin, A, Dalglish, C & Miller, P 2006, *Leadership: 2nd Asian Edition*, Wiley, Australia.

Fisher, R & Ury, W 1981, *Getting into yes: Negotiating agreement without giving in*, Houghton Mifflin, Boston.

Goleman, D 2004, 'What makes a leader?', *Harvard Business Review*, The best of HBR edition, January, Article first published 1995.

Hofstede, G 2001, *Culture's Consequences* 2nd edn, Comparing Values, Behaviors, Institutions and Organizations Across Nations, Thousand Oaks, CA: Sage.

Huber, G 1980, *Managerial Decision Making*, Scott Foresman, Glenview, Illinois.

Hughes, R, Ginnett, R & Curphy, G 2006, *Leadership: Enhancing the lessons of experience*, McGraw Hill, New York.

Humes, J 1991, *The language of leadership: Sir Winston Churchill's Five Secrets of Public Speaking and Leadership*, Business Library, Melbourne.

Lussier, R & Achua, C 2004, *Leadership: Theory, application, skills development*, 2nd edn, Thomson, USA.

O'Hara-Devereaux, M & Johansen, R 1994, *Globalwork: Bridging distance, culture and time*, Jossey-Bass, San Francisco.

Robbins, S, Bergman, R, Stagg, I & Coulter, M 2003, *Management*, 3rd edn., Prentice Hall, Frenchs Forest.

Trompenaars, F & Hampden-Turner, C 1998, *Riding the waves of culture: Understanding cultural diversity in global business* 2nd edn, McGraw-Hill, New York.

Tropman, J 2003, *Making Meetings Work: Achieving High Quality Group Decisions*, Sage Publications, Thousand Oaks, California.

Chapter 10

LEADING TEAMS

CHAPTER CONTENTS

Spotlight: Michael K. O'Loughlin

Michael K. O'Loughlin was born on 20 February 1977. He is a high profile Indigenous Australian Rules football player with a very successful record with the Sydney Swans.

His senior career commenced with his selection in the third round of the 1994 National Draft. He played twelve senior games for the Swans in 1995, earning a 'Rising Star' award nomination. The following year he was a key player in the team that won the minor premiership. Michael is currently the games record holder for the Swans, having passed John Rantall's record in round 14 of the 2007 season. He has a chance to be the first Swans player to pass the significant 300 games milestone.

In 2005 he was selected alongside Swans teammate Adam Goodes in the Indigenous Team of the Century. Along with the grand final win against the West Coast Eagles in 2005 (breaking a 72 year premiership drought for the Swans), he described his selection as the highlight of his career

Since 2006 Michael has continued to be a key part of the Swan's line-up, including playing a decisive role in the qualifying and preliminary finals that put the Swans into the Grand Final for the second consecutive year. In the 2006 grand final, Michael played well, kicking 3.1 (19) for the afternoon. He continued to play consistently well for Sydney through the 2007 and 2008 seasons, returning from ankle surgery mid-way through the 2009 season when he announced his retirement from the game.

Michael is an acknowledged team member and leader. He learnt many of his team values from his mother and grandparents (whom he regards as important role models in his life), including the need to sacrifice individual wants for the benefit of others and to be willing to do whatever it takes to attain team success. As an elite high profile sportsman, he understands the importance of being a role model for this team and for younger players and fans. As such, he endeavours to do the 'right things', abide by team rules and discipline codes, and to learn from his mistakes. Michael understands that to be an effective leader, you must first be an effective team member.

The Swans have a particularly interesting and unusual 'shared leadership' model. Unlike other teams, there is no single team captain. Rather, there is a leadership group with co-captains (Adam Goodes, Brett Kirk and Craig Bolton) who work closely with other senior team members to lead the team.

The leadership model used by the Swans may have applications in organisations, as many leadership theorists believe that everyone in an organisation (or work group) can exercise leadership and that leadership should not just be the concern of top management.

According to Michael, the shared leadership model of the Swans works because each of the leaders has earned the right to lead, there is a culture of honesty at the club where opinions are valued, and there is an emphasis on continuous improvement for individuals and the team.

According to Michael, if you want to lead a team well, you need to build good relationships with all personalities, conduct yourself in a way that generates the respect of others, be open to honest feedback from others, be approachable, and listen to constructive criticism.

The shared leadership model utilised by the Swans and Michael's description of good leadership is working well for the Swans. This model of leadership compares well with the way effective leadership is supposed to work in modern organisations. If organisational leaders are able to build a culture in their organisations similar to that existing at the Swans, high performance might be expected follow.

Source: Interview with Michael O'Loughlin 15 April 2009.

The spotlight on Michael O'Loughlin provides practical examples of two significant issues in team dynamics—team values and shared leadership.

Team leaders must have team values, be role models, and conduct themselves according to team rules and norms. The significance of this is summed up by Michael's statement that '... to be an effective leader, you must first be an effective team member'.

The Swans also provide a good example of how shared leadership can work for teams. Shared leadership of teams is becoming a more accepted form of team leadership. Effective leaders often adopt this approach, even if only informally.

Introduction

Over the last few decades, as economies have moved from primarily manufacturing or industrial bases to service industries or knowledge bases, we have witnessed an increase in the formation of teams. Most of the work undertaken in modern organisations is done by or through teams. Extensive research has demonstrated superior teamwork to be the most consistent strategy for producing superior services and products.

Teams and team work are in evidence at all levels of organisation — from board room to factory floor. There are also many different types of teams, with a trend in modern organisations to the development of self-managed teams. We will not, therefore, spend time justifying the need for teams or discussing their advantages and disadvantages: these are well known and accepted. We will concentrate on the leadership of teams and the need for leaders to understand the role they play in developing successful and effective team work in organisations.

As you read through this chapter, keep this question at the back of your mind — do teams make leadership an irrelevant concept?

Groups and teams

The words, *team* and *group*, are often used interchangeably. Groups are a collection of individuals working together. Teams, however, are committed to a common purpose. They are task focused. They have performance goals for which the team and management hold the team accountable. In the work situation, a team may even contain members who are reluctant to work together. Sub-cultures can develop within a team and this requires special skills on the part of the leader. In a team, structure is often more overt and directed than it is in groups in general. So while a team is a group, not all groups are teams.

Types of teams

Organisations are generally fluid in the way they are structured. They often change the way they are organised in response to environmental pressures. There are many different ways of creating teams; flexibility enables organisations to continue to respond to these pressures. This flexibility has led to a variety of names for teams—e.g. project teams, quality control teams, management teams. In this section we examine four types of teams generally used to respond to competition and global trends. The four types of teams are:

- functional teams,
- cross-functional teams,
- self managed teams, and
- global and virtual teams.

They are distinct in their membership, their duration, and in the way they can influence their mission.

Functional teams

As the name suggests, a functional team is a team created in a functional department of an organisation—e.g. finance, human resources or marketing. It usually consists of a line manager (who is the team leader) and team members. It is probably the most popular form of team structure in organisations, as most organisations are structured along functional lines.

The functional team typically exists for long periods and its membership is relatively stable. Due to these factors, functional teams may be less responsive to changes in the external environment of the organisation, often having a tendency to focus on the department's objectives at the expense of the overall mission of the organisation. This can lead to a less than effective overall organisational performance. Too many functional teams in any organisation can lead to the 'silo effect'—a lack of co-operation between functional teams. This makes leading overall change in the organisation more difficult; sub-cultures tend to develop in each functional team at the expense of the overall organisational culture.

Research on functional teams has shown that team performance will be higher when:

- team members share the objectives of the team,

- team members have the necessary skills to perform their tasks and understand their roles,

- the team leader can promote cohesiveness,

- the team leader has the required support and resourcing of the organisation, and

- the team has good relationships with other functional teams in the organisation.

While still popular as an organising entity in large organisations, functional teams are in decline generally as organisations look for more effective ways to improve customer service, processing times, and quality.

Cross-functional teams

Cross-functional teams are teams made up of members from different functional departments of an organisation. In large modern organisations they are increasingly being used as the basis for team creation to improve the coordination of activities.

These teams may be temporary (for particular projects) or a permanent part of the organisation. Most cross-functional teams exist only for the life of the project—e.g. a team to implement a new system or product for the organisation. Functional teams and cross-functional teams are established for different purposes, and while some literature suggests that functional teams might 'evolve' into cross-functional teams over time, in practice it is not a reality.

Bringing in team members from different functions gives the cross-functional team more expertise and experience than can be expected in functional teams. The issues facing the team can be viewed from the different perspectives of its cross-function team members. Team members bring organisational networks with them that assist them to solve problems that functional teams might find either more difficult or impossible. On occasions, cross-functional teams also include members from outside the formal organisation— e.g. customers, suppliers, or joint venture partners. By participating in the team, individuals often get a different perspective on the organisation—they learn new skills, get a wider organisational perspective, and take back broader networks to their functional departments.

Members of cross-functional teams are also usually members of functional teams at the same time. This often brings about role conflicts for team members, requiring the leader of the team to be highly skilled at facilitation and the development of trust.

Research on cross-functional teams has shown that they are less likely to be successful if they are self managed (Cohen & Bailey 1997). They are therefore unlikely to 'evolve' into self managed teams. The selection of leaders for cross-functional teams is a critical factor in the likely success of the team's mission. While many styles of leadership may succeed in functional teams, cross-functional teams require a leadership style more akin to a facilitator or consultant. Only experienced leaders are usually trusted with the leadership role.

Self managed teams

As a response to increasing global competition and greater customer expectations, many organisations around the world are turning to self managed teams (sometimes referred to as semi-autonomous work groups). Self managed teams may be either functional or cross-functional, but it is usual for self managed teams to perform the same task repetitively and to have a relatively stable membership.

The main factor distinguishing self managed teams from other teams is that the team is given the authority for operational decisions in achieving the team's goals. There is, therefore, no direct supervisor for the team.

Depending on the overall philosophy of the organisation, the organisation usually sets the mission, the scope of the team, and the budget under which the team operates. Operating decisions are left to the team, which sets performance goals, quality standards, allocation of work and other matters to do with team performance. The degree of delegation to the team varies between organisations and there is no prescriptive model for the self managed team. Some teams, for example, are delegated responsibility for recruitment and human resource issues while in others they are left to a central or corporate human resources department.

Irrespective of the degree of delegation given to the self managed team, the concept requires the organisation to make a number of adjustments to traditional organisational practice. For example, the organisation's incentive schemes, performance management and general leadership practices will need to change from a policy framework supporting functional and cross-functional team practices to that required to support the self managed team. If the organisation does not make the required adjustments to implement self managed teams, providing the appropriate conditions and framework for the team to succeed, the concept can be a total failure.

Self managed teams are gaining increasing attention in large organisations. The advantages of self managed teams include a stronger commitment from team members to the work undertaken, better quality, and more job satisfaction. As team members are often cross-trained to perform many of the team roles, it increases their flexibility, makes the work more interesting and enriching, and assists the organisation in dealing with turnover and absenteeism.

While self managed teams have no direct supervisor, there are still two important leadership functions that must be attended to in order to secure their success. One is *internal* and the other is *external*.

Internally, the team must decide how it will handle the leadership function. Self managed team members often elect a 'coordinator', rotating the position among the team members on a regular basis. The heads of faculties in universities are often appointed in this manner. An alternative is for team members to share leadership. In this case, various team members take responsibility for certain activities of the team, depending on who has the expertise for the task. In the spotlight section at the commencement of this chapter, we saw how the Sydney Swans utilise a shared leadership model for the leadership of the team, with three experienced players responsible for the team rather than one 'captain'.

The external leadership function is shown symbolically at the right of Figure 10.1. The leader is positioned outside the formal self managed team. The role of the external leadership function is to serve the team as its coach, consultant and facilitator rather than to supervise the work of the team directly. The person in this role will usually serve several self managed teams in the one organisation. A key activity of the role is to serve as a 'blocker' or 'negotiator' of issues coming down from senior management or from other teams in the organisation that might affect the team's performance.

The success of self managed teams in any organisation will depend on how the organisation puts in place structures to support the concept. Given the emergence of self managed teams as a significant form of organisation, there are several conditions (suggested by Stokes [1994]) that top management must consider if the potential of self managed teams is to be realised. These include:

- top management support and commitment,
- clearly defined goals and objectives,
- appropriate rewards structures and policies,
- meaningful tasks and measurement systems,
- substantial authority and discretion,
- experienced facilitation,
- small size and stable membership, and
- strong information systems.

Top management support and commitment

The strong support of top management is necessary to ensure that all members of the organisation support the implementation of self managed teams. This will include making the resourcing available for the implementation and dealing with the inevitable politics at play when functional departments lose power over the self managed teams.

Clearly defined goals and objectives

The organisation must put into place clear objectives to guide the decisions of the self managed teams. It must provide the basis for evaluating their performance.

Appropriate rewards structures and policies

The traditional reward systems emphasising individual performance will need adjustment to reward team performance. It is usual for self managed teams to have considerable discretion over how team rewards and bonuses are distributed to team members.

Meaningful tasks and measurement systems

The tasks set for the team must be meaningful and can be accomplished only if the team members work together. There must be a performance measurement system that provides timely and adequate feedback about the progress of the task and the outcomes of the team.

Substantial authority and discretion

The team requires sufficient authority to carry out its task without interference from top managers or other managers. Such authority is important if the team is to feel empowered and remain motivated.

Experienced facilitation

Team members must have good interpersonal skills to perform its internal leadership functions and to facilitate team meetings.

Small size and stable membership

The size of the self managed team must be limited only to those members necessary to undertake the task. Small teams are known to be more productive than large teams, some research suggesting that self managed teams cannot be successful if they have more than 12 team members. Membership should also be relatively stable — stability aids team cohesiveness and learning how to manage the team's tasks.

Strong information systems

Self managed teams must have access to information if they are to make sound decisions on processes and services. Teams, therefore, need access to information once the prerogative of line managers — and not readily shared with operating team members.

Many experienced and successful team leaders are taking a 'step back' from overt leadership of their functional or cross-functional teams (sometimes referred to as leading from behind). They are allowing their teams to operate as if they were self managed. Such a change in leadership style can be very empowering to team members. While this practice is occurring in many team environments, the leader is still technically responsible for the team, so the situation does not meet the definition of a self managed team. As explained earlier, self managed teams require top managers to provide the appropriate conditions and framework for self managed teams to succeed.

Global and virtual teams

Many large organisations are global enterprises with employees scattered across many nations around the world. Nationally based organisations often also have many work sites that are geographically spread around the country. While employees are geographically dispersed, they remain members of teams, both functional and cross-functional. Due to the distances involved, team members and their leaders often do not meet face to face, relying on communications technology like the internet, email, phone and video conferencing to keep the team heading in the same direction.

Leaders of global and virtual teams face many of the same challenges as leaders of cross-functional teams. In fact, cross-functional global teams are used extensively for new product development and are the dominant form of virtual team. However, a few of the leadership challenges increase in degree due to the distances involved. These include:

- greater difficulty in gaining commitment of team members due to the diversity of members,

- special problems exerting influence over team members at a distance,

- greater difficultly in establishing and maintaining trust within the team as its members are seldom or never actually together,

- different value sets or ways of understanding or behaving resulting from cultural differences of team members,

- frustrations created by time differences when virtual team meetings are called,

- problems with communication technology not working effectively—especially in poor countries or in isolated areas where infrastructure is underdeveloped,

- the difficulties of building on team-member strengths at a distance and mitigating team member weaknesses,

- the psychological distance between team members created by geographic distance,

- greater difficulty facilitating team learning and knowledge management,

- the inability to observe the nuances and body language in meetings run electronically—available to facilitators of face-to-face meetings, and

- special issues regarding performance management of underperforming team members.

What can leaders of global and virtual teams do to militate against these increased challenges? The most important factor is that the team must have a clear vision—a vision of where it wants to be in the future, and of how it relates to the overall organisation. A clear vision that is communicated frequently by the leader is the glue that holds the team together, notwithstanding the differences and distances between its members.

How teams develop and decline

Most teams progress through a number of different stages as they become more cohesive and productive. There are two accepted theories for describing the stages of development:

- punctuated equilibrium, and

- Tuckman's four-stage model.

Punctuated equilibrium

The first, lesser known theory, is called the 'punctuated equilibrium' process (Gersick 1988). Gersick posits that teams do not progress through the widely accepted series of stages. Rather, they spend considerable energy and time talking through a series of ideas and strategies to achieve them. Once these ideas have been widely discussed in the team, the team exudes full energy towards achievement of its goals, also re-examining its strategy to see whether it will complete the task. The theory suggests that a team's progress towards its goal is triggered more by the team members' awareness of the amount of work to be completed and the time available for its completion.

Tuckman's four-stage model

The second—and most widely accepted view of how teams develop—was first proposed by Tuckman (1965). It consists of four stages. Tuckman and Jensen (1977) later added a fifth stage, but as this stage ('adjourning') happens when the team terminates and leadership is no longer required, it is not considered here.

As many factors may impede the progression, it cannot be guaranteed that a team will progress through the four stages of team development. However, the theory is widely accepted due to its practicality (and also for the rhyming of the four stages). It is the responsibility of the team leader to assist the team to progress through the stages so that the team performs to its potential. As we will see later, the team will require different styles of leadership throughout the process. The four team stages (Tuckman 1965) are:

- forming,
- conforming,
- storming, and
- performing.

Forming

When a group first comes together, members need to establish a sense of direction and security. They will be uncertain about their own roles and goals in the new team. Sometimes, the team vision will yet to have been established. Self-consciousness and silence will tend to dominate interpersonal relations. Effective team leader behaviours will centre on establishing introductions, answering questions, and clarifying goals, rules and expectations.

Conforming

Once the team has resolved the issues in the forming stage, team members start to interact. They begin to conform to emerging team-member expectations and norms. Styles and norms of team communication and interpersonal relations develop. Team goals become important and different roles for team members become clear. Effective team leader behaviours in this stage include providing feedback to team members, facilitating role differentiation and articulating a vision for the team.

Storming

When team roles have been differentiated, team members feel more comfortable with participating openly in the team. Team members often also test the boundaries and norms now existing in the team. This invariably leads to some conflict — which the team must learn to deal with if it is to continue to develop. Effective team leader behaviours in this stage include a focus on team processes, reinforcement of the vision, identification of common threats, and fostering win-win thinking among team members.

Performing

In this stage the team is functioning as an effective unit. Questions about continuous improvement and innovation dominate the thoughts of team members. Effective behaviours for team leaders include advancing a quality culture in the team and providing ongoing feedback on team performance.

Teams are not able to reach the performing stage unless they have progressed through the other three stages. During the progression, the role of the team leader changes — as shown in Figure 10.1.

As shown in the figure, the role of the leader changes from one where, in the traditional group model, the leader is the sole director of the team to one where, in the self managed team, the leader is 'outside' the team. As the team progresses through the stages, the leader also needs to move from a solo or directive leadership style to an empowering style. Not only does the role and style of leadership need to change during the four stages, but so also do the skills that the leader requires to be effective in the role.

Figure 10.1 Changing team leader style and roles as a team develops

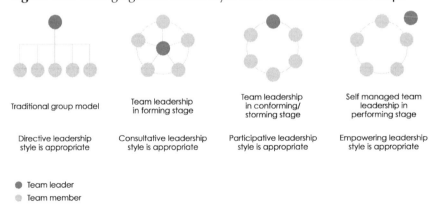

Traditional group model	Team leadership in forming stage	Team leadership in conforming/ storming stage	Self managed team leadership in performing stage
Directive leadership style is appropriate	Consultative leadership style is appropriate	Participative leadership style is appropriate	Empowering leadership style is appropriate

● Team leader
◌ Team member

Source: Adapted from Dubrin, Dalglish & Miller (2006, p. 271).

As interaction between team members increases with team progress through the stages, so does the potential for conflict. If the team does not deal appropriately with conflict and other group dynamics, the team may regress to the former stage—or plateau where it is. Accordingly, as the team progresses, the need for the leader to have conflict resolution and communication skills increases.

Leaders of successful teams understand where their team is positioned in each stage and at any point in time. They need to work towards moving the team to the next stage. It is an unfortunate reality that teams often do not move through the stages sequentially, the stages overlapping and the team moving backwards and forwards through the stages as internal and external forces influence the team. For example, if a critical team member leaves the team or is replaced, the team will often revert to the previous stage for a short period. Teams also often decline to the point that the team is no longer functional.

Following a comparative and historical analysis of prior research studies (Collins 2009), the researchers developed a descriptive model to illustrate how previously successful organisations decline. The model consists of five sequential stages of decline. Part of the research demonstrated that the way managers and leaders interact can predict the state of an organisation and the teams within it. While the research concentrated on the most senior leadership teams in organisations, it can apply equally to teams at any level of the organisation.

Teams can start heading down a decline curve because they exist in a fluid environment and, like the organisation they are a part of, must face internal and external forces for change. Sometimes the teams or their leaders make poor decisions that impact on the long-term viability of the team. Often, high performing teams become arrogant or insulated by their own success to the signs of decline – or they lose the ability to see the underlying factors that made the team successful in the first place. Some teams become undisciplined or cannot fill vacated positions with appropriate people. Complacency is a normal part of organisation success, and even fast changing teams can become resistant to change.

Accordingly to Collins (2009, p. 77), teams in decline demonstrate these behaviours:

- people shield those in power from unpleasant facts, fearful of penalties and criticism for shining light on the rough realities in the team;

- people assert strong opinions without providing data, evidence or a solid argument;

- the team leader has a very low questions-to-statements ratio, avoiding critical input and/or allowing sloppy reasoning and unsupported opinions;

- team members acquiesce to a decision but do not unify to make the decision successful – or worse, the team members undermine the decision after it has been made;

- team members seek as much credit as possible for themselves, yet do not enjoy the confidence and admiration of their peers;

- team members argue to look smart, or to further their own interests, rather than argue to find the best answers to support the overall cause;

- the team conducts 'autopsies with blame' seeking culprits rather than wisdom; and

- team members often fail to deliver exceptional results and blame other people or outside factors for setbacks, mistakes, and failures.

On the other hand, teams progressing through the development stages demonstrate these behaviours (Collins 2009, p. 77):

- people bring forth grim facts or harsh realities to be discussed in the team without fear that the team leader will criticise them or 'shoot the messenger';

- people bring data, evidence, logic and solid arguments to team discussion;

- the leader employs a 'Socratic' style, using a high questions-to-statements ratio, challenging team members and pushing for penetrating insights within the team;

- team members unify behind a decision once made, then work to make the decision succeed, even if they vigorously disagreed with it during discussion;

- each team member credits other people for success, yet enjoys the confidence and admiration of his or her peers;

- team members argue and debate, not to improve their personal position, but to find the best answers to support the overall cause;

- the team conducts 'autopsies without blame', mining wisdom from painful experiences; and

- each team member delivers exceptional results, yet in the event of a setback, each accepts full responsibility and learns from mistakes.

By observing the signs of decline in teams, team leaders can detect declining team situations and take action to reverse the curve or prevent the decline from establishing itself in the first place.

Activity 10.1

Using the described behaviours, diagnose your team and evaluate where the team is positioned in the four stages of development. Remember that the team's position may overlap more than one stage. Use the descriptors of each stage to identify the level of its functioning. Now list the strategies you will adopt to move the team to the next stage of development and/or prevent it from declining.

Characteristics of effective teams

There is a diversity of research on why some teams are effective and others are not. It is not uncommon in organisations to find that teams that are practically identical have significantly different outcomes in terms of success or failure. So what is it that makes some teams successful and other teams not?

One issue often overlooked by senior managers when evaluating team performance or team leadership should be intuitively obvious. People in organisations always look up the hierarchy to more senior leaders for clues about how to behave. Therefore, for lower-level team leaders to be effective, the executive team needs to demonstrate and role-model the team work and behaviours desired within the lower-level teams. This is a foundational principle for effective team work in organisations and extends, not just to teams and teamwork, but to many other facets of organisational behaviour. For example, if the senior management team acts in unethical ways or not in accordance with the stated values of the organisation, this dysfunctional leadership behaviour will be emulated — it will cascade to lower levels of the organisation.

According to Hughes, Ginnett and Curphy (2006), a team's failure can often be traced to the moment it was established. From the establishment of the team, attention must be paid to four characteristics — namely:

- task structure,
- team boundaries,
- norms, and
- leadership.

Task structure

Has the team a clear idea of the team's task? Is the task unambiguous and congruent with the overall mission of the organisation? Has the team got a clear mission and articulated performance standards? All team members should know what the team is trying to achieve and how well the team and individuals in the team are performing.

Team boundaries

Has the team the correct number and composition of members to undertake the task? Have the members the technical skills and knowledge necessary to perform the work? Do team members have the interpersonal skills to resolve conflict and the appropriate level of diversity to work together? Have team responsibilities and relationships been clearly defined?

Norms

Does the team share a set of 'norms' which set the acceptable standards of behaviour? Norms influence how team members perceive and interact with each other. Norms establish the team culture. Norms are different to team rules in that rules are openly discussed and are set by the organisation. Norms are not discussed and if they were, they would become rules.

Leadership

Has the leader established a climate where team members feel empowered and free to offer their opinion or assistance to other team members? Do team members feel comfortable questioning team and team leader decisions?

If the above four team characteristics are not in place appropriately during the formation process, the team leader should modify these factors in the design of the team. Once the team is established and the above characteristics are in place, the team leader needs to turn attention to three other characteristics:

- team cohesiveness,
- high levels of communication, and
- organisational support.

Team cohesiveness

Team cohesiveness is the extent to which team members band together and remain committed to achieving team goals. According to Lussier and Achua (2004), team cohesion is said to increase when:

- team members agree on a common purpose or direction,
- there is high praise and recognition for the team,

- the organisation encourages and motivates teams to compete with each other for rewards, and

- members find they have common ground and similar attitudes and values, and enjoy being on the team.

High levels of communication

The team leader needs to be concerned with group maintenance and the interpersonal aspects of the team. Good communication assists team members to stay focused on the team goals and to take advantage of the resources available to the team.

Organisational support

Effective teams have high levels of support from management and the organisation generally. Does the organisational culture support team work and have reward programs that reinforce team behaviours?

Activity 10.2

Use the characteristics of effective teams described above to diagnose your own team. Tick the appropriate box for each characteristic. Where the characteristic is not fully in place, develop some strategies to meet the deficit.

Characteristic	Needs attention	Fully in place
Task structure	☐	☐
Team boundaries	☐	☐
Norms	☐	☐
Leadership	☐	☐
Team cohesiveness	☐	☐
Communication	☐	☐
Organisational support	☐	☐

All the boxes in the 'fully in place' column should be ticked if team success is to be maximised.

Leader in action: André Smit

Dr André Smit has had an international management career spanning 30 years, working as a leader of teams and as a developer of people. He had a successful managerial career working in a variety of roles with diverse global organisations including 3M, Westfield and The Venetian in Macau. In late 2009, André took up an associate professorship in the School of Management, Leadership and Government at the Macau Inter University Institute to teach and research in areas where previously he had been a successful practitioner.

Working mostly in the areas of sales, human resource development and organisational development, André is acutely aware of the importance of developing high performance teams and of the need for teamwork generally in organisations.

His experience working in Asia, where he was responsible for developing the talent pool in an organisation with over 20,000 staff with 40 different nationalities, made him sensitive to the fact that cultural awareness is critical in developing teams and for team leaders. To assist staff to be fully developed as team members, André implemented development programs at all levels, including internships for undergraduates, foundational management programs for graduates, advanced management programs for postgraduate students, and executive development courses for directors.

According to André, leading a team is about transforming the team from what it is to where it wants to be. If this is to occur, the leader of the team must have a very clear vision of what needs to be achieved to transform the individual and team to the next performance level. This is only possible when the individual and team's values are aligned with such a vision.

Part of leading high performance teams is to ensure team incentives and rewards are in place rather than individual incentives and rewards:

Successful organisations become "employers of choice" through motivating diverse teams, and creating a team environment where the teams willingly want to exceed expected performance standards. This can be achieved by focusing on human resource policies that address the team members' needs and where individual team members are rewarded only by nomination of their team peers.

André provides the following strategies for leaders who need to lead teams that comprise of people from diverse nationalities:

- Encourage ownership and empowerment. Leaders need to understand how team members from some cultures value the power relationship between them and the leader, and who they sometimes consider should be the ultimate decision maker for the team. Transforming diverse teams through a talent development program enables the leader to create an environment that encourages all team members to take responsibility and allows individual team members to lead themselves — to be empowered and take ownership for decision and team outcomes.

- Leverage experiences. Provide developmental opportunities to all team members. Use the different cultural experiences and educational backgrounds from the team members to resolve potential problems and to target new opportunities.

- Promote from within. Organisations need to be good corporate citizens and to develop local talent into senior management. Not only does this strategy save the cost of importing leaders from outside the organisation or outside the country, it also ensures the future supply of local executives for expansion.

Sources: Interview with Dr Smit on 26 June 2009.

The profile on Andre Smit above shows the importance of having teams that share the organisation's values and the importance of a vision for the team so that team members are aware and inspired to go in the same direction. The organisation must also ensure that policies and rewards are team based and not individual based if teams are to prosper and be successful in the organisation.

Measuring team-member strengths and weaknesses

After working with teams all over the globe, Margerison and McCann (1995) developed 'Team Management Systems', a team-based assessment protocol used extensively around the world to design teams and to assist teams to have a better understanding of the strengths and weaknesses of the team and its members.

Margerison and McCann's research examined the nature of work carried out in teams. They identified eight core 'work functions' (different types of work underpinning teamwork) and one central activity that integrates the work functions. The underlying proposition of their system is that people tend to assume the role they naturally prefer and therefore perform better in those areas that match their work preference.

Understanding work preferences is a critical component in developing team performance. Team Management Systems' Team Management Profile Questionnaire (TMPQ) is a 60-item assessment focused on enhancing understanding of an individual's approach to work. Based on the responses to the TMPQ, a Personal Team Management Profile provides constructive, work-based information outlining an individual's work preferences and the strengths that an individual brings to a team. The nine functions or roles within the system include:

- *advising* — gathering and reporting information,
- *innovating* — creating and experimenting with ideas,
- *promoting* — exploring and presenting opportunities,
- *developing* — assessing and testing the applicability of new approaches,
- *organising* — establishing and implementing ways of making things work,
- *producing* — concluding and delivering outputs,
- *inspecting* — controlling and auditing the working of systems,

- *maintaining* — upholding and safeguarding standards and processes, and

- *linking* — coordinating and integrating the work of others.

For a team to be effective, it is important to concentrate on each of these team functions and roles. If any function is not adequately covered by at least one person in the team, the team needs to analyse the deficiencies and put plans into place to strengthen that activity. The system provides leaders with a good conceptual understanding of what roles are needed to ensure team effectiveness and the tools to assist in diagnosing the team strengths and weaknesses.

Activity 10.3 Self assessment

Diagnose your team by evaluating each of the team member's strengths and weaknesses against the nine roles. List the team member or team members that appear naturally to assume each of the roles identified.

Team roles	Name of team member who undertakes this role
Advising	
Innovating	
Promoting	
Developing	
Organising	
Producing	
Inspecting	
Maintaining	
Linking	

A practical framework for team improvement

All teams, no matter what type or size, can benefit from a practical framework to assist the leader in how to develop the team to its full potential. Most teams in organisations are at the lower levels of the hierarchy and are functional teams. Many leaders of these teams would like to move the team to the next stage of team development but are not sure of the steps involved. The steps outlined below are recommended for leaders who are newly appointed to teams. Few leaders get the opportunity to create their own teams from the ground up (unless the team is a cross-functional team). Most often, people assume leadership of an existing functional team.

When a new leader takes responsibility for a team, there is a window of opportunity for the leader to move the team forward, to make a change to the culture of the team. Leaders who have been in the team for some time can also use this practical framework, but it is much more difficult for them as the culture of the team will more than likely resist any significant efforts for change.

There are two types of change programs:

- major change programs and
- small-scale, incremental programs.

Major change programs are usually directed from above. They involve all or most of the functional teams in an organisation. Systems changes or changes in strategic direction fall under this category.

Incremental, small-scale change accounts for most team change. While it may be small scale, it is equally important if the team is to progress to its full potential. All teams, no matter of their level of productivity and performance, can improve in some areas. This framework is designed to assist leaders to commence the journey on the road to continuous improvement in their teams.

Step 1

In consultation with all the team members, use your arrival as team leader to consult widely with the team's stakeholders, clients and customers (both internal and external). Use this technique in conjunction with formal advice to the stakeholders of your arrival as team leader. This could mean utilising a questionnaire or informal interviews with the stakeholders to find out their views on the team's performance, customer service standards, expectations etc.

Step 2

Hold a brainstorming session with your team to find out what improvements could be made to improve team performance. Present the exercise as a look into the future—do not criticise the team's current performance. Get each staff member to list three issues they would improve in the team if they were team leader for a day. Write down your own ideas for improvement based on what you know about the team in your short period with the team, and your experience in other teams. Use the term 'continuous improvement' as the general philosophy for the initiative. Paint a picture of what the team will be like when the improvements are in place. This will be become the 'vision' for the team. As leader, you should communicate this vision frequently to the team so that all team members know where the team is heading.

Step 3

Once you have collected all the data from your stakeholders and the team members, prepare a list of the improvements suggested during steps 1 and 2. Then call a team meeting to discuss the suggestions and issues, and to see what is achievable. Try to get the team to prioritise the suggestions into an action plan. It is important during this phase that team members feel some ownership of the issues raised. Blend in your own suggestions. It is better that the team feels that the suggestions and issues come from them or other stakeholders rather than from you.

Step 4

Once you have a list of priorities, consult with your supervisor to ensure that the items on the action list are appropriate and can be resourced. Most continuous improvement activity in teams can be achieved within the team's normal resources and budget. Additional resources are usually only required for major changes in systems. Try to develop a list of actions that can be completed in less than one or two years. Plans that are more grandiose, or cover lengthy periods, are often too overwhelming for the team. It is important that the initial action items are achievable so that your team can taste early success and accomplishment.

Step 5

With your supervisor's support, go back to your team and build the action plan. Include not just the prioritised list of actions, but also strategies to achieve them, timelines, and who will take responsibility for each of the actions. Don't try to rush the action items. The team will continue to have its operational responsibilities and the additional work will require additional enthusiasm. It will be up to you as team leader to model the behaviour and passion for the change in your language and actions. Remember to communicate the vision at every opportunity.

Step 6

Hold regular meetings with your team—at least once per week. Ensure that the action list and the current status of action items are discussed. Develop strategies with the team to overcome any barriers that are impeding progress to achievement. Celebrate the completion of each and every action item.

Step 7

Ensure the improvements your team are implementing are both widely known in the organisation and throughout the organisation at designated periods in the improvement process. Encourage top leaders in the organisation to visit the team to encourage the actions being taken. It is important to maintain the team's energy and that they get recognition from outside the team. It is important that they perceive that they are being rewarded for tackling the improvement program. Get the team to give presentations to more senior leaders in the organisation on what the team is doing and where it is going. Take a back seat during these presentations. Allow team members to make the presentations and take the credit. When your team looks good so do you!

Step 8

Once the improvement program is fully implemented, celebrate the achievements in a meaningful way. Allow the team a period of consolidation before starting the process again.

Summary

Groups and teams are not synonymous terms. A team is a group but not all groups are teams. Teams are task focused. They are different from groups in that teams are committed to a common purpose. They have established performance goals for which the team and management holds the team accountable.

There are many forms of teams, with a trend in modern organisations for cross-functional teams to address the need to improve coordination. Many cross-functional teams are also virtual, bringing new leadership challenges to those charged with their leadership. Self managed teams are also gaining popularity as a form of organisation as senior managers look for ways to empower employees, create greater flexibility, and more commitment.

Teams progress through a number of stages of development. The best known theory and description of the stages is referred to as 'forming, conforming, storming and performing'. Teams are not able to reach the performing stage unless they have progressed through the other three stages. If the team does not deal appropriately with conflict and other group dynamics in the team, the team may either regress to its former stage or plateau where it is. There are a number of behaviours that are said to indicate whether a team is in decline or moving through the development stages.

Characteristics of successful teams include well designed task structure, defined team boundaries, development of acceptable team norms, effective leadership, team cohesiveness, high levels of communication, and top management support.

All teams, no matter what their type or size, can benefit from a practical framework to assist the leader in how to develop the team to its full potential. Although most organisations have moved to team-based structures, and self managed teams are a significant trend in organisations requiring high levels of team-member participation and leadership, leaders do, and will, continue to play a critical role in leading all types of teams.

Reflection on your leadership practice

In the introduction to this chapter, you were requested to keep a question at the back of your mind:

Do teams make leadership an irrelevant concept?

Having now read this chapter and diagnosed your own work team, is your role as a leader of the team effective. That is, are you an effective leader of your team. If your answer is yes, then write a few words why you consider yourself a successful team leader. If your answer is qualified, then make an effort to improve your team leadership by adopting some of the practices outlined in this chapter.

References

Cohen, S & Bailey, D 1997, 'What makes teams work: Group effectiveness research from the shop floor to the executive suite', *Journal of Management*, vol. 34, pp. 239-290.

Collins, J 2009, *How the mighty fall and why some companies never give in*, HarperCollins Publishers, New York.

Dubrin, A, Dalglish, C & Miller, P 2006, *Leadership: 2nd Asian Edition*, Wiley, Australia.

Gersick, C 1988, 'Time and transition in work teams: Toward a new model of group development, *Academy of Management Journal*, vol. 31, no. 1, March.

Hughes, R, Ginnett, R & Curphy, G 2006, *Leadership: Enhancing the lessons of experience*, 5th edn, McGraw-Hill, New York.

Lussier, R & Achua, C 2004, *Leadership: Theory, application, skill development*, 2nd edn, Thomson, USA.

Margerison, C & McCann, D 1995, *Team Management*, Management Books 2000 Ltd, England.

Stokes, L 1994, 'Moving toward Self-Direction: An action plan for self-managed teams', *Information Systems Management*, vol. 11, Winter, pp. 40-46.

Tuckman, B 1965, 'Developmental sequence in small groups', *Psychological Bulletin*, vol. 63, pp. 384-399.

Tuckman, B & Jensen, M 1977, 'Stages of small-group development', *Group and Organizational Studies*, vol. 2, pp. 419-427.

Chapter 11

LEADING CHANGE

CHAPTER CONTENTS

Spotlight: Professor Peter Farrell

Peter Farrell has served as ResMed's Executive Chairman of the Board since January 1, 2008. He has been a director of the company since June 1989 and from July 1990 until December 2007 he served as Chief Executive Officer. Professor Farrell was also ResMed's President from its inception until September 2004.

From July 1984 to June 1989 Professor Farrell served as Vice President, Research and Development at various subsidiaries of Baxter International, Inc. From August 1985 to June 1989 he also served as Managing Director of the Baxter Center for Medical Research Pty Ltd, a subsidiary of Baxter. From January 1978 to December 1989 he was Foundation Director of the Centre (now Graduate School) for Biomedical Engineering at the University of New South Wales where he currently serves as a visiting professor. He provided a commitment to the university of $500,000 to establish the Centre for Innovation and Entrepreneurship at the Australian School of Business based on a contribution of $100,000 per annum on the achievement of milestones. The university has received $300,000 to date.

He holds a BE in chemical engineering with honours from the University of Sydney, an SM in chemical engineering from the Massachusetts Institute of Technology, a PhD in chemical engineering and bioengineering from the University of Washington, Seattle, and a DSc from the University of New South Wales.

Professor Farrell was named 1998 San Diego Entrepreneur of the Year for Health Sciences, Australian Entrepreneur of the Year in 2001, and US National Entrepreneur of the Year for 2005 in Health Sciences. In August 2000 he was named Vice Chairman of the Executive Council of the Harvard Medical School Division of Sleep Medicine. In addition to his responsibilities with ResMed, he is a director of NuVasive, Inc. (a NASDAQ-listed company that develops and markets products for the surgical treatment of spine disorders) a director of Pharmaxis Limited (an ASX and NASDAQ-listed specialist pharmaceutical company), and the non-executive chair of QRxPharma (a specialty pharmaceutical company involved in pain management listed on the ASX). He is Fellow or Honorary Fellow of several professional bodies.

In 2006, Forbes recognised ResMed as one of the best small companies in the US for the 10th year in a row.

When asked about change and being entrepreneurial, Professor Farrell said he thought the following skills and abilities were necessary:

- a certain knowledge of physics, chemistry and mathematics,

- good communication skills to present ideas,

- the ability to think clearly and express oneself clearly,

- a good grounding in finance (being able to read a balance sheet and understand an income statement) plus an ability to recognise a value proposition,

- a love for technology (a deep understanding of technology is a sine qua non and how it can be can be used as a true game-changer),

- a fetish for making a contribution and achieving outcomes,

- a sense of urgency is needed; nothing worthwhile gets done without a sense of urgency.

'To be an entrepreneur one also needs large doses of persistence and determination, as well as a high tolerance for bad news. Organisations need to be focused. Focus is about choice and the choices need to be realistic and aimed at innovation. Too many get distracted by saddling up too many horses in the barn at once. The best undergraduate education for an innovator or entrepreneur is a basic degree in engineering; short of that a good grounding in technology is beneficial, including exposure to physics, chemistry, mathematics, computing and statistics. One must attempt to quantify risks and opportunities; proper metrics are vital.'

According to Professor Farrell, if a leader wishes to develop a culture of innovation and change in their organisation, there is a set of personal qualities that should characterise all employees. These qualities are listed in the statement of ResMed's corporate values. They include:

- Ethics and integrity. There is no alternative to being ethical and having integrity—the *sine qua non*—an indispensable element of any business.

- An apolitical team player. A successful organisation is an effective team. Collectively, the organisation makes better and more informed decisions—and politics have no place in the company.

- Initiative. The motto of the company is 'just get on with it'—provided you have covered all the bases that need to be covered and that appropriate people are kept in the loop.

- A sense of urgency. Problems should be defined and then solved with a sense of urgency in execution.

- Instinct and resourcefulness. If you have a worthwhile problem and you are willing to roll up your sleeves to address it, there are people who will be willing to help.

- Creativity. Always think how things can be done better and differently.

- Proactive communication. Never assume that someone who ought to know actually does; tell them, even if it means telling them something they already know.

- Commitment to quality and continuous improvement. We need to have an obsession with doing things better. If we are not moving forward, we are actually moving backwards.

- Self esteem. We all need sensible and rational inputs so don't be afraid to stand up and be counted.

- Value-consciousness. Every project and use of company resources should be subjected to a cost/benefit analysis.

- Customer focus. We must be externally focused rather than internally focused.

- Concern for co-workers. Nothing can come to fruition without people making it happen, so we need to provide an environment that fosters the well-being of each employee, where each of us treats the other honestly and fairly.

Sources: ResMed website <http://www.resmed.com/au/>, interview with Professor Farrell on 30 July 2009 and *The Australian Financial Review*, 27 April 2009.

The spotlight on Professor Farrell presents a picture of the way important elements of the organisational culture must be if innovation and change in the organisation are to thrive. It also provides a very good example of a coherent, practical, corporate values statement. Corporate values statements are often broad and general. For example, they may list words like, 'teamwork', 'honesty', 'trust', and 'equity'. While these values are worth pursuing, single words are open to interpretation, especially by diverse groups within the organisation. Having values that are defined and well articulated means that those reading them cannot misinterpret the meanings attached to each word. ResMed's values statement reported here is an abbreviation of the actual statement. It is still specific and detailed, however, so the organisation's staff and stakeholders are left in no doubt as to the importance of the values and the behaviours that are expected in the organisation.

Introduction

For many people change is painful, anxiety-provoking, and just plain difficult — whether it be personal change or organisational change. It has been said that 'people only like the change that jingles in their pockets' (Robbins 2002).

For others, change is stimulating. It is a challenge to be savoured. The reality of life for both kinds of people is that change, both personal and organisational, is inevitable. It is indicative of growth and progress. Why some people meet the change effort with less enthusiasm may be due, in part, to the way the path to change is planned, communicated and directed by leaders. This chapter examines the role leadership plays in the implementation of change.

Change is also a complex, customised process. What works well in one change implementation or in one organisation may not be replicated automatically in another. A variety of organisational dynamics and variables play an important role in determining how change might be successfully implemented.

There are four types of organisational change discussed in this chapter. We will concentrate on change in organisational processes and change in organisational functions. Factors to be considered for cultural change are discussed in chapter 7. Changes to power distributions relate more to the concept of strategic leadership. They are discussed in chapter 12.

Leaders of organisations need to manage change effectively. This chapter provides frameworks for the way leaders can successfully implement change in their organisations. There is little point, however, in addressing organisational change without first addressing personal change. In reality, people in organisations do the changing that brings about organisational change. Leaders, therefore, must first develop an understanding of the effects of change on individuals — and then extend that understanding to the affect change has in the organisational context.

To lead planned change, leaders require a *change plan* that recognises the known stages of personal and organisational change. The plan must be sufficiently flexible to allow adaptation as variables not anticipated at the commencement of the change program emerge. Leaders must be accomplished at leading change in organisations. The ability to lead change successfully assists leaders to be categorised by others as 'transformational leaders' (see Chapter 6). This is a desirable characteristic to cultivate.

The nature and speed of change

Organisations of every size and type are part of a complex, dynamic, changing global world where change is part of everyday life. Technology and the need to be competitive in this environment mean that change is continuous and rapid. Continued globalisation of markets and supply chains will lead to change intensifying.

While change takes place all around us, each change in an organisation is unique. Like leadership itself, there is no single approach to ensure success. Leaders often think they can implement change without disruption to individuals. Individual resistance to change, however, is one of the primary reasons why change programs fail at both the individual and organisational level.

Organisations must continue to change, responding to their environment. If they do not adapt continually, it is evitable that organisational decline or organisational death will follow. According to Collins (2009), decline of organisations is largely self-inflicted by poor leadership and change management. There is also strong research evidence suggesting that change programs in organisations are subject to very high failure rates. Accordingly, leaders must be skilled at leading change if they are to achieve the objectives of their change programs.

Types of organisational change

There are four different types of organisational change. The four types include (Cao and McHugh 2005):

- change to organisational processes,
- change in organisational functions,
- change in organisational culture, and
- change in power distribution in organisations.

Process change

Process change includes attempts by leaders to transform the flow of inputs to outputs in an organisation. It is often referred to as 'process improvement'. It can apply to information, products, and services. This type of change can be large or small scale, and may involve changes to activities across functional departments in the one organisation.

Functional change

Functional change refers to attempts to change horizontal or vertical structures within an organisation. Examples could be changes to policy or systems, changes to the way people are organised in teams or in the way departments relate to each other.

Changes to organisational culture

Organisational cultural changes are attempts to change the values, norms and behaviours of people in the organisation.

Changes to the distribution of power

Changes to the distribution of power involve changes to the way an organisation makes decisions—and which group (if any) should be the dominant coalition in the organisation.

These four types of change are interconnected. They interact within the systems of an organisation. A change in any one dimension will likely result in a change in the other dimensions. Change programs designed to address issues in any of the dimensions may require different or multiple approaches to meet the consequential changes in the other dimensions.

In this chapter we will concentrate on change in organisational processes and change in organisational functions. Factors to be considered for cultural change are discussed in chapter 7. Changes to power distributions relate more to the concept of strategic leadership. They are discussed in chapter 12.

Individual and personal change

There are numerous books about organisational change—what it means and how to do it. Organisations, however, are no more than the people in them. If all the people in an organisation gathered in a park, the organisation would be in the park, not in the empty buildings left behind. Organisational change, therefore, commences with personal change; it is about people change. In other words, *people change, organisations don't.*

People change by being led, not by being told to change. As discussed so far in this book, leadership concerns influence and building strong team relationships. The best way to get people to consider changing, therefore, is to influence them by leading by example. Leaders who have strong, supportive relationships with their teams will be more successful in implementing change because team members will trust and follow them.

There is a significant amount of research relating to the way change affects individuals at the psychological level, and the stages individuals move through when experiencing change. To discuss this transition we have chosen the Transitional Cycle Model (Scott & Jaffe 2004) as it best represents the change process for individuals and for organisations. The transition curve is illustrated in Figure 11.1.

Figure 11.1 The Transition Curve

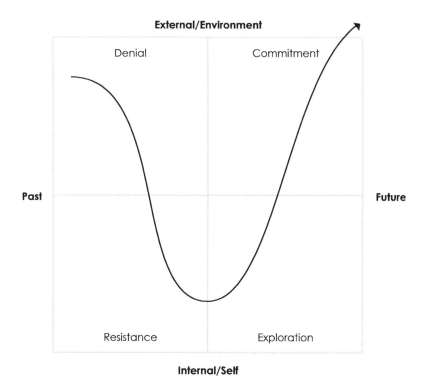

Source: Scott, C & Jaffe, D 2004, *Managing change at work: Leading people through organizational transitions*, 3rd edn, Crisp Publications, Boston, p. 35. Used with permission of Changeworks Global, San Francisco.

The four stages of change

Individuals confronted by change typically move through four stages. Most people move through these four stages for each and every change or transition in their lives. Some people move quickly and unconsciously through each stage whereas some get stuck at one or more of the stages. According to Scott and Jaffe (2004), the four stages are:

- denial,
- resistance,
- exploration, and
- commitment.

Denial

During change, people focus on what they are doing at the present. They often deny the need for change. Often, during large-scale change programs like organisational restructuring, the first response is shock and numbness. People in the organisation often simply get on with their jobs as if nothing had happened or been announced. They refuse to explore the need for change. Common responses by people affected by change in this stage include 'this cannot be happening' or 'it won't really be implemented'. The denial phase is harmful both to the individual and the organisation because it impedes healing for the individual and progress for the organisation. To get people through this stage, leaders need to confront employees with information (e.g. a change meeting), seek questions, and give feedback. Some team members may need significant time to work through the stage.

Resistance

Resistance occurs when people are no longer numb, when they begin to feel self doubt, anxiety and uncertainty, or negativity about the change. In the first instance, all employees focus on how the change affects them personally; in the second instance, they focus on how the change affects their team members. Common responses in this stage are high levels of stress and anxiety, mourning the past, or pretending the change is not really happening. Sometimes team members can even slip back into the denial stage. To make this stage pass more quickly, the leader must encourage team members to air their views and to express their feelings openly.

Exploration

When people have moved through the resistance stage, their energy often turns to the future. This burst of energy can lead to the generation of many new ideas. People will often engage in searching out and testing new ways of doing things. A lot of uncertainty continues to prevail during this stage. This uncertainty can generate stress if the leader does not guide the employees towards the vision for the future. Leaders should resist pushing team members through this phase too quickly. They should not accept less than an optimum outcome for the organisation.

Commitment

The commitment stage has been reached when team members have accepted new ways of doing things and are ready to commit themselves to the change plan. The stage will last until a new change is suggested and the transition begins again.

Leaders need to understand the Transitional Cycle Model and assist team members to move through the stages at a reasonable rate. If the team or individual members get stuck in any of the stages, the change process can be prolonged or jeopardised.

Activity 11.1

Think about a major change you have faced in your personal or organisational life. How did you handle the transition? Did your emotions follow the Transitional Cycle Model?

The organisational change leader

Organisational change may be either a planned or unplanned response of the organisation to internal and/or external pressures exerted upon it. Sources of these pressures can be individuals, interest groups, factions, cliques or teams. External sources include regulatory requirements, new competition, changing social values, and changing philosophies and practices. Internal forces include new business practices, different leadership practices or 'bottom-up' demand for a cultural change. At any rate, the effort will embody new and different relationships and functions among team members. It will create new allegiances and attitudes. It will create new opportunities and vulnerabilities in the organisation.

There are three kinds of leaders in organisations. Those who:

- watch things happen,
- make things happen, and those who
- ask 'What happened?'

We're interested in the second group of leaders—those who make things happen.

Change plans

The leaders of organisations at all levels are most responsible for change in organisations. They are charged, by virtue of their positions, to ensure that any change effort brings maximum benefit to the organisation. Most often, leaders are required to lead a planned change effort. A planned change effort requires the leader to develop a *change plan*.

Organisations often use generic change plans as the basis for implementing change within their organisations. Examples of generic change plans are outsourcing, total quality management, restructuring, and delayering. While these generic programs are used worldwide and are popular with consultants, there is little empirical evidence to support their effectiveness (Yukl 2002). Change is a complex, customised process in organisations. What works well in one organisation may not work well in another.

Generic solutions to organisational change can often make things worse rather than better. Leaders, therefore, need to be very clear about the nature of the issue being addressed by the proposed change and the objectives of the change program.

The need for diagnosis

All change programs should start with a careful and extensive *diagnosis* of the organisation and the problems to be addressed in the change program. One of the principles underlying planned change includes the notion of interdependence. That is, a change in one part of a system of interrelated parts (an organisation) affects other parts of the system. It follows that when change upsets the system's equilibrium, resistance won't be far behind. Change leaders must, therefore, know how to identify and manage forces operating for and against the change. This knowledge is part of the organisational diagnosis when planning change.

In summary, leaders should begin with a clear understanding of the need for change and the likely effect the change will have on all aspects of the organisation. By providing specific details concerning the nature and context of the change effort, the leader can keep everyone focused on the direction of change.

Focus on action

When preparing the change plan, leaders need strategies specifying action steps for each phase of the effort. When establishing this focus, three specific issues will need to be addressed — namely:

- people issues,
- resourcing issues, and
- getting the change effort to stay on track.

People issues

Leaders need to remind themselves that people change for *their* reasons, not those of the leader. So in deciding what needs to be changed, leaders must take into account how the people most affected will benefit or gain. To hear what fears or concerns have arisen, they must involve those affected by the change early in the process; they must build their change plan around minimising these fears and concerns. One of the best tools to motivate people for change is skilful communication (addressed in chapter 9). The objectives and rationale for change must be communicated clearly before anyone can begin to accept and own them.

Clear communication strategies will need the right kind of information. Strategies to explore ideas will be essential. How one manages the process of inquiry is important to generate useful information. In order to gain their full commitment, this process should engage participants in dialogue about change. Such a process requires the leader to be skilled in all areas — that is, skilled in verbal, written and small- or large-group communication. The plan should include strategies to handle the inevitable personal, structural and systemic conflicts.

Resourcing issues

Leaders must ensure that appropriate resources are provided at the right time. Appropriate resources include financial, human and material resources. Not every change requires large-scale resourcing. Each effort will need a list of the critical resources needed, their potential cost, and source(s) for obtaining them.

Staying on track

Making the change effort stay on track is a crucial responsibility of every change leader. Communicating a vision is not enough. Keeping on track requires expert planning with well-defined strategies. The strategies must be coordinated at each phase of the change process. Complicated plans have to be broken down into small, manageable chunks. When strategies are rooted in specific activities that individuals currently perform, they become an anchor for goal-directed action.

A systems perspective

The plan should also identify the specific change management issues needing to be addressed. Leaders need to recognise that any organisational change effort is multidimensional. A systems perspective is useful to view the change. The aim is to understand the interactions, interconnectedness, and independence of the sub-systems in the organisation.

A blueprint for success

Change leaders recognise the importance of working from a well thought-out, well-defined, written change plan. This becomes their blueprint for success. Along the way, the plan is modified as a result of the collaborative efforts of others. Open discussions, information sharing, and problem solving keep everyone's feet on the ground and avoid potential oversights. The dialogue involves attention to complaints that serve as legitimate sources of information.

Monitoring and tracking

Once the plan has been developed and the change implemented, the change leader needs to monitor and track all aspects of the planned and unplanned events of the change. Change leadership encompasses looking for hidden, not easily predictable barriers or consequences that are beyond the intended goal. Some of these effects may be due to oversight, poor communication, lapses in persistence, and/or personal vulnerabilities.

In order to let the momentum of the change build, the plan needs to ensure that team members who are the subjects of the change are allowed to experience the pressures of the change. The pressures, however, need to be kept in a range that team members can handle. One of the leader's most important steps for executing large-scale change is to cut the change program into smaller, more manageable chunks. Bringing the general terms to specific terms allows this management to occur.

Organisation culture

The organisation's culture is pervasive; it influences everything the leader must achieve to implement the change. Organisation culture, therefore, must be acknowledged as part of the change plan. Issues of organisation culture are addressed in chapter 7.

Frameworks for implementing change

There are several personal and organisational frameworks that leaders should pay attention to when implementing change. These frameworks describe the typical patterns associated with change. Change leaders can utilise them to develop an effective change plan. The frameworks are outlined later in this chapter.

Activity 11.2

Identify two people in your organisation (or one you know of) who you know from your experience are able to lead successful change. Observe what they do. Draw up a list to describe the behaviours you see. Now discuss the list of behaviours with at least one of them. In your discussion, look to confirm your observations and find out if they do things that you have not observed to bring about change?

Models of planned change

There are two well-known, generally accepted models describing the pattern that typically occurs when a planned change is implemented:

- Lewin's force-field analysis, and

- Kotter's eight-stage model.

Change leaders can use these models to assist them to conceptualise the way change happens and to ensure that each of the phases in the models is given appropriate attention in the development of the change plan. Leadership in each phase is critical to the success of the change effort.

Lewin's force-field analysis

Lewin's force-field analysis (Lewin 1951) proposed that the change process can be divided into three phases:

- unfreezing,

- changing, and

- refreezing.

Unfreezing

In the unfreezing phase, the subjects of the change are convinced of the need for the change; they are given evidence showing why the 'old way' will no longer sustain the organisation. In times of crisis, there is little need for the leader to convince organisational members of the need for change. Change is often incremental, however, and the need for it may not be obvious. It is important for leaders to take an active role in this phase to assist in bringing about the attitudinal change required to make the next phase successful. Without this phase as a pre-requisite, attempts to implement change are likely to result in strong opposition, anger and ongoing resistance.

Changing

The change phase involves the consideration and selection of the change option to be implemented. Building consensus for the selected option is a critical role for the leader; the option selected must be appropriate and must have the full support of those involved.

Refreezing

In the refreezing phase, the planned change is implemented. The leader's concerns are to ensure that the new way of doing things is properly established and that the organisation does not slip back into doing things the old way.

To achieve planned change, Lewin (1951) proposes two types of actions by leaders using his model. One action is to increase 'driving forces' — i.e. incentives or other methods that encourage change. The other action is to reduce 'restraining forces' like fear of failure, economic loss or opponents to the change. It is essential that these forces be identified as part of the initial organisational diagnosis for the change.

Lewin's model is simplistic and somewhat static. It was developed at a time when change in organisations was experienced in short bursts followed by a period of stability. Change is now a way of life. It is continuous rather than occurring in discrete or specific events. The model is still relevant, however, as it provides leaders with a simple conceptual framework for thinking about change generally, it assists leaders to identify the driving and restraining forces for a change, and is a reminder that there is much work to be undertaken both before and after the change program if it is to be successful.

Kotter's eight-stage model

Kotter's model (Kotter 1996) passes through eight stages. The role of the leader is critical to each of the stages. Again, this framework is helpful for leaders to gain understanding of the dynamics of change. Often this model is applied only to major change programs but it can work equally well for smaller-scale change programs.

The model has eight stages — namely:

- Establish a sense of urgency,

- Create a guiding coalition,

- Develop a vision and strategy,

- Communicate the vision,

- Empower actions,

- Generate short-term wins,

- Consolidate gains and produce more change, and

- Anchor new approaches in the culture.

1. Establish a sense of urgency

This stage is similar to the 'unfreezing phase' in the Lewin model. It requires the leader to ensure that people in the organisation accept that the proposed change is both necessary and desirable. While such an action might seem self-evident, many change programs fail at this stage because leaders do not spend the required time convincing employees that a change is necessary. In order to reduce later resistance to the change, the acceptance of the need for it must be genuine and complete; employees must have moved through the 'denial' stage of the Transitional Curve mentioned earlier in this chapter.

2. Create a guiding coalition

No one leader can single-handedly lead a successful change initiative—but one leader alone can assuredly lead the program to failure. Organisational change is a complex dynamic. There are many forces at play, some outside the control of the leader. Having the right people on the change team, all of whom share the same objective for the change, will improve its chances of success. Also having some 'change champions', that is, people who are not part of the leadership team but accept the need for change and are enthusiastic about it, will assist in guiding others towards the desired outcome. Their enthusiasm excites others.

3. Develop a vision and strategy

A vision is a picture of where the organisation will be after the change has been implemented. It provides people with a direction and a goal; it allows all actions to be measured against its attainment. Those subject to the change must accept this vision and want to be a part of it. It must become their own. However, a vision without action plans or strategies on how to get there can be frustrating and confusing for those who are the subject of the change. The strategies provide the clear path towards the vision.

4. Communicate the vision

People cannot accept the vision unless there is coherent communication about it. People must be encouraged to question and seek feedback on how the organisation will look and function after the change. Communication does not only mean talking by the leaders. Leaders must 'live' the vision in their actions and deeds. Often, for very large change programs, the amount of information can be overwhelming, so it is better to communicate in coherent 'chunks' of information while keeping the vision of the future clear.

5. Empower actions

Researchers have identified that people resist change if they feel threatened, are uncertain about the change, their self interests are under attack or they do not share the perceptions of the change leaders. In this stage, the leader needs to remove these possible barriers to change by ensuring that the people affected can join in the change effort. A consultation process with all those involved can ensure that concerns are responded to and that people get the knowledge and resources they need to feel empowered about what is happening.

6. Generate short-term wins

All change programs need to let the participants feel success early in the program. Success breeds further success. With success, people see the benefits and the validity of the change and the progress towards the vision. Wise leaders, therefore, ensure that the change effort includes small, achievable milestones early on, where success is easier to achieve than milestones further down the change path.

7. Consolidate gains and produce more change

Short-term wins generate momentum for change programs. They attract people who may not initially have agreed with the change. This stage and the next one can be compared to the 'refreezing phase' in the Lewin model. Old ways of doing things are replaced permanently by the new way; a different culture, one more relevant to the new vision, is born.

8. Anchor new approaches in the culture

Kotter argues that people will generally not share the leader's beliefs at the start of the change process—that a change in culture comes at the end of the change process. A successful change program will produce a significantly different organisational culture, where the old ways of doing things are long forgotten and people regard the new ways to be superior.

Leader in action: Dr Dennis Richards

After completing a science degree in physiology at the University of New England, Armidale, Dennis Richards qualified as a chiropractor from Palmer College of Chiropractic in Iowa, USA.

After graduating with a Doctor of Chiropractic, he experienced life in Europe, working with the STATIC group chiropractic clinics in Italy. He then travelled extensively in Africa, Europe, the USA and Canada before returning to Australia to open up his own clinic in Tweed Heads, NSW.

Dennis is highly regarded as a leader in the field. Since 1998 he has held board positions with the Chiropractors' Association of Australia (CAA), specifically representing its members in NSW and the ACT. In 2001 he was awarded the prestigious 'Chiropractor of the Year' award. In 2005 he was elected president of the Chiropractors' Association of Australia.

Following his appointment in 2001 by the CAA to be Pacific Regional representative on the Council of the World Federation of Chiropractic (WFC), in 2006 Dennis was elected Secretary and Treasurer of the world body. The WFC meets annually in exotic locations like Paris, Toronto, Orlando, Sydney, Johannesburg, Montreal and Vilamoura, Portugal.

In 2003, the CAA appointed Dennis to be its representative on the Sydney 2005 WFC World Congress Planning Committee. This involved two years of intense work involving close liaison with WFC and CAA staff to create an event which eventually attracted a record attendance of chiropractors from Australia and around the world, producing a financial surplus for both organisations.

Over the last few years, Dennis has implemented significant governance and operational changes in the CAA and the WFC. In the CAA, he has worked to re-develop and focus the board on the achievement of the CAA Strategic Plan. The plan has necessitated cultural and operational changes in the way the CAA operates as it shifts strategic tasks from board members to the CEO and its organisational wing. The strategies used in the change plan included wide consultation to gain the support of stakeholders, changing the composition of the board to increase diversity, employment of consultants to conduct an operational audit, streamlining of board meetings to enable more matters to be addressed in less time, and diverse communication strategies.

According to Dennis, barriers to the changes were overcome by 'relentless communication with members via attendance at meetings around the country, regular President's Reports in the CAA magazine, email blasts to members, and a series of five papers published in the *Chiropractic Journal of Australia* documenting board and association strategies and activities'. He also stresses that 'finding talented people, including directors, who would assist in concrete ways to address the action items of the strategic plan, rather than just talk about them, can help drive change — a task which can be lonely without solid supporters'.

Things are somewhat different in the WFC, given that it is an international body with its Secretariat in Toronto, Canada, and that the thirteen council members are scattered around the world, meeting only once a year.

As the WFC had been founded twenty years previous (and had been working according to bylaws developed that long ago), Dennis worked to convince the council that the twenty-year anniversary was an opportune time to carry out a 'visioning consensus' to develop core values and core purposes for the organisation, and a vision statement detailing where it wanted to be in a further twenty years time.

He did this by written material and oral presentation, sharing with the council evidence of how such efforts had been productive for other organisations. He showed them how the organisation's stakeholders (its national chiropractic association members), could take part by email even though they were located in different places around the world. Fear of what the outcomes might be had to be overcome by convincing the council to trust the members they represented.

As he had done with the CAA, Dennis also worked to focus

and shorten meetings of the WFC council; he sought to introduce a requirement limiting the length of oral presentations of reports that previously had been submitted in writing. The survival of this requirement needed constant vigilance—council members were often eager to share the developments in the regions they represented.

Making changes such as these required careful lobbying and the support of other members of the council. It required the development of a comprehensive change plan. Dennis offers the following suggestions for others wishing to implement change.

1. Be crystal clear in what change you think should be implemented, and why. Share this with stakeholders over and over again so they understand the need.

2. Do not try to impose change on others. Invite them into the process of determining what change needs to take place and why. This will increase the likelihood of their participating in making the change happen.

3. Be patient and persistent. Creating change requires changing minds and cultures. This can take time.

4. Occasionally review your plan for change. The environment and subsequent need for the originally planned change may itself have changed. Your plan may need modification.

5. Relentlessly and repetitively communicate the need for change. This can attract others who are inspired to help you and build the support networks needed to make the change happen.

6. Mentor others into carrying the change forward when you have gone.

Source: Interview with Dr Richards 19 June 2009.

Change in organisations of any size can be difficult. The profile of Dennis Richards demonstrates that change is possible even in large organisations if the change is led well. It also shows that no change in an organisation should be attempted without a change plan.

Dennis's suggestions for change leaders are insightful hints for all leaders who will at some point in their careers, have to face and lead a major change program.

The adaptive leadership change framework

Contemporary leadership theorists such as Lowder (2009) argue that due to the constantly changing and increasingly complex environment in which organisations operate, there is a need to challenge many of the leadership theories that focus on traits, behaviours and situational factors (outlined in chapter 5). Instead, leadership should focus on the needs and demands of stakeholders. As was discussed earlier in this chapter, change management is also often thought of as a planned, linear process similar to Kotter's eight-stage model of change.

A model for sustainable leadership

Heifetz, Grashow and Linsky (2009) propose a model for sustainable leadership. The model provides a framework for determining when and how to lead change resulting in creative problem solving fostering successful and sustainable change in the relationships between the organisation and its stakeholders.

Known as *adaptive leadership,* it is based on the premise that leadership is more a process than a collection of personal capabilities. The process requires all those connected to a change to focus on the specific problems at hand and to modify the way they have worked in the past to arrive at new solutions.

Adaptive leadership is a practical leadership framework that helps individuals and organisations to deal with change in a way that is non-threatening to those responsible for making the change happen. By including all stakeholders in the change process, adaptive leadership offers a model of change different to the way change is traditionally implemented. It is essentially about experimentation and learning, and allowing people to deviate from the plan as learning takes place.

According to Heifetz, Grashow and Linsky (2009), leaders confront two types of problems:

- technical, and
- adaptive.

Technical problems

Technical problems are well defined; the solutions to the problems are usually well known. An example of a technical problem might be increasing the efficiency of a process. Technical problems may therefore be likened to a process change type.

Adaptive problems

Adaptive problems are not well defined and the solutions are not known in advance of attempts to address them. Large- and small-scale change programs of all types in organisations are often categorised like this. The leader may have a plan but the outcome of the plan may not be a certainty.

Many different stakeholders are usually involved in the solution of adaptive problems because the attitudes, priorities and behaviours of the stakeholders are usually part of the problem.

Change programs often fail because leaders apply known or standard solutions (for example, total quality management or six sigma) as if the problems are technical, failing to recognise that the problems are adaptive in nature.

The seven stages of adaptive leadership

The seven stages of adaptive leadership that can be used to implement complex change are outlined in Table 11.2.

When interpreting Table 11.2, it should be noted that the seven steps are not meant to be undertaken in a linear way but are a cyclical process.

Adaptive leaders thrive in challenging environments brought about by adaptive problems. They are willing to:

- entertain diverse and divergent views before making major decisions,
- admit when they are wrong and alter or abandon a non-productive course of action, and
- experiment and take reasonable risks.

These characteristics are not new in leadership. What is new is the speed of change organisational leaders now face and the need for organisations to adapt successfully at a time when the more traditional models of leadership and change management may not be appropriate.

Table 11.2 Stages of adaptive leadership

Steps in process	Dimension	Activity/issues for adaptive leaders
One	Identify the type of problem	Is the problem a technical or adaptive problem? Many problems have both technical and adaptive elements that must be addressed by different interventions.
Two	Focus attention	Put the key issues before the stakeholders and secure commitments from stakeholders that they will engage with the problem.
Three	Frame the issues	Stakeholders need to understand that problems present opportunities as well as difficulties. Find common ground and ensure that the time is right and ripe for presenting the issue to be addressed.
Four	Secure ownership	Allow stakeholders to take responsibility for the problem. Ensure involvement and that the right people are on key teams.
Five	Mediate stakeholder conflict	Different stakeholders hold keys to different parts of the solution. Ensure conflicts between stakeholders are quickly resolved in order that forward progress is maintained.

Steps in process	Dimension	Activity/issues for adaptive leaders
Six	Generate and maintain productive distress	Adaptive problems take long periods to resolve and progress is often incremental. Stress needs to be harnessed so that people feel the need for change, but kept at a level where it does not overwhelm participants.
Seven	Create a safe haven	If issues become counterproductive, the pace of change needs to be slowed so that a safe place is created to discuss divergent perspectives

Sources: Adapted from Heifetz, R, Kania, J & Kramer, M 2004, 'Leading boldly', *Stanford Social Innovation Review*, vol. 2, no. 3, Winter, pp. 21-31 and Randall, L & Coakley, A 2007, 'Applying adaptive leadership to successful change initiatives in academia', *Leadership & Organization Development Journal*, vol. 28, no. 4, pp. 325–335.

Activity 11.3

Compare the seven stages of adaptive leadership with the Kotter eight stages of planned organisational change outlined earlier in this chapter. Synthesise the two models into one larger model to provide guidance for your next change project.

Resistance to change

Individual resistance to change is one of the primary reasons that change programs fail at the personal and organisation level. Research shows that strong resistance to change can even occur when the change is to the individual's best interests (O'Toole 1996).

Leaders also need to remember a basic axiom about change. That is, *any change in one part of a system will result in associated effects in other parts* of the system. This leads to increased complexity and difficulty in accomplishing the intended results of the change effort. In short, change is always tougher than it looks. Understanding resistance to change therefore means that leaders must go beyond the issues listed below as reasons why people resist change. They must look for resistance at the group and organisational levels.

According to Connor (1995) people may resist change because of:

- previous negative experience with change,
- a lack of understanding of the rationale for the change,
- a lack of trust of the people who propose the change,
- contentment with the status quo and belief that the change is not necessary,
- the change has not been clearly communicated,
- a belief that the change is not feasible or workable,
- economic threats to their job security, pay and promotion potential,
- fear of personal failure,
- loss of job status and personal power,
- concern that change will be for the benefit of the change designers only, rather than in the best interests of the organisation,
- concern about their abilities to learn a new system,
- concern about managing change-related technical problems,
- a high need for security, and
- the possibility of threatening existing networks and personal relationships.

Leaders may also resist change because they:

- don't properly understand their role in reducing resistance to change,
- are unable to demonstrate personal support for the change because they do not agree with it,
- forget to obtain the ideas and opinions from the people most affected by the change and try to force it on others,

- are concerned they do not have the necessary skills or competencies to lead the change,
- are not confident that more senior leaders understand the culture of the organisation, and
- do not get sufficient resources to implement the change program.

Resistance to change is a fact of life in all organisations. As discussed earlier in this chapter (in the section dealing with personal change), it is a natural reaction of most people. Leaders should therefore view resistance to change as a given. They should redirect the energy and emotion created by the resistance to improve the change effort— and as a source of commitment once opponents are converted to followers.

Activity 11.4

Interview two senior colleagues in your organisation about a change effort in which they were involved. Ask them to list the key concerns they had during the change process. Keep a frequency count of those issues listed above which were present in their descriptions. What does it say about the need to build trust in organisations?

Summary

Leaders of organisations confront change on an unprecedented scale. Change is now a way of life in organisations; it is continuous rather than occurring in discrete or specific events. Leading change of any scale is therefore a balancing act for the leader.

When the leader has identified the type of change required in the organisation, the leader needs to understand how change affects individuals. Individuals affected by change move through a transitional curve consisting of four stages:

- denial,
- resistance,

- exploration, and

- commitment.

An understanding of the stages of personal change can assist the leader to extend that understanding to the organisation.

Organisational change may be planned or unplanned. Leaders need to be able to develop a change plan. Generic change plans (e.g. total quality management) are used extensively to implement change. They have face validity but there is little empirical evidence to suggest that they are effective.

Customised change plans commence with an organisational diagnosis to establish the people issues, resourcing issues and objectives of the change. Clear communication strategies need to be a part of the plan. The practical framework for team improvement outlined in chapter 10 can also be adapted to assist a leader to develop a change plan.

A number of models can be used by leaders to understand and plan change in organisations. These include Lewin's force-field analysis model and Kotter's eight-stage framework. The eight-stage model includes:

- establishing a sense of urgency,

- creating guiding coalitions,

- development of a vision,

- communicating the vision,

- empowering actions,

- generating short-term wins,

- consolidating gains, and

- anchoring the new approaches in the culture.

Contemporary leadership theorists argue that the constantly changing and increasingly complex environment in which organisations operate challenge existing leadership and change management theories. As a result, the concept of adaptive leadership has emerged. Adaptive leadership offers a framework for determining when and how to lead change in a way that results in creative problem solving fostering successful and sustainable change in the relationships between the organisation and its stakeholders.

Individual resistance to change is one of the primary reasons that change programs fail at both personal and organisation levels. Resistance to change is a fact of life in all organisations; it is a natural reaction by most people. Leaders need to use the inevitable pressures and stress generated by change to maintain a state of distress that is bearable by team members but strong enough to move the change plan forward effectively.

Reflection on your leadership practice

Think about your experience with organisational change programs. Your experience may be as a participant in the change or as a leader of the change. If any of the change programs failed to meet their objectives, list why you think that happened. If any of the change programs achieved their objectives, comment on why you think these changes were successful. What have you learned from reading this chapter about implementing change in organisations and how will you implement and apply that learning in your next change program?

References

Cao, G & McHugh, M 2005, 'A systemic view of change management and its conceptual underpinnings', *Systemic Practice and Action Research*, vol. 18, no. 5, pp.475-490.

Christensen, C 1997, 'Making strategy: Learning by doing', *Harvard Business Review*, vol. 75, no. 6.

Collins, J 2009, *How the mighty fall and why some companies never give in*, HarperCollins Publishers, New York.

Connor, D 1995, *Managing at the speed of change: How resilient managers succeed and prosper where others fail*, Villard Books, New York.

Heifetz, R, Kania, J & Kramer, M 2004, 'Leading boldly', *Stanford Social Innovation Review*, vol. 2, no. 3, Winter, pp. 21-31.

Heifetz, R, Grashow, A & Linsky, M 2009, *The Practice of Adaptive Leadership*, Harvard Press, Boston.

Kotter, J 1996, *Leading Change*, Harvard Business School Press, Boston.

Lewin, K 1951, *Field Theory in Social Science*, Harper and Row, New York.

Lowder, Tim M 2009, *Change Management for Survival: Becoming an Adaptive Leader*, viewed May 29, 2009, <http://ssrn.com/abstract=1411492>.

O'Toole, J 1996, *Leading change: The argument for values based leadership*, Ballentine Books, New York.

Randall, L & Coakley, A 2007, 'Applying adaptive leadership to successful change initiatives in academia', *Leadership & Organization Development Journal*, vol. 28, no. 4, pp. 325 – 335.

Robbins, S 2002, *The truth about managing people and nothing but the truth*, 3rd edn, Prentice Hall, USA.

Scott, C & Jaffe, D 2004, *Managing change at work: Leading people through organizational transitions*, 3rd edn, Crisp Publications, Boston.

Yukl, G 2002, *Leadership in Organizations*, 5th edn, Prentice-Hall, New Jersey.

Chapter 12

STRATEGIC LEADERSHIP

Cutting edge ideas about leadership must face the test of applicability to real life. Yet they must also pass the test of ethics and values, because in the end, ideas will be effective weapons only if they are productive of happiness. (Burns 2003)

CHAPTER CONTENTS

- ☐ Spotlight: Kevin Rudd
- ☐ Introduction
- ☐ Thinking strategically
- ☐ Creating a vision
- ☐ Corporate social responsibility
- ☐ Leader in action: Olivia Lum
- ☐ Globalisation
- ☐ Technology and innovation
- ☐ Summary
- ☐ Reflection on your leadership practice
- ☐ Individual skills profile

Spotlight: Kevin Rudd

Kevin Rudd, the former Prime Minister of Australia once described himself *as a very determined bastard* <www.theage. com.au>.

One of the first things Kevin Rudd did on becoming Australian Prime Minister was to make a formal apology to the 'Stolen Generation' — indigenous children who were taken from their homes and parents to assimilate them into the white community. It was an election promise carried out as the first action of the second sitting of the 42nd Parliament of Australia <www.smb.com.au>. Around Australia thousands of people from all walks of life listened to the speech.

It was very moving to see the Prime Minister with a bit of heart. I loved it when he said he was sorry. There was just something personal about it. It's very hard for a prime minister to be personal. (David Price, indigenous composer, www.smb.com.au)

On the international stage while holding the position of Prime Minister, Kevin Rudd also made a symbolic gesture — ratifying the Kyoto Agreement on Climate Change — something the previous Australian Government had refused to do. Through a number of gestures, Rudd indicated his willingness to engage with the challenges that face the global community and to take a leadership role.

Born in Nambour in 1957, the youngest of four children, Kevin spent his early childhood on a dairy farm. In 1969, when he was 11, his father was killed in a car accident. Rudd graduated as dux of Nambour High School in 1974. His love of all things Chinese started at the age of ten when his mother gave him a book on ancient civilisations <www.theage. com.au>. Kevin attended the Australian National University (ANU) where, in 1981, he graduated with a First Class Honours in Chinese language and history.

Rudd's interest was in ideas as the basis of action — and actions as the basis of bringing about change. After graduating he joined the Department of Foreign Affairs and Trade. He had early leadership responsibilities overseas, including serving in Australian embassies in both Stockholm and Beijing in the mid 1980s. He was on the diplomatic 'fast track' and could have expected his next overseas posting to be as first secretary in a major embassy or as a junior ambassador.

Rudd took a leave of absence from the foreign office — stepping off the career fast track to join the Labor opposition in Queensland. In 1988 he became chief of staff to Wayne Goss, the Queensland opposition leader, helping to guide the ALP to government after decades out of power. In 1991 he was appointed Director General of the new Office of the Cabinet. Rudd's direct approach was a shock. He was nicknamed Dr Death — a man who pushed himself very hard and expected others to follow. He had the same reputation while he was Prime Minister of Australia.

He decided to stand for Federal Parliament and in 1998 he finally won the seat of Griffith with a 2% swing. In December 2006 he became Labor leader and Leader of the Opposition.

Kevin is not a particularly jovial politician. He is not someone who exudes charisma and character, but he worked hard to supplement his intellectual capacity. He grew into the various roles — politician, Leader of the Opposition and finally, in 2007, Prime Minister of Australia. He fell spectacularly from the position on 24 June, 2010 in an overnight coup and Julia Gillard was appointed Prime Minister in a dramatic turn of events over a 24 hour period.

Was Kevin Rudd an unlikely Australian Prime Minister? He brought with him experience and the skill set of a diplomat, an international business person, and a change-making public servant in state politics. He was not universally popular in federal politics. Kevin appeared to enjoy having power. He justified power as a means to change things to benefit individuals, communities and the welfare of Australians. While his leadership as Prime Minister ended as a failure, he did have one of the aspects of leadership known to be necessary – he had a clear **vision** of Australia and its role in the world.

This is an enlarging vision that sees Australia taking the lead on global climate change, rather than continuing to play the role of saboteur. This is an Australia that takes the lead on the Millennium Development Goals both in word and deed and leads by example in dealing with the chronic poverty in our own region. This is an Australia that becomes a leader, not a follower, in the redesign of the rules of international order we helped to craft in 1949 to render further genocides both intolerable under international law and impossible through international resolve. This is an Australia which takes the values of decency, fairness and compassion that are still etched deep in our national soul and breathes them afresh in the great debates now faced by our country and the international community. The time has well and truly come for a vision for Australia not limited by the narrowest of definitions of our national self interest. Instead we need to be guided by a new principle that encompasses not only what Australia can do for itself, but also what Australia can do for the world. (Rudd 2006)

Rudd expressed his well-articulated vision for Australia in the early stages of his journey towards the Prime Ministerial role. This assisted in elevating him into the public eye and in gaining the support of his colleagues to lead the then Labor opposition. Having an exciting and achievable vision for your followers is an essential skill for leaders. But as history records for Kevin Rudd, having such a vision is only one aspect of effective leadership and will not itself, guarantee leadership success. The successful leader must maintain the support and respect of followers and have the skills necessary to implement the vision. If this is not achieved, then the leadership is no more than symbolic, or a façade that will crumble when tested.

Sources: Currie Petersen, E 2007, 'Kevin Rudd' in Dalglish, C & Evans, P, *Leadership in the Australian Context*, Tilde University Press;
Macklin, R 2007, *Kevin Rudd: The Biography*, Penguin;
Walker, J 1995, *Goss: A Political Biography*, University of Queensland Press;
<http://www.smb.com.au/news/national/rudd.says.sorry/2008/02/13/120276034290. html>;

<http://www.theage.com.au/news/national/kevin-
rudd/2006/12/02/ 1164777852646.html?pa;
<http://www.pm.gov.au/media/interview/2008/interview_05
80.cfm>; <http://www.pm.gov.au/>.

In today's changing world, all leaders require strategic leadership
skills whether it be for a head of a government or a mid level
managerial position in an organisation. To become such a leader
takes many skills, one of which is strategic ability. Kevin Rudd took
risks with his career, worked extremely hard, and had a clearly
articulated vision both for himself and for Australia. The extent of
his government's strategic implementation processes was often
questioned as slowing down action— while he might have had a
vision acceptable to the Australian population, he and his
government failed to implement many key parts of that vision.
However, there is no doubt that vision, an ability to scan a complex
world environment, is one of the important components of
leadership.

Introduction

Strategic leadership deals with the major purposes of an
organisation. Its perspective, therefore, is often different from that of
leadership at other levels in an organisation. We study strategic
leadership as a separate function because in practice it is the
province of top-level executives and politicians who are exposed to
the full range of challenges and uncertainties that the global
environment offers.

Strategic leadership defined

For the purposes of this chapter, strategic leadership is defined as
'the process of providing the direction and inspiration necessary to
create and sustain an organisation, business or country in a
globalised environment'. So far in this text the emphasis has been on
the nature of the leader and their relationship with followers—the
behaviours and tactics used to bring about the desired outcomes.
This chapter focuses on the third dimension of the leadership
process—the external environment. It explores how leaders interact
with this external environment and the challenges they face. The
chapter provides a more detailed look at the leadership

environment and the crucial importance of strategic thinking in today's rapidly changing environment.

Historical context

Strategy is a term that can be traced back to the ancient Greeks where its focus was on military operations. For the next two thousand years strategy remained the domain of the military; it only started to be applied to business in the second half of the nineteenth century (Ghemawat 2006). Strategy then became the province of large corporations, particularly in the United States.

World War II provided a stimulus to strategic thinking in business as well as in the military domain. Peter Drucker, a pioneer in the definition and understanding of the practice of management, identified that management was not a passive behaviour — it was the taking action to ensure results. Large businesses could therefore take on the responsibility for shaping their environment, rather than simply responding to it. This became a key rationale for business strategy — i.e. consciously using formal planning to exert positive control over the environment.

The environment of business

Strategic thinking, therefore, requires the leader be able to understand the dynamics of the environment; it enables the organisation to respond positively and — where considered necessary — take action that changes the environment in a way that is positive for the organisation.

This process applies not only to governments and non-government agencies but also to business. Business is not separate from the context it inhabits. Business has the capacity not only to respond in a variety of ways to external stimulus but also to have an impact on its environment — both positively and negatively.

In a global world where many businesses are richer than countries, where business extends across national boundaries and where the behaviour of business can have a dramatic impact on people around the world, the ability to think strategically, to see the business, organisation or country in the context of its environment and impact is essential — not just for the success of the organisation, but for the planet as a whole.

At the end of this chapter, we will again take a pause to allow you to build your *individual skills profile.*

Thinking strategically

We have already discussed the impact of values and culture on the behaviour of leaders. These obviously have an impact on the way leaders think and act. Here we explore the component parts of strategic leadership.

High-level cognitive activity

Thinking strategically requires high-level cognitive skills — the ability to think conceptually, the ability to absorb and make sense of a multitude of trends, and the ability to use this information to plan for the future. A number of the leadership models examined in this text (e.g. transformational leadership and servant leadership) include this aspect of strategic thinking.

Gathering multiple inputs (listening)

Strategic thinking requires leaders to be in touch with those who influence the future. The best strategy is democratic in its formulation; it includes as many points of view and sources of information as possible. This is becoming more important as technology brings about rapid change and globalisation opens up not only new markets but new ideas and new challenges. Those involved in delivering the strategy may have very different priorities. Understanding these differences enables the development of strategies that can and will be implemented, because they reflect an understanding of issues of importance to those involved in implementing the strategy.

Anticipating and creating a future

Perhaps the most important and most obvious component of strategy is direction setting. Followers expect leaders to create the future, rather than simply responding to the present. Strategic leadership is about telling the organisation what it should be doing, where it is going. To do this the leader must accurately forecast or anticipate the future. More than ever, insight into tomorrow is the difference between success and failure (Harrison, cited in Dubrin *et al.* 2006).

Creating the future is more forceful than anticipating the future. It retains control within the organisation and creates a world that is desirable rather than one that is simply survivable. The organisation must ask questions about the shape of the industry (country) in the future and decide what needs to be done in the present to get the most benefit from future circumstances. This may need a special emphasis on the development of skills and capabilities that are 'ahead of their time'.

Revolutionary thinking

Hamel (1996) believed that incrementalism, i.e. making small changes over time, may not be the best response to current global changes. He believed that success lies with a number of revolutionary practices — namely:

- re-conceiving a product or service,
- redefining market space, and
- redrawing industry boundaries.

Re-conceiving a product or service

Re-conceiving a product or service involves radically improving the value equation to the customer. What new technologies are available? What are the appropriate technologies for particular situations (contexts)? What works in North America may not work in South East Asia or North Africa.

Redefining market space

There are a number of ways in which existing products and services can be taken to new markets. This can mean making products that are universally applicable, or as the global market grows, identifying niche markets that require specific adaptations.

Redrawing industry boundaries

Many big retail companies in Australia are doing this in a number of ways. One way is by compressing the supply chain so that what was originally a retail operation integrates wholesale and production under its control. The same retail sector has grown by taking on the traditional functions of other industries such as banking (EFTPOS) and the sale of fuel.

An outstanding strategic leader creates jobs and growth rather than focusing on ways to eliminate jobs. Strategic leaders look for ways to have a positive impact on their organisation and the society in which the organisation exists.

Activity 12.1

With a group of your peer mangers, think about the organisations in which you work, or the countries in which you live. What strategies are being used to benefit from the current global environment? What evidence is there that the leadership is thinking strategically?

Look for evidence of strategic thinking on the part of leadership and how this is used to develop plans and actions for the future.

Creating a vision

We have discussed vision in several chapters of this text, including its role in charismatic leadership. Vision is an integral part of strategic leadership. It describes what is possible, and provides direction and aspiration. A shared vision is not an idea. It is a force in people's hearts, something tangible and real. Few, if any, forces in human affairs are as powerful as a shared vision (Senge 1990).

Senge (1990) places great emphasis on shared vision. Many corporate vision statements, however, are not part of the democratic process Hamel suggests is necessary for successful strategic thinking. They are the vision of a small group who will benefit from the outcomes identified. The power in shared vision lies in the listening that has occurred and the personal commitment to achievement of those responsible for implementing the vision.

There are number of characteristics to an effective vision. It should be:

- brief,
- clear,
- focused,

- supportive of decision-making, and
- inspirational.

Brevity

An effective vision statement is brief. It will not be read if it is not. It needs to encapsulate what is important.

Clarity

An effective vision statement is understandable. Can those given responsibility for implementation understand what is sought? Can they understand how their contribution fits the vision?

Focus

An effective vision statement is focused. It must identify what is most important in the image of the future presented, rather than rest on broad generalised statements.

Support to decision making

An effective vision statement supports decision making. Does understanding the vision make it easier to make practical decisions, to choose between different possible courses of action?

Inspiration

An effective vision statement is inspirational. Those people responsible for achieving the vision should be inspired to use all their skills and be committed to the outcomes. It is difficult for those employed in a company to be inspired by strategies that benefit only a small group of stakeholders such as shareholders.

Olivia Lum (later discussed under the heading *Leader in action*) provides an example of strategic leadership, responding with new solutions, with innovation, and with new technology in new markets. Her vision and mission statements, including the values statement, reflect a very different world to that seen in many corporate vision statements.

Activity 12.2

Find the vision/mission statements for your organisations. Evaluate these vision statements against the criteria listed above.

Do they:

- Encapsulate what the organisation wants to achieve?

- Inspire commitment?

- Provide guidance for decision makers?

Are they:

- Brief?

- Easy to understand?

- Focused?

Give examples of where the vision statements are effective and where they could be strengthened.

Corporate social responsibility

The global context

As we have discussed, strategy grew from a military context where the objectives were clear and the 'enemy' known. This allowed for detailed planning where winning was the only acceptable outcome. When large corporations took to strategic planning, many of these attitudes went along with the processes. The planning process was detailed and often time consuming, the desired goals clear, and little consideration was given to 'collateral damage' — the unplanned consequences of success.

In the 21st century this relatively simplistic approach to business is being challenged. The enemy is not clear. Technology is changing the way the world operates so fast that long-term planning is increasingly complex; a prolonged planning process may be overtaken by events and the outcomes out of date before they are fully developed. Stakeholders, including shareholders, are increasingly concerned about collateral damage—the impact of business practices on the social end ecological environment.

Social responsibility

With the increasing awareness of the interconnectedness of business and society, the question is now asked—what is the responsibility of business (or any organisation) to the community in which it operates? Is it, for example, responsible for the impact it has on the environment and the lifestyle of the surrounding community? Businesses are responsible to multiple stakeholders. Whilst the extent of their responsibility is often hotly debated from an economic perspective, business must use its power responsibly or risk losing it—and power rests with multiple stakeholders, be these employees, board members or consumers. There are those who argue that business has an ethical responsibility that goes beyond avoiding economic harm; that there is a positive duty whether or not there is an economic reward.

Dubrin, Dalglish and Miller (2006) identify four aspects of social responsibility—namely:

- legal,
- ethical,
- economic, and
- philanthropic.

Legal

Legal responsibility is obedience to the laws and regulations wherever the organisation operates.

Ethical

Ethical responsibility is adherence to the standards of acceptable behaviour as judged by stakeholders.

Economic

Economic responsibility is the maximisation of stakeholder wealth and value.

Philanthropic

Philanthropic responsibility is 'giving back' to society.

There are arguments against these definitions of social responsibility. For example, there is the argument that increasing shareholder value is the only thing that matters. Another argument claims that social responsibility places an individual at a disadvantage. These arguments appear simplistic in today's business context, where stakeholders are well-informed and reputation is vital to long-term business success.

Economic responsibilities

Economist Milton Friedman is the best known proponent of the argument that management's sole responsibility is to maximise profits for shareholders. Yet even he states:

Make as much money as possible while conforming to the basic rules of society, both embodied in the law and those embodied in ethical custom. (Friedman, cited in Hartman 1998)

This view can present interesting challenges as companies operate across legal and cultural boundaries. What is clear is that corporations are expected to make decisions which advance the profitability of the business. Some of the corporate collapses that have occurred in the early 21st century (including ENRON and the collapse of large financial institutions) suggest that they failed in this most basic of responsibilities. Many of these collapses left shareholders financially impoverished and entailed massive corporate losses.

Legal responsibilities

In addition to economic responsibilities, business is expected to carry out its work in accordance with the law and government regulations. Individuals are equally expected to comply with the law. Different countries have quite different legislative frameworks—e.g. the consumption of alcohol in some Gulf countries is forbidden. For some expatriate managers who come from different legal frameworks, this law may seem foolish. How does one make a decision whether or not to obey the law?

If a business is operating in a number of different countries, with different legal requirements (many of which are less onerous than those impacting on the 'head office' operation), which set of legal responsibilities applies? Do they apply to everyone equally?

Ethical responsibilities

There are societal expectations that have not been codified into law. Increasingly, customers are becoming concerned not only with legal compliance but with the impact of the operations of a business on the society in which it operates. The advance of communication technology has meant that shareholders are much more aware of what is being done in other parts of the world, and the impact of particular practices. There has been a rise in 'ethical investing' where investors make decisions about what companies they will invest in on ethical, as well as financial grounds. Increasingly, consumers are looking for products that enhance the society in which they operate rather than exploit it. Forest Alliance and Fair Trade Products are two of the movements that have seen consumers use their spending power to support more ethical trading.

Philanthropic responsibilities

Philanthropic responsibilities engage the corporation in activities that promote human welfare and goodwill. Because philanthropy is generally considered voluntary, failure to be philanthropic is not considered unethical. Philanthropic activity is often considered the domain of successful companies and that these activities will be the first to disappear in times of hardship. The Tata Group in India provides an interesting model for philanthropic activity.

> *No success in material terms is worthwhile unless it serves the needs and interests of the country and its people, and is achieved by fair and honest means. (J.R.D. Tata)*

The Tata Group is perhaps unique in the world—63% of the capital of the parent firm, Tata & Sons Ltd., is held by Tata Philanthropic Trusts. The trusts are best known for establishing a number of institutions—e.g. The Tata Institute of Social Sciences. The trust also continues to promote projects in the management of natural resources, health, and other areas of social development. Here philanthropic responsibility is built into the business model (Dubrin, Dalglish & Miller 2006, p. 137).

Environmental responsibility

It is almost impossible not to be aware of environmental issues. In some countries there is strict legislation with regard to emissions and pollution. But this is not the case all over the world. Standards are very different; in some case there are no standards. And yet emissions and pollution anywhere in the world impacts on everywhere in the world. It is worth exploring whether those companies which comply with environmental legislation in their home countries operate to the same standards in other, less regulated, economies.

Parker (2007) argues that the cost of no action with regard to responding to environmental concerns brings only difficulties. He articulates them as:

- higher insurance premiums,

- penalties for contravening environmental regulations,

- expenditure on clean-up and remediation,

- claims and payouts for major environmental damage, and

- loss of market share due to the organisation's reputation regarding environmental impact.

Activity 12.3

In a group of peer managers, discuss how corporate social and environmental responsibility impact on the development of strategy in your organisation. What additional questions have to be asked in the strategic thinking process? What are the potential benefits of responding positively to the challenges presented by social and environmental issues?

Leader in action: Olivia Lum

Hyflux Ltd began in 1989 as Hydrocem (s) Pte Ltd., a trading company selling water treatment systems n Singapore, Malaysia and Indonesia. In 2001, a little more than a decade later, Hyflux became the first water treatment company to be listed on the Singapore Stock Exchange.

Oliva Lum, the entrepreneur who started and now heads Hyflux, never knew her biological parents. In Kampar, a poor Malaysian mining town, she was adopted at birth by an elderly woman she called grandma. At nine she became the sole breadwinner when her grandmother became too old to work. She made her money from odd jobs such as selling fruit, sandwiches, ice cream and jeans in school, and weaving rattan bags and playing the clarinet in funeral processions. By the time she was 12 she had earned enough money to move them to better housing.

Despite difficulties at home, Lum was a top student. Her school master at Pei Yuan Secondary School advised her to go to Singapore, where there were more opportunities. In 1977 she gained admission to Tiong Bahrun Secondary School. She went on to study at the National University of Singapore where she majored in chemistry. She supported herself by selling insurance, cosmetics, flower pots and souvenirs. In 1986 she graduated with honours.

After graduating she worked as a laboratory chemist at Glazo. Here she learnt about environmental control. She also saw the potential of water treatment and recycling in water-scarce Singapore. In 1989 she left her well paid job at Galxo and founded Hydrochem, the forerunner of Hyflux, selling her apartment and car to raise $20,000 capital for the start-up. In 1993 Lum brought new water treatment technology to Singapore. By 1997 the company had secured contracts from major companies; the company's reputation and business took off. Today, Hyflux is one of the hottest firms in the Asian water market; under Lum's leadership it has scored a number of research and development breakthroughs.

In 2003 her enterprise and drive to succeed earned her Singapore's Ernst and Young Entrepreneur of the Year for Manufacturing and Industrial practices. In 2004 she was named Businessman of the Year at the Singapore Business Awards—the first woman to be so honoured.

Olivia Lum has a clearly articulated vision for the company.

Our vision

To be the leading company that the world seeks for innovative and effective environmental solutions.

Our mission

To provide efficient and cost effective solutions to meet our clients' needs through innovation and technological advancement.

Our values

Boldness Dare to dream, dare to do and dare to excel.

Entrepreneurship Nurture the entrepreneurial spirit, embrace challenge and master change.

Satisfaction Exceed internal and external customer satisfaction, take pride in work and deliver excellence.

Testimony Be the face behind the brand, excel in business conduct and embrace best practice in corporate governance.

In 2008/2009 Hyflux won contracts to design, build and operate seawater desalination plants in North Africa, a region that has great need of the technology but a market not yet tapped by many Western corporations.

Besides being the most competitive quote, our proven track record in delivering large-scale desalination contracts coupled with our proprietary membrane technology and our ability to offer total integrated solutions are the keys to winning the bid. (Olivia Lum, Hyflux CEO)

Sources: Singapore's Hyflux to develop seawater desalination plants in Libya,

<www.themalaysianinsider.com/index.php/business/30426-singapore-hyflux-to>, accessed 23/9/209; Hyflux gets $468m Algerian desal contract, <http://cleantech.com/news/2750/hyflux-gets-468m-algerian-desal-contract>, accessed 23/9/09; Vision Mission Values, <http://www.hyflux.com/vision.htm>, accessed 23/9/2009; Jake Lloyd Smith, 'The Moisture Merchant—Dealing in Liquid Assets', *Time Magazine*, 5 April 2004, <www.time.com/time/2004/innovators/200404/stroy.html>; Shivaranjanei Subramaniam,'Olivia Lum', National Library of Singapore, <http://infopedia.nl.sg/articles/SIP_1535_209-06-232.html>, accessed 23/9/09.

The profile above on Oliva Lum demonstrates how different experience can be turned to activity to build leadership character and perseverance, two highly prized qualities for leaders. Her own values have been clearly cascaded throughout the organisation and now drive its strategy.

Globalisation

From their different perspectives (economist and political scientist respectively), Jeffrey D. Sachs (2003, 2008) and James McGregor Burns (2008) have identified the impact of globalisation to be one of the most significant challenges of the 21st century.

The twentieth century saw the end of European dominance of global politics and economics; this century will see the end of American dominance (Sachs 2008). New powers such as China, India and Brazil will continue to grow; they will make their voices increasingly heard on the world stage.

In an interdependent world, cooperation may well take the place of competition as the scramble for power and resources becomes more than a 'game'. No part of the world can be abandoned to extreme poverty, or used as a dumping ground for toxic waste, without it having a negative impact on the whole.

Poverty – the greatest of the strategic leadership challenges

Poverty probably presents the greatest of the strategic leadership challenges. One third of the world (2 billion people) remains trapped in extreme poverty, unrelieved by the global economic growth which has benefited so many. Not only does this cause hardship for the poor, it creates great risks for the rest of us. At best, these people exist on $A2 dollars a day. Half of the world's total wealth goes to 10% of the world's population. In 1998 the world's 200 richest people had more wealth than the combined incomes of the world's poorest 41% – about 2.3 billion people.

Burns (2003) argued that 'no leader can truly lead if they cannot respond to the wants of followers, if they fail to elevate and empower them'. No leader can truly lead if lacking in the ability to produce intended change through creative innovation.

Need for new leadership strategies

Burns goes on to argue that new leadership strategies are required, that the failed strategies of the past must be left behind and new ways offered to solve the problem lying at the very root of most of the world's other problems – the vastly uneven distribution of resources and opportunities.

The new leadership strategies would provide a host of listeners who would hear the voices of the poor. Here is the first step in any strategy of leadership – to listen. For it is leadership, listening closely to the wants of the poor and recognising them as actionable needs, that can marshal and direct resources, both material and psychological, and answer them.

Efficacy

A leader not only speaks to the immediate wants of followers but elevates people by vesting in them a sense of possibility – a belief that changes can be made and that they can make them (p. 239). The crucial factor in the dynamic comes into play at the outset – the building of efficacy. Whilst leadership is necessary at every stage, beginning with the first spark that awakens people's hopes, its vital role is to create and expand the opportunities that empower people to pursue happiness for themselves.

This text has been about building self efficacy. It has provided you with the opportunity to enhance you knowledge and skills and increase your confidence as a leader.

Technology and innovation

Burns (2003) argues that the strategic failure central to past approaches rose from the assumption that money and technology constituted the essential—and even total—keys to overcoming poverty.

This strategy has been used in many countries around the world—including Australia, with its multiple failed policies to help its indigenous people. It did not overcome the vicious circle of interrelated poverties, lack of education, health care, access to resources, and self efficacy.

Appropriate technologies

It is by listening that appropriate technologies can be used to help individuals and groups solve their own problems in their own ways. The developing world may well be better prepared to accept new technologies or alternative power sources than those countries that have for a hundred years depended on carbon-based fuels. If you have always driven a petrol-fuelled car and generated electricity using coal, the barriers to change can be substantial. If you have never had electricity, or a car, solar and wind technologies present opportunities rather than threats.

Innovation

Innovation is not the sole province of the rich. Visit any city in Africa—where infrastructure is limited—and you will find mobile phone technology being used, not just as a means of communication but as a means of overcoming the lack of infrastructure and creating business opportunities. Even in very poor communities there are people building businesses around their mobile phones—selling time to those who cannot afford a phone of their own (Dalglish & Matthews 2009).

Strategic leadership in the 21st century

Matching the appropriate technology with the needs of the community is where innovative, strategic leadership has such a significant role to play. The ability to listen, to be aware of the trends—and be able to match the appropriate technology, old or new, to the needs of followers—will be the cornerstone of strategic leadership in the 21st century.

Summary

Strategic leadership deals with the major purposes of an organisation. Its perspective, therefore, is often different from that of leadership at other levels in an organisation.

In a world where many businesses are richer than countries, where business extends across national boundaries and where the behaviour of business can have a dramatic impact on people around the world, the ability to think strategically, to see the business, organisation or country in the context of its total environment is essential, not just for the success of the organisation, but for the planet as a whole.

Strategic leadership is comprised of a number of capabilities. They include:

- high-level cognitive activity,
- the ability to gather multiple inputs (listen),
- anticipating and creating a future,
- revolutionary thinking, and
- creating a vision.

An effective vision statement should be:

- brief,
- understandable,
- focused,
- supportive of decision making, and
- inspirational.

With the increasing awareness of the interconnectedness of business and society, the question is now asked whether business, or in fact any organisation, bears responsibility to the community in which it operates. Four aspects of corporate social responsibility were discussed:

- economic responsibility,
- legal responsibility,

- ethical responsibility, and

- philanthropic responsibility.

It is almost impossible not to be aware of environmental issues. Emissions and pollution anywhere in the world impact on everywhere in the world. Parker (2007) argues that the cost of no action with regard to responding to environmental concerns brings only difficulties. He lists them as:

- higher insurance premiums,

- penalties for contravening environmental regulations,

- expenditure on clean-up and remediation,

- claims and payouts for major environmental damage, and

- loss of market share due to the organisation's environmental impact reputation.

Poverty in a globalised world presents probably the greatest challenge to strategic leadership. One-third of the world (2 billion people) remains trapped in extreme poverty unrelieved by the global economic growth which has benefited so many. Not only does this cause hardship for the poor, it creates great risks for the rest of us.

Burns (2003) argued:

> No leader can truly lead if they cannot respond to the wants of followers, if they fail to elevate and empower them ... No leader can truly lead if lacking in the ability to produce intended change through creative innovation. (p. 239)

Reflection on your leadership practice

The reflection for this chapter is to pause your reading and complete the *individual skills profile* at the end of this chapter.

References

The Age, <http:www.theage.com.au/news/national/kevin-rudd/2006 /12/02/ 1164777852646.html>.

Burns, JM 2003, *Leaders who changed the world*, Penguin, New Delhi.

Cape York Institute, <http://cyi.org.au/director.aspx>.

Currie Petersen, E 2007, 'Kevin Rudd' in C Dalglish, & P Evans, *Leadership in the Australian Context*, Melbourne, Australia, Tilde University Press.

Dalglish C & Matthews J 2009, Designing self-sustaining support for micro-enterprises in sub-Saharan Africa – a pilot, World Forum on Business as a process for World Benefit. Cleveland USA.

Dubrin, A, Dalglish, C & Miller, P 2006, *Leadership 2nd Asia Pacific Edition*, Milton, Qld: John Wiley and Sons Australia England.

Ghemawat, P 2006, *Strategy and the Business Landscape* 2nd edn, Pearson/Prentice hall, Upper Saddle river, New Jersey.

Hyflux gets $468m Algerian desal contract, viewed 23 September 2009, <http://cleantech.com/news/2750/hyflux-gets-468m-algerian-desal-contract>.

Hamel, G 1996, 'Strategy as revolution,' *Harvard Business Review*, July-August, pp. 69-82.

Indigenous Stock Exchange: people – Noel Pearson, viewed 30 August 2009, <http://www.isx.org.au/people/ 1026013663_2590.html>.

Macklin, R 2007, *Kevin Rudd, the Biography*, Penguin Group Australia.

Pearson, Noel, Walking in Two Worlds. *Australian*, viewed 30 August 2009, <http://www.theaustralian.news.com.au/story/0,20867, 20656108-7583,00.html>.

Pearson, Noel, Hand up preferable by far to a handout, *The Australian*, viewed 19 May 2007, <http://www.theaustralian.news.com.au/ story/0,20867,21755316-7583,00.html>.

Pearson, Noel, Five steps to get them off welfare, *The Australian*, viewed 30 August 2009, <http://kooriweb.org/foley/resources/pearson/ aust9aug2008html>.

Sachs, J 2005, *The End of Poverty*, Penguin Books. London.

Senge, PM 1994, *The Fifth Discipline*, Random House, Sydney.

Singapore's Hyflux to develop seawater desalination plants in Libya, viewed 23 September 2009, <www.themalaysianinsider.com/index.php/ business/30426-singapore-hyflux-to >.

Shivaranjanei Subramaniam, *Olivia Lum' National Library of Singapore*, viewed 23 September 2009, <http://infopedia.nl.sg/articles/ SIP_ 1535_209-06-232.html>.

Smith, JL, The Moisture Merchant Dealing in Liquid Assets, *Time Magazine*, 5 April 2004, <www.time.com/time/2004/innovators/ 200404/stroy.html>.

Vision Mission Values, viewed 23 September 2009, <http://www. hyflux.com/vision.htm >.

Walker, J 1995, *Goss, a Political Biography*, St Lucia, Queensland, University of Queensland Press.

http://www.smb.com.au/news/national/rudd.says.sorry/2008/02/1 3/1202760342960.html.

http://www.pm.gov.au/media/interview/2008/interview_0580.cfm.

http://www.pm.gov.au/.

INDIVIDUAL SKILLS PROFILE

Use a pause in your reading to complete this skills profile as a moment of reflection and to view the level of your current leadership skill and knowledge.

The format for the profile is straightforward. Under each heading there is a brief explanation of what is required; it is up to you to fill in the details.

Your power profile (from Chapter 8)

Insert your scores from Activity 8.1 into the space in the table below:

Coercive	Connection	Information	Legitimate	Reward	Expert	Referent

A score of 6 or greater on any of the seven power types is high and implies that you prefer to influence others by utilising that particular type of power. A score of 2 or less is low and implies that you prefer not to utilise this particular type of power to influence others.

What do your scores in each of the power types reveal about your use of power?

....
....
....
....
....
....
....

Your influence tactics (from Chapter 8)

Insert your scores from Activity 8.2 into the space in the table below:

Influence tactic	Score for each dimension
Rational persuasion	
Apprising	
Inspirational appeals	
Consultation	
Exchange	
Collaboration	
Personal appeals	
Ingratiation	
Legitimating tactics	
Pressure	
Ingratiation	
Coalition tactics	
Total score	

Your total score will range from 11 to 55. The higher your score, the more influence tactics you use. The more influence tactics you use, and the more often you use them, the more influential you probably are.

What do your scores in each of the influence tactics reveal about your ability to influence?

....
....
....
....
....
....
....

Your listening behaviours (from Chapter 9)

Insert your scores from Activity 9.1 into the space in the table below:

Active listening behaviour	Score for each dimension
Making eye contact	
Affirmative nods	
No distracting gestures	
Asking questions	
Paraphrasing	
No interrupting	
No talking over the top	
Smooth transitions	
Total score	

Your total score will range from 8 to 40. The higher your score, the more effective you are as an active listener.

What do your scores for each dimension of active listening reveal about your ability to communicate effectively?

....
....
....
....
....
....
....

Your MBWA (from Chapter 9)

How often do you get out of your office and talk informally with your team members in their space? Rate yourself on the scale below by circling the word(s) that best represents your behaviour:

Never   Not often   Often   Very often   All the time

What does your MBWA behaviour imply about your relationship building skills?

....

....

....

....

....

....

....

Your conflict management style (from Chapter 9)

Insert your scores from Activity 9.7 into the space in the table below:

Conflict management style	Score for each style
Avoidance	
Accommodation	
Force	
Negotiation	
Collaboration	

It is recommended that leaders use the first four styles (avoidance, accommodation, force and negation) infrequently. The conflict style recommended for most conflict situations is the collaborative style. It is very useful when the leader initiates the conflict resolution process.

What do your scores for each style reveal about your ability to resolve conflict successfully?

....

....

....

....

....

....

Your rating of other key skills and concepts

Now that you have read this book, and having been exposed to a number of concepts that are important to effective leadership, respond to each statement about your understanding for each of the following concepts. Respond honestly. Your response is not a reflection of you, but a reflection of your current skill level.

	Strongly disagree		Neither agree nor disagree		Strongly agree
I understand the need for my experience and learning to be reflective.	1	2	3	4	5
I understand the need for self-awareness to improve my leadership.	1	2	3	4	5
I understand the ethical issues involved in leading others.	1	2	3	4	5
I understand the gender issues involved in leading others.	1	2	3	4	5
I understand the cultural issues involved in leading others.	1	2	3	4	5
I understand the approaches available for my own professional development as a leader.	1	2	3	4	5
I am skilled at giving both positive and negative feedback to others.	1	2	3	4	5
I understand the dynamics of teams and how to use them to improve teamwork.	1	2	3	4	5
I understand the issues around leading and implementing change.	1	2	3	4	5
I am able to create a vision that will inspire and motivate my followers.	1	2	3	4	5

Improving your leadership involves responding to these statements in an honest way, identifying skill and knowledge gaps and making a plan to close those gaps. The Summary section of this book provides assistance to develop a plan for your development.

Summary

Now that you have arrived at this point in the book, you would have undertaken the activities and reflections in each chapter and read about the leadership practices of other successful and notable leaders who have been profiled. You should have completed the *individual leadership profile* at the end of Chapter 4 and the *individual skills profile* at the end of Chapter 12.

The early chapters of the book emphasised the importance to leaders of being reflective. It has been noted that reflection is possibly a leader's least favourite activity. Leadership development is based on the premise that self-learning and reflection are fundamental to improving leadership effectiveness. If you are to improve your leadership skills and practice, then it is important that you are aware of your current level of skills, your values and behavioural patterns and the predominant ways you attempt to influence others. Self-awareness is therefore a key to being a more effective leader. Self-awareness is really about self-discovery and our aim in this book has been to assist you to move along the path of self-discovery.

The latter chapters of the book raised skill areas and contextual factors that are important to leaders. All leaders lead in a cultural context, and by this we mean both organisational culture and national culture. These issues are particularly important as organisations are impacted by globalisation. Issues of culture, power, communication, teamwork, change and strategy ensure leadership is a complex process.

Throughout the book we have endeavoured to emphasise that there is not just one type of personality or leadership style that makes a leader effective. The leadership styles and personalities of effective leaders at all levels vary widely. This makes leadership and leadership development a very personal phenomenon that is context specific and situational in nature. Notwithstanding, the emphasis in the book is that a prime obligation for all leaders is that they are morally obliged to serve first the organisation and its people rather than serve their own interests.

Despite the fact that most leadership styles can be effective, some forms of leadership that are now common in our organisations inevitably give rise to crises – for the people who work with the leader and for organisational risk, governance and performance. And as we have witnessed in the Global Financial Crises (GFC), the results of this type of dysfunctional leadership often manifest around the globe and affect people and areas not clearly related or imagined previously.

One lesson of the GFC is the need for good quality, sustainable and effective leadership in our society. What the globe requires is good quality leadership at every level in society and right throughout its organisations. The quality of the leadership can only be judged by how well leaders empower and bring out the best in others, not by short-term profit maximisation and other unsustainable economic models.

This book is in itself, a leadership development program. The program uses experiences (through participation in the activities and reflections) and education as a means of assisting leaders to take control of their own development. We have attempted to provide you with a conceptual framework for understanding leadership and a way of facing the future requirements for quality leadership.

So what of your future? We trust that we have communicated to you throughout this book that your leadership style and skills require constant attention, maintenance and can always be improved and refined. The final exercise is a tool to assist you with this refinement. We provide below a process to enable you to develop a 2–3 year leadership development plan.

A 2–3 year leadership development plan

What is provided here is the outline for a leadership development plan. It provides a framework for a development plan that will help you develop your own leadership skills and style. You can use this to choose the appropriate style of leadership for you, in your particular employment and cultural context.

The format for the plan is straightforward. Under each heading there is a brief explanation of what is required, and then it is up to you to fill in the details about the leader you know best — yourself. You will find that the answers will change over time, but the format allows you to add and take away content whenever it is appropriate to do so and to continue to refine your own leadership.

Before you commence, keep these issues in mind:

- Plan only 2–3 years ahead. The plan is a work-in-progress and will change as your career, skills base and circumstances change.

- Keep your goals modest. Do not try to improve in more than 2 or 3 areas at any one time.

- Be specific and not general in your statements and about your goals. Set time lines for yourself.

- Use your *individual leadership profile* from Chapter 4 and your *individual skills profile* from Chapter 12 to assist in building your development plan.

Now work through the steps below responding to each of the questions as you work your way through.

Step 1 – How do you want to be remembered as a leader?

This exercise will assist you to focus your attention on what really matters to you and to engage with the values you articulated earlier in Chapter 2 and in your *individual leadership profile* from Chapter 4.

Write in the space provided below responses to the following questions:

If you were to leave your current position tomorrow, what would you like to be said about you, your contribution to the organisation and your leadership at the farewell function?

....
....
....
....
....
....
....

What do you think would *actually* be said?

....
....
....
....
....
....
....

If there is not a good coherence between what you would like said about you and what you think might be said about you, explain why you think the difference exists.

....
....
....
....
....
....
....

What are you going to do about the difference if one exists?

....
....
....
....
....
....
....

Step 2 - What leadership style or position do you aspire to?

Perhaps you see one particular leadership style or model explained in this book, or a style of a leader you admire, that you feel would be most effective in your current position or the positions to which you aspire. Think about the model or style of leadership that you are drawn to. What characteristics and behaviours are required for this style to be successful?

....
....
....
....
....
....
....

If it is a particular position you aspire to, obtain a job description.

- Find out as much as possible about what the position involves.
- Examine exactly what knowledge, skills and attitudes are required to be effective in this position.
- List the critical elements for success.

The position may be one you aspire to at some time in the future. This activity gives you time to work on the capabilities and attitudes you will need to be successful in that position. It provides a target for you to focus on.

Step 3 – Analyse your own strengths and weaknesses

Each chapter in this book will help you do this. You first commenced the list of your strengths and weaknesses when you developed your *individual leadership profile* at the end of Chapter 4. The outcomes of the Reflective Best Self exercise in Chapter 4 will also be helpful for this step. Refer back to these and also include the knowledge gained in Chapters 5–12 of the book.

What do you see as your current leadership strengths?

....
....
....
....
....

What do you see as your current leadership weaknesses?

....
....
....
....
....
....
....

Are you technically competent but with little experience developing teams or partnerships?

....
....
....
....
....
....
....

Are you an outgoing person, or do you prefer to work on your own?

....
....
....
....
....
....
....

Step 4 – Compare your current attributes with those you desire in the future

Now is the opportunity to compare your knowledge, skills and attitudes with those of your aspirations.

Do you need to develop your communication skills? If so how?

....
....
....
....
....
....
....

Do you need mentoring or coaching in any areas? If so, how will you do this?

....
....
....
....
....
....
....

Now identify the two or three areas you believe you need to work on most to move you towards your desired position or style. Set timelines to attain these.

....
....
....
....
....
....
....

Step 5 – Develop capacity

Now that you have identified the areas you need to work on to become the sort of leader you want to be, you need to explore ways to develop these capacities. How to do this is always a challenge.

Do you need to expose yourself to new and different experiences? If so list them here.

....
....
....
....
....
....
....

Do you need to attend training and, if so, what sort of training?

....
....
....
....
....
....
....

How will you ensure that your new skills are used in the workplace? If you don't use your newly developed skills they will fade away. Think of some ideas and list them here.

....
....
....
....
....
....
....

Would a coach or a mentor be the way to go? Why or why not?

....
....
....
....
....
....

Find out the ways available for you to develop the knowledge and skills you have identified as necessary to your leadership development. Explore how possible these are and how effective they might be. Try to gain the support of your employer and your family as you set out on the developmental journey.

Step 6 – Success

How will you know your leadership has improved?

What will be different in relation to the way you interact with others?

....
....
....
....
....
....

What will be different in relation to the way you feel?

....
....
....
....
....
....

What will be different in relation to the outcomes you achieve?

....
....
....
....
....
....

It is important that you put timelines on the changes you make. Try to be specific about what you hope will change.

When the changes occur, celebrate, then move on and develop or refining a new plan.

INDEX